Internal Sec

# Internal Security Beyond Borders

## Public Insecurity in Europe and the New Challenges to State and Society

Olivier Brenninkmeijer

Programme for Strategic and International Security Studies

The Graduate Institute of International Studies, Geneva

HEI

PETER LANG

Bern · Berlin · Bruxelles · Frankfurt am Main · New York · Oxford · Wien

Die Deutsche Bibliothek – CIP-Einheitsaufnahme

**Brenninkmeijer, Olivier :**
Internal security beyond borders : public insecurity in Europe and the new challenges to state and society ; programme for strategic and international security studies / Olivier Brenninkmeijer. The Graduate Institute of International Studies, Geneva. – Bern ; Berlin ; Bruxelles ; Frankfurt am Main ; New York ; Oxford ; Wien : Lang, 2001
ISBN 3-906765-64-4

British Library and Library of Congress Cataloguing-in-Publication Data:
A catalogue record for this book is available from *The British Library*, Great Britain, and from *The Library of Congress*, USA

Cover design: Thomas Jaberg, Peter Lang AG

ISBN 3-906765-64-4
US-ISBN 0-8204-5302-1

© Peter Lang AG, European Academic Publishers, Bern 2001
Jupiterstr. 15, Postfach, 3000 Bern 15, Switzerland; info@peterlang.com

Printed in Germany

This work is dedicated to Benjamin
and to all teenagers who care for the future of our society.

# Table of Contents

# Preface

Crime and violence seem to be everywhere nowadays. That at least is the widespread impression many people particularly in industrialised societies have. They feel nowadays less threatened by the possibility of aggression from without than by a seemingly increasing number of criminal acts from within. It seems that war and conflict, in short: insecurity has become "internalized". And so have, as a consequence, the security concerns. It is today's society as a whole, and the citizens individually, who fear to be the most likely and vulnerable target of acts of violence and criminal behaviour ranging from simple robbery to physical attack, from terrorist blackmail to financial banditry.

The conclusion from all this is that our concerns about what "security", or rather "insecurity", actually means have shifted from the seemingly remote level of interstate war to the very close one of personal vulnerability. This development is cause for deep and widespread concern for governments and society, for the international community no less than for individual citizens.

The present book addresses itself not just to the still small number of experts. Its main addressee is the public at large. To the best of my knowledge this is the first study of its kind that provides a wide-ranging overview of the manifold challenges to what the author calls "objective" and "subjective" security, the former meaning actual, identifiable threats or illegal acts directed against individuals, society, private and official institutions; the latter referring to an environment which people perceive to be insecure, unpredictable if not outright dangerous. Or, to put it differently, the objective reality of crime and violence finds its complement in people's subjective feeling or insecurity.

This study examines both sources of insecurity. They are those with which we are generally quite familiar. Thanks to the media and political discourse they have become part of our daily life and concern. There are two different kinds of security threats that nowadays worry people most. On the one hand there is the delinquent behaviour of ever younger children, of young people and, of course, of adults, be they citizens or foreigners. There are, on the other hand, the immigrants and asylum seekers as well as the criminal acts by foreigners, often called "tourist-offenders", who enter the country one evening and leave it with the stolen goods a few hours or days later.

The search for greater security or, at least, less insecurity has therefore moved dramatically up on the local, national and even international agenda. It is common to practically all countries in Europe – East and West, North and South, and well beyond. Such "internationalization" can be at least partly explained by the manifold links that tie crime to migration, terrorism to fundamentalist movements, and cross-border travels of sport fans to acts of hooliganism in foreign towns.

The field of both concern and investigation of its causes has therefore become very wide indeed. It calls for more, and more systematic, international cooperation as well as for a better understanding of the root causes of this plague of modern society and the possible remedies to eliminate or at least identify them.

I am very happy that the author, Olivier Brenninkmeijer, has undertaken the difficult and delicate task to investigate as thoroughly as possible the manifold ramifications and consequences of our new and widening security environment and the concerns that it raises. Given the great complexity of the topic, the study does not, and indeed cannot, claim completeness, let alone infallibility. But it provides, in my view, a highly welcome and necessary guide through the complex and emotion-filled situation in which modern society finds itself today. The study calls rightly and convincingly for common solutions and cooperation. This call is all the more persuasive as it clearly shows that the objective threats to security as well as the subjective feelings of insecurity are becoming ever more and everywhere the same.

Mr. Brenninkmeijer was, for two and a half years, research assistant at the "Programme for Strategic and International Security Studies" (PSIS) of the Graduate Institute of International Studies in Geneva. As the principal concern and interest of the PSIS is security, both national and international, this study fulfills a truly pioneering role in tackling the less traditional but increasingly central concern of personal and societal security.

We hope that the present volume will stimulate a growing interest in what unexpectedly turned out to be a highly demanding but worthwhile undertaking, i.e. to contribute to our better and more balanced understanding of these new security dimensions. They are likely to remain a major concern to our society for any foreseeable future.

Geneva, June 2000

Professor Curt Gasteyger
Graduate Institute of International Studies, Geneva,
Former Director of the
Programme for Strategic and International Security Studies

# Foreword

During the last thirty years many diverse factors have contributed to fundamental changes of security. Security is, first, a sum of various more or less objective criteria: political and social stability, clear and accepted legal provisions and their effective enforcement, absence or remoteness of dangers like war, terrorism, and other forms of violence, serious crime or devastating economic threats. But security is, second, also a reflection of subjective perception by groups or individuals of all these factors - or of their absence, including deficiencies in law enforcement, thus creating feelings of insecurity.

In some ways the beginning of the 1990's brought the most dramatic and palpable changes with regard to security. Shortly after the stunning and much cheered breakdown of the eastern bloc, the Warsaw Pact and the Iron Curtain, the former balance of nuclear terror (which had disciplined many violent powers) vanished and opened the world to some sort of omnipresence of the evil or terrible. Several states provided themselves with nuclear, chemical and possibly bacteriological weapons. Ever more criminal organisations use the vacuum of power to establish their own structures even linking with "homologues" in other countries. The "technological explosion" of immediate communication available world-wide offered previously unimaginable potential of use and misuse. Other globalisation effects have facilitated complex and therefore hard to detect criminal activities including corruption. International criminal investigation has become less effective and successful due to the limited reach of national legislation in a globalised world and due to the expansion of legal defence possibilities as opposed to more and more sophisticated criminal *modi operandi*.

On the regional level, the generation of those brought up by parents who admired the "revolution" of 1968 has grown to adolescence or young adulthood. They show a totally different attitude towards society as a whole and observance of the law in particular. For them solidarity and responsibility, rights and duties, have radically different meanings than for older people. Permissiveness rather than consistency seems to prevail, at least where it promises personal gain. In addition, great numbers of immigrants in Europe from countries with other cultures and religions, many of them marked by the terrible experiences of violence, have contributed to a highly diversified multicultural population with very disparate values. All of this, together with media reports on disasters, crime and violence from the world over that flood peoples' living-rooms, deeply influence the perception of increasing insecurity.

The author, Olivier Brenninkmeijer, has undertaken the huge task of analysing the many challenges and dangers of what is still called "internal security" in a wider theatre. His merit is that he does not present one factor after and beside the next, but shows their many complicated interdependencies. Furthermore, he does not shy away from philosophical issues such as the contradictions between the demands for perfect security on the one hand and maximum freedom (civil liberties) on the other, or between the demands for impenetrable walls (as for the EU or Swiss outside border) and freedom of movement. Yet another complication in his view is the widespread enjoyment of violence for entertainment and its condemnation when perceived as a threat. In various contexts, particularly in the chapter on Switzerland, he shows clearly that no nation is capable anymore to safeguard its "internal" security alone. Under the given European, even global, conditions the term "internal security" has become misleading. The history of the nineties, especially of the Balkans, and its implications and consequences have proven that the distinction between external (defence) and internal (police, criminal justice) security is obsolete and dangerous, yet still widely used.

That the author addresses also the very crucial subject of crime prevention by suggesting new approaches adds to the high value of his work. Brenninkmeijer's monograph offers many most interesting insights. I hope that it will not be read by experts only, but will find a much wider public, including politicians, especially those who have so far failed to share responsibility for the security of the people, in whatever field of politics they may be active.

June 2000

Dr. Markus H.F. Mohler
Commandant, Cantonal Police of Basel-Stadt, Switzerland.

# Acknowledgements

This study could not have been conducted without the much appreciated help and advice of numerous institutions and experts of many European countries. Our particular thanks for their helpful comments on parts of this study go to Dr. Adam C. Bouloukos, President, United Nations Staff Council Vienna, Mr. Urs von Daeniken, Head of the Swiss Federal Police, Dr. Thomas Feltes, Professor at the Fachhochschule für Polizei, Villingen-Schwenningen, Germany, Professor Frank Gregory, University of Southampton, Mr. Stephan Gussmann, Swiss Federal Office for Police, Mr. Christoph Häni, Swiss Federal Co-ordinator for Internal Security, Professor Imre Kertesz, Advisor at the Chief Public Prosecutor's Office, Budapest, Hungary, Mr. Helmut Koetzsche, Criminologist, Mr.Thomas Köppel, Swiss Federal Police, Derek Lutterbeck at the Graduate Institute of International Studies, Dr. Markus Mohler, Commandant, Cantonal Police of Basel-Stadt, Mr. Roger Sauvain, European Liaison Office at Interpol, Ms. Renate Storz, Scientific Adjunct at the Swiss Federal Statistical Office, as well as many others who freely gave of their advice.

Finally, we owe particular gratitude to the Sophie and Karl Binding Foundation in Basel for having so generously funded this project. Its realisation would not have been possible without this support and the farsightedness of the Foundation's late president, Mr. David Linder who supported it from the very beginning.

Curt Gasteyger
Olivier Brenninkmeijer

# Summary

European security appears to be less stable today than it was a decade ago. Challenges to internal security are changing in nature and scope to such an extent that they increasingly affect public perceptions of safety in European society. Crime, violence and clandestine migration are most often mentioned today by politicians and in the media as having become intensified or critical problems for public security.[1] These problems are not new, however. Violence and crime by adults and youth have existed since the beginning of history. What has brought these forms of human behaviour to wide public attention through the 1990's are the numerous inter-ethnic wars around the world, reports of international organised crime, transnational banditry and the exploitation of migrants by traffickers. Public sensitivity to security problems has also risen because of anti-foreigner sentiments in Europe as well as a growing feeling of helplessness with regard to juvenile delinquency, violence among Europe's children and among the not-so-young hooligans and *casseurs* at large public events.

The abundance of information available today on crime and violence committed by local youth or by travelling offenders as well as on the international mobility of the latter and the growth of organised crime leads many to fear that internal security is seriously threatened. This is particularly so where the public is losing confidence in state institutions responsible for public safety (police, border guards, the military, secret intelligence services and the criminal justice system). The loss of confidence is to some extent expressed through a rising polarisation of opinions among political parties and the public debate they nurture as well as in the potentially dangerous trends which give rise to protectionism, isolationism and xenophobia.

---

1   The terms "internal security" and "public security" or "public safety" are here taken to mean the same thing. "Internal security", however, is more often taken to imply the security of society in a country while the word "public" often refers to the security or safety of individual people.

19

How Europeans perceive their personal safety or the security of their society depends on whether a loss of control is feared over social, political and economic changes. Phenomena such as the globalisation of economic trade, of consumer-driven values or of crime are not initiated by individual governments nor are they globally controlled. Rather, they are consequences of a mixture of often isolated political, economic and social changes which characterise European society and the global environment of which it is part. Public expectations for more safety as well as objective measures to prevent a rise of crime and violence in society oblige us to think about the possible challenges to internal security in Europe. What are the challenges and what can be done to address the subjective nature of public insecurity in a positive way?

Feeling unsafe results from a subjective assessment by each person of three broad phenomena: (1) unforeseen changes in society due to political, social and economic influences; (2) uncertainty about whether threats and risks are real or merely imagined; and (3), whether counter-measures, such as crime prevention and law enforcement are effective. In this context, data on objective security in society (the risk of becoming a victim of crime, indicators of economic performance, statistics on health and social welfare) do not necessarily correspond to subjective insecurity feelings among the public (fear of losing a job, of serious disease or of being robbed).

Changes in our social, economic (including technological), political and security environment affect our lives almost daily. This appears unavoidable, especially as today's globalised and highly industrialised society seems to produce these changes faster than ever before. Public feelings of insecurity may thus arise due to a variety of unforeseen experiences which can at times even seem contradictory. For example, our quality of life may not appear to improve as we expected even though we benefit more and more from sophisticated technological advances. Because of these advances and of political changes over the past years, our global mobility has become a highly valued aspect of personal freedom for holidays and for trade. However, this same freedom also allows criminals to travel freely. At the same time, global population pressures combined with political and economic instability in less industrialised countries push many migrants and refugees to travel to Western Europe in search of temporary safety, a job or a new home.

Europeans have no choice but to participate in an increasingly interconnected society. All government functions that deal with economic policy, education, social welfare and the protection of human rights are affected. In the domain of internal security, law enforcement and policing methods must continuously be updated to maintain or improve the social order needed for the public to feel safe. All of this inevitably implies a willingness to learn, share and co-operate across jurisdictional and political borders. Most important is that both the objective challenges to security and subjective public perceptions are addressed at the same time. To neglect how people feel about their safety will prove counterproductive even to the most sophisticated local or international policing efforts.

Education and public awareness-raising about how security and public safety can be developed is one necessary element. Crime prevention and anti-violence coping methods can be taught in schools and through participatory community policing projects. They directly improve feelings of safety as well as objective security conditions (better neighbourhood watch schemes, public empowerment and responsibility, closer contacts with the police or with drug-abuse counsellors). At national government levels, another necessary element is the development of new crime and violence prevention programmes. These require institutional reforms in various ministries and police agencies. The aim is to prevent subjective insecurity as it is felt by the public and to improve objective security conditions locally, nationally and across international borders.

In this sense, the development of internal security must reach beyond the traditional confines of police jurisdiction, municipalities, cantons, Länder, départements, counties or national territories. Rather, this effort should address both: (a) the international security challenges as they affect Europe's internal security and (b) local challenges to public safety as they influence the subjective security feelings of individual Europeans. In other words, internal security is no longer an internal affair of individual countries. It is today an international concern that requires at once small and local as well as Europe-wide and global attention. This study is intended as a contribution to the debate on the expansion of internal security concerns beyond national borders.

# Chapter 1

# Introduction: Internal Security in its new Context

What are the most feared challenges to security? Some might respond by pointing at nuclear weapons arsenals, the huge world-wide legal and illegal trade of military hardware, global pollution, or the volatility of international trade and financial markets. However, for most Europeans, these rather remote military, environmental and complex economic considerations seem to have little significance in their daily lives. Rather, for them security implies public safety in society. This includes a stable job, the protection of human rights and individual freedom, an improvements of daily living conditions and an absence of crime and violence.

Through the last ten years, Europeans experienced some dramatic changes affecting political stability, industry, employment, social security and public perceptions of safety in society. The following chapters provide an overview of the issues, challenges, questions and problems that fuel the ongoing security debate in Europe. It centres on violence, crime, un-civil or deviant behaviour in society. It also relates to the question how the state, Europe in general, the European Union as well as individual people can deal with these phenomena. While it is true that other debates on unemployment, political extremism or health-care also affect how Europeans feel about their security, crime awakens the strongest feelings. The same may also be said with regard to war or natural catastrophes. However, this study will concentrate on the challenges to security which stem principally from different kinds of offending behaviour and individual perceptions of safety. At the same time, ideas for the prevention of insecurity will be introduced in a later chapter. These may help us to recognise that perceptions of insecurity are not predetermined or permanently fixed. Insecurity feelings are liable to increase in situations where fear dominates public discourse and diminish within a context where confidence in public security is facilitated.

We begin with a brief overview of how the concept of security, particularly "internal security", has undergone considerable change since the end of the Cold War. A principal reason is that challenges to security, as they are commonly perceived, have become either more numerous or greater in their impact on public feelings. One indication of this is the frequent mention of juvenile delinquency, violence and other forms of anti-social behaviour in daily newspapers and television programmes. This introductory chapter also explains why Europe is singled out for this study. One reason is that most European countries share not only common political values and economic ambitions, but they are also concerned with two significant challenges that are often included in discussions on internal security. These are immigration and crimes committed by foreigners – topics that are loudly debated in several European countries today.

## Recent developments in internal security

At the end of the Cold War, many Europeans hoped that the days of burdening international security problems were over. However, security became a concern in a very different form. Now, juvenile delinquency, crime and violence are causing many more people to worry about their safety than they did a decade ago.[2] During these years, the public came to realise that factual (objective) security was something very different from (subjective) feelings of insecurity. While for the majority of Europeans actual personal safety has not worsened, a change in the nature and scope of various kinds of crime and violence occurred. It was particularly felt by those living in lower socio-economic conditions who suspect immigration in Europe to

---

2   A crime is defined here as an act punishable by law. However, there are many deviant forms of behaviour which are unacceptable, but not necessarily a crime when defined legally. For example, "delinquency" is behaviour which may or may not be a crime in a criminal court, but which is an act punishable under different types of regulations. It may be damaging either to things or to people, but it may also simply be a neglect of duty. Similarly, the term "offence" is used here as the general notion for all violations of commonly accepted regulations; i.e. legal rules, official procedures or unwritten civil norms of behaviour which we learn through education. Finally, the word "deviance" is the most general term which implies all behaviour that offends other people because it is not considered decent, proper or appropriate.

contribute to their situation.[3] Immigrants are seen by many as competitors for jobs, housing and welfare services – a challenge that is sometimes considered as equal to violence, crime and delinquency. This implies that the spectrum of actors perceived as causing security problems has become much wider. Their activities have more complex causes and the consequences which they produce in European society appear increasingly difficult to understand. This is in part because of the greater political openness among countries in Europe, freer trade and industrial competition around the world as well as the enormous technological advancements that facilitate communication.

Transnational crime, juvenile delinquency and violence have not only undergone considerable change in the minds of individual Europeans, but are also becoming a concern for governments individually and international organisations collectively such as the United Nations. They find it increasingly difficult to cope with security problems because of the aggravation of objective challenges and a seeming multiplication of subjective expectations for more public safety. Governmental departments responsible for security have become aware of new and growing demands for security and are under constant pressure to improve their services. This is especially the case in urban or industrial regions where the discrepancy between the wealthy and the economically less fortunate or marginalised residents is obvious or where economies in transition create large unemployment. This is the case in almost all of Europe's larger cities. Their residents are also exposed to the greatest stress from increases in theft, violent robbery and juvenile delinquency.[4]

The growing awareness among the public and respective state agencies, such as the police, of the development of deviant and criminal behaviour raises concerns that crime, incivility and violence reflect some characteristics of modern industrialised societies. Indeed, crime trends indicate that

---

3 Expressions such as "lower socio-economic condition", "lower socio-economic neighbourhood", "poorer socio-economic class", "economically less fortunate" or "communities with lower than average income" are mentioned without any kind of moral or political judgement and are used here for the sake of simplicity.
4 KANGASPUNTA, K., M. JOUTSEN and N. OLLUS, *Crime and Criminal Justice Systems in Europe and North America 1990–1994*, Helsinki: European Institute for Crime Prevention and Control, affiliated with the United Nations (HEUNI), 1998; p. xii–xiv.

some types of offences have increased and that most have also changed in character.[5] Particularly noticeable, perhaps, has been the rise of juvenile violence from the mid-1980's and early 1990's onwards in many parts of Europe. Official figures of aggression by youth show an increase of 50 to 100 percent.[6] Some police agencies even claim that the threshold of inhibition to use violence on the part of the young has lowered. The term violence implies both, the criminal use of violence against other persons (bodily injury, robbery, mugging or the threat of violence) and violent behaviour against property (vandalism or arson).[7]

Besides the more common forms of violent behaviour, transnational crime by individuals and organised groups has also grown world-wide.[8] This can be explained in part by the increasing facility for people to communicate and to travel across national borders or over large geographical distances. Technological developments that facilitate new and less expensive means of transportation and communication are a boon not only for global trade and travel, but also for international crime. Thus, the openness of East and Central European countries to travel provide for new trading and illegal trafficking routes for goods and services of all kinds.

5    Recent reports provide evidence of increases of different types of crime. However, most studies warn against taking crime data at face value as statistics are based on offences added up by police who do not establish their records in the same manner across different administrative units and countries. See for example: UNITED NATIONS, *Global Report on Crime and Justice*, Graeme NEWMAN, ed., Office for Drug Control and Crime Prevention, Centre for International Crime Prevention, Oxford: Oxford University Press, 1999; and, KANGASPUNTA, K., M. JOUTSEN and N. OLLUS, *Crime and Criminal Justice Systems in Europe and North America 1990–1994*, Helsinki: European Institute for Crime Prevention and Control, affiliated with the United Nations (HEUNI), 1998.
6    PFEIFFER, Christian, "Jugendkriminalität und Jugendgewalt in europäischen Ländern", Hannover: Kriminologisches Forschungsinstitut Niedersachsen, 1997; and summarized as: "Trends in Juvenile Violence in European Countries" by the National Institute of Justice, U. S. Department of Justice, May 1998.
7    "Robbery" and "mugging" imply theft with the use of violence or the threat of violence.
8    See for example: GODSON, Anna, "EU Enlargement and Organised Crime", in *Outlook 99*, London: Control Risks Group Ltd., January 1999; pp. 62–65; Von DAENIKEN, Urs, "Organisierte Kriminalität in Osteuropa, Einflüsse auf die Schweiz", in STAHEL, Albert A., ed., *Organisierte Kriminalität und Sicherheit*, Bern: Verlag Paul Haupt, 1999.

The entry of Eastern organized crime in the international market, together with the conflict in the Balkans has changed the routes traditionally used. Russia and other East European countries are increasingly becoming the new transit routes for drug trafficking as well as for other criminal purposes, such as car theft in Germany, UK and the Netherlands, and illegal alien smuggling from Southeast Asia.[9]

Most offences that are easily perpetrated by travelling criminals have increased.[10] They are burglary, the theft of cars and trucks, the trafficking of migrants, of drugs, of illegal industrial goods and of women for prostitution. These types of crimes thrive because stolen goods from the West sell profitably in Central and Eastern Europe while, at the same time, Western consumers buy illegal products or pay for services in the grey or black market imported from the East and from developing countries. The result is that there exists an unregulated market in Europe that is difficult to control. It offers, for example, narcotic drugs from around the world, prostitutes from Eastern Europe or from developing countries, very cheap labourers, money laundering services, tax shelters or high profits for shipping companies that export and illicitly dump industrial waste elsewhere.

## Globalisation and perceptions of insecurity

The security debate is closely linked to what is commonly called "globalisation". It has become a much debated and even contested issue since the

---

9  SAVONA, Ernesto, "European Money Trails", in *Transnational Organized Crime*, Vol. 2:4, 1996; p. 3.
10  Studies on the developments of offences by traveling criminals are increasingly being prepared. See for example: SAVONA, Ernesto U. with A. DI NICOLA, and G. DA COL, "Dynamics of Migration and Crime in Europe: New Patterns of an Old Nexus", *Transcrime*, Working Paper No. 8, Trento: Research Group on Transnational Crime, University of Trento, School of Law; October 1996. KREVERT, Peter, "Europäische Einigung und Organisierte Kriminalität: Konzequenzen für Polizei und Nachrichtendienste, Wirtschaft und Gesellschaft", in *Europäische Beiträge zu Kriminalität und Prävention*, Vol. 1, 1998, Münster: Europäisches Zentrum für Kriminalprävention. For Switzerland, see: KILLIAS, Martin, "Immigrants, Crime and Criminal Justice in Switzerland", in: TONRY, Michael, ed., *Ethnicity, Crime, and Immigration: Comparative and cross-national perspectives*, Chicago: The University of Chicago Press, 1997; pp. 59, 63.

second half of the 1990's. One reason that the topic of security figures in many discussions on globalisation is because "we live in a global economy, but the political organisation of our global society is woefully inadequate".[11] We simply do not know (yet?) what the effects of globalisation will be. This development is not merely a post Cold War phenomenon. Trade, the mobility of people and of information began with the first days of commerce across continents. It is only in recent years, however, that globalisation has become a household word. It does not merely imply a boon for industry and trade in some parts of the world, but also a potential force of less desirable changes in society.

> The processes of globalisation have been driven by a number of forces. Worldwide expansion of capitalism and technological progress are at the core of the dynamics [...]. These forces have been in operation for centuries but have increased in scale and intensity in recent decades. [...] The collapse of communism in Europe is only the most dramatic manifestation of this global phenomenon.[12]

One may thus welcome the globalisation of certain political values, such as democratic governance or respect for human rights. They contributed to the end of Soviet-style communism and surely influence societies kept unfree. However, the word globalisation is increasingly used to describe the spread of economic interests around the world which appear to challenge local needs for social security, employment as well as cultural identity. Global trade inevitably affects forms of social, economic and political interaction in both the West and less industrialised parts of the world. Marketing practices and commerce around the world, for example, affect consumption patterns, fashion trends, musical tastes, communication habits and entertainment. All of them influence not only the way we live and work, but even how we identify ourselves and think about our security.

How does globalisation affect internal security? There are essentially four explanations: First, globalisation promotes the spread of values, especially economic ones which shape consumption patterns, desires, expecta-

---

11 Soros, George, *The Crisis of Global Capitalism*, New York: Public Affairs, Perseus Books Group, 1998; p.xix.
12 Ghai, Dharam, "Economic Globalization, Institutional Change and Human Security", Discussion Paper 91, Geneva: United Nations Research Institute for Social Development, 1997; p. 2 & 3.

tions and needs. At the pinnacle of these values is that of personal success especially through wealth. Second, the free movement of information influences not only commerce-induced values, but also the worry about security. Such worry is particularly acute when information on crime, the movements across national borders of clandestine migrants and the trafficking of illegal goods and services are part of daily fare in the media. Third, thanks to international mobility, criminals can more easily engage in transnational crimes and hide themselves or their activities in countries where legal loopholes exist. Finally, the free flow of information reinforces greater and more liberalised economic competition. Combined with the dream of personal wealth, it encourages people almost everywhere to become rich as quickly as possible. But when wealth cannot be obtained easily through legal ways, then illegal means are often chosen.

Most of us are every day exposed to commercial advertising and entertainment. A frequent mention of crime in them can create a more acute sense of awareness of potential dangers and cause feelings of insecurity. This is especially the case for people who already suffer from other forms of stress: insecurity on the job, discrimination, hostility or violence at home, peer pressures at school or at the work-place, or high expectations that, because they are unfulfilled, cause personal disappointment.

What, then, challenges security perceptions most among Europeans? Most often, economic instability combined with high unemployment and insufficient state welfare services are mentioned.[13] Furthermore the European public, especially people who live in poorer socio-economic conditions, increasingly express anxiety about a society that is less secure.[14]

13  In 1998, there was widespread consensus among the public in the European Union with regard to policy priorities: 92% believed that the fight against unemployment should be a priority and 89% of people living in the EU wanted their governments to fight poverty and social exclusion. Other priorities are to maintain peace and security in the greater European region and to fight against organised crime and drug trafficking (both 89%). Taken from: *Eurobarometer 50*, Brussels, March 1999. See further: http://europa.eu.int/comm/dg10/epo/eb/eb52/highlights.html
14  Insecurity feelings have indeed increased with regard to crime and delinquency. A German study confirmed this already in 1994 where comparisons were made with earlier years, see: DÖRMANN, Uwe, *Wie sicher fühlen sich die Deutschen?*, Wiesbaden: Bundeskriminalamt (BKA-Forschungsreihe Band 40), 1996. Regarding France, see: ROBERT, P., R. ZAUBERMAN, M. L. POTTIER and H. LAGRANGE, "Mesurer le crime, entre statistique de police et enquêtes de victimation (1985–1995)" in

The debate on internal security comes alive most clearly where economic and social insecurity are perceived as acute and where the commercial media and politicians are able to capitalise on fears. Crime and violence in the news becomes at once also a source of entertainment and insecurity. Europeans in their majority, however, do not experience violent crimes themselves. Usually, people hear or read about crime and then assess their own situation. In this respect, the news media and the entertainment industry may contribute unintentionally to a sense of insecurity.

Other causes of public insecurity are complaints and debates by politicians who accuse the government of not fighting crime sufficiently or of not responding to public fears. The claim that a national or local government is not providing adequate security for its citizens (whether real or not) implies that the public is not adequately protected. When such claims are made by political opinion-leaders, they may reinforce anxieties and encourage expectations for more government security services. This is mostly visible in election times. Politicians who make internal security or crime fighting a theme of their campaigns can capitalise on public fears to gather support for their cause. More problematic is when political campaigning includes images of asylum seekers and clandestine migrants. Mixing these two social phenomena – public security and migration – lends itself easily to a mix of otherwise distinct issues that can lead to either protectionist fears or more radical anti-foreigner sentiments. This can be observed in the political discourses of several West European political leaders since the early 1990's.

## Internal security

What do we mean by the term "internal security"? It traditionally referred to the territorial state and its geographic border beyond which "inner" should become "outer" and where security is traditionally one-dimensional, i.e. that of military security. In recent years, priorities have changed. The kind of political interests that dominate today's security concerns have little in

*Revue Française de sociologie*, Vol. 40:2, April/June, 1999; pp. 255–294. See also: ROHMER, Hartmut, "Kriminalprävention in NRW als gesamtgesellschaftliche Aufgabe", in *Europäische Beiträge zu Kriminalität und Prävention*, Münster: Europäisches Zentrum für Kriminalprävention, 1998, No. 2; p. 15–16.

common with those up to the late 1980's. Previous security priorities focussed on the prevention of war between the superpowers and their allies, on defence strategies against military invasion and the fight against political subversion. Today, security priorities have shifted. In the forefront, they encompass the prevention of crime, of illegal transnational trafficking and smuggling, the control of clandestine migration and the fight against urban juvenile delinquency. More than merely policing is implied if the new and more complex security concerns are to be addressed. Affected are obviously state authorities responsible for security, but also other ministries and departments. For example, police forces and border guards are obliged to collaborate with asylum and immigration authorities while the integration of new immigrants has become a concern for education ministries and employment services. At the same time, crime prevention implies that police offices must increasingly work together across regions and national borders. Similarly the harmonization of national penal laws and the exchange of criminal intelligence information become necessary among national authorities.[15]

> We must answer to the Europe of Crime with a Europe of Police and a Europe of Judges. In ten years, the regional aspect of criminality and the internationalisation of crime have grown considerably.[16]

Europeans are becoming ever more heterogeneous, multi-cultural and diverse. Consumption habits and life-styles are shared across national borders and every generation seeks to express and identify itself in ever-more liberal ways. The security conditions in one state inevitably affect the safety of the populations in neighbouring countries. Combating both, international crime and local forms of criminality and delinquency implies that national governments cannot avoid any longer to collaborate with each other and with specialised multilateral institutions. Europe's future internal security can only exist when it is developed and maintained across national borders.

---

15 In part from a report prepared by the Swiss Federal Office for Foreigners, 20 August 1998, Die Schweiz und die europäische Sicherheitszusammenarbeit aus der Sicht des Eidg. Justiz und Polizei Departements (EJPD).
16 From an interview with RAMSEYER, Gérard, "Security in Geneva", in: *Geneva News*, February 2000, Vol. 21, No. 1; p. 7.

## Not all challenges to security are assessed equally

There is little doubt that human beings evaluate their safety or security in as many different ways as there are individual persons. Each one assesses his or her own safety depending on factors such as place (a public park, a dark alley), time of day or the possession of valuable items that could be stolen. Insecurity is a feeling based on numerous criteria. These include the impact of violence on society which is strengthened through its wide mediatisation; the ageing of the European indigenous population; growing urbanisation; economic instability particularly among the less well-to-do; local and "visible" criminality; and the effects which wars and poverty in countries not far from Western Europe have on society through the influx of asylum seekers and immigrants.[17]

How people perceive problems related to their safety also depends on personal experiences, the social environment in which they grew up and live as well as what they hear from others or learn from the media. We have all seen vandalised public or private property and graffiti sprayed on walls. We are familiar with the problems caused from excessively loud or reckless behaviour by drunken people or the sight of desecrated grave sites. We have all heard about aggression in schools and violence among emotionally charged crowds at football matches or at political rallies. Furthermore, there are also threats to safety, law and order which are less visible and may not create the same sense of public insecurity. Violence in families, corruption in industry, in government or in sports, as well as fiscal fraud could be counted among the "less visible" challenges to internal security.[18]

This implies that not all challenges to internal security are easy to identify. In fact, many security issues that concern us here are more subjective than objective. What is a security problem to one person may not be so for another. For example, poor lighting in city streets may represent a problem for an elderly person who fears being mugged. For a young man, however,

---

17 In part from an interview with RAMSEYER, Gérard, "Security in Geneva", in: *Geneva News*, February 2000, Vol. 21, No. 1; p. 7.
18 The topic of violence is discussed here only in the context of crime and aggressive behaviour in public. Violence in the family is a serious matter which can influence offensive behaviour among children and adults. However, family violence is not discussed here as it does not directly affect peoples' confidence in public safety or in the internal security of a country.

street lighting is not an issue. Instead, the availability of jobs is far more important. Similarly, some Europeans believe that transnational crime is a very serious problem while for others it is merely a minor consequence of the globalisation of trade, social trends and economic values.

An issue often linked to security is migration and immigration.[19] Many Europeans see the arrival of ever more foreign labourers and immigrants as a potential security problem. This is often because migrants compete for jobs with indigenous workers and contribute to changes in the local or national social and political climate. Indeed, the end of the Cold War has been a catalyst for migration towards Western Europe. Through the 1990's, ever more people in poorer regions of the world have sought better living conditions in the West. However, opportunities for migrant labour in Western Europe have been reduced through the past decade due to higher unemployment figures and economic pressures. One consequence has been that migrants began to opt for clandestine travel. Whether they choose to migrate and live in secret or apply for asylum in the hope to obtain a residency permit largely depends on why they emigrated in the first place.[20]

The arrival of ever more immigrants has many Europeans feeling uneasy. An increasing number of them fear that their countries are becoming the new homes for more and more foreigners (official labourers, clandestines migrants or permanent immigrants).[21] While European goverments individually and the EU collectively have elaborated more stringent asy-

19  For the purpose of clarity, migrants are defined here as persons who have left their home country, who do not have residency permits in any other country. Immigrants are defined as persons who are legally or illegally (clandestinely) in the host country of their choice and have the intention to settle, if not permanently, then at least for an undefined period. This usually implies a time-span in which they can try to acquire a long-term residency permit and/or citizenship (naturalisation).

20  MÜNZ, Rainer, "Phasen und Formen der europäischen Migration", in ANGENENDT, Steffen, ed., *Migration und Flucht*, Bundeszentrale für politische Bildung, Schriftenreihe Band 342, München: Verlag R. Oldenbourg, 1997; pp. 43–44.

21  For example, Swiss citizens judge the role of foreigners in their country as less and less positive since the mid-1970s. (GILOMEN, Heinz: "Die Situation der Ausländischen Bevölkerung in der Schweiz". In BAUHOFER, S. & N. QUELOZ, eds., *Ausländer, Kriminalität und Strafrechtspflege*, Zürich: Verlag Rüegg, 1993.; p. 70). Similar results are also found in Germany where the majority of citizens in the East and the West believe that there are too many immigrants and asylum-seekers. On average since 1989, 64 % of Eastern Germans believe that there are too many immigrants and over 50 % of Western Germans agree with that impression today.

lum regulations and tightened immigration policies, the belief is fairly widespread that they are not taking social indicators, such as political extremism and xenophobia, seriously enough. This impression is evident in several countries where extreme sentiments, political lobbying and violence against foreigners have been part of public expressions. Animosity towards foreigners is growing, even in some countries of Central Europe and in Eastern Germany. This is felt particularly towards immigrants, asylum seekers and clandestine migrants who are not from the same linguistic and cultural background as is the host community.[22]

Regardless of the identity of migrants, the potential security challenges as perceived by the public are rarely the same as problems which affect the stability of a state or of government institutions. Those offences which challenge the state are the kind that affect the reliability of chains of command in administration, in the military or in the police. Minor crimes and infractions, juvenile delinquency and violence in society do not directly threaten government institutions. Rather, the stability of institutions is harmed when their leaders or staff collude with organised crime, criminal trafficking or financial crime. A real danger for security exists when civil servants are involved in corruption which becomes endemic and enmeshed in the day-to-day operations of government offices. Among such practices are: falsifying government documents, licences or personal identification or selling government property for personal profit. These activities invariably undermine a government's administrative operations, its democratic legitimacy and discredit the transparency needed for decision-making and financial accounting. While these offences can represent a serious challenge for the security and stability of a state, they are often remote and of little relevance to ordinary citizens. The public is far more concerned with juvenile violence in school yards, vandalism of public property, a lack of order in public places, or increasing reports of property thefts and burglaries.

Clearly, the sources of public insecurity are as complex as are the reasons for why people engage in offending behaviour and crime. In order to come to grips with these, the causes of deviant, criminal, violent and other forms of offensive behaviour must be identified. It is useful here to mention

---

22 PFEIFFER, Christian, "Guppendrill und Fremdenhass" in *Schweizer Monatshefte*, Vol. 79 / 80, No. 12 / 1, December / January 1999 / 2000; pp. 61–65.

that these causes as well as the sources of subjective insecurity can be found in the following broad phenomena:

(1) Stress of dislocation and instability in families. This may particularly be the case in families that experience difficulties as a result of a divorce or violence in the home. Further stress appears where great differences in behaviour between generations render communication difficult. This is often the case in situations where the younger generation follows trend-setting activities with which parents cannot identify. In families where parents, often immigrants, have not been able to integrated or become familiar with the local society, dislocation between them and their off-spring can also add considerable stress.

(2) Social disintegration among segments of the population has become a serious problem. It has security implications in several large urban areas. This is especially so for communities who find themselves separated from the well-to-do economic and cultural environment in which they want to live. The economically least prosperous communities of indigenous Europeans and immigrants are most affected by the stress from social disintegration. Among them, youth from marginalised indigenous and immigrant communities are the most vulnerable. They often lack a social and educational context that provides them with a sense of purpose. The attitude that reflects such a development of socio-economic disintegration in these sectors of our society can be portrayed as follows:

> If there are no jobs, why not smoke pot, go to rave parties, steal cars to go on joy rides, mug old women, beat up rival gangs and, if need be, kill. [...] Young men, increasingly young women too, and many who are not so young see no reason to abide by allegedly prevailing rules which for them are the rules of others. They opt out of a society which has pushed them to the margin already. They become a threat. Those who can afford it, pay for their protection. [...] Those who cannot afford protection become victims.[23]

(3) An aspect of dislocation and disintegration which may contribute to marginalising still more people is the accelerating pace of technological developments as driven by the free market economy. It affects some

---

23 DAHRENDORF, Ralf, "Economic Opportunity, Civil Society and Political Liberty", Discussion Paper No. 58, Geneva: United Nations Research Institute for Social Development, 1995; p. 12.

families and communities more than others. Those fortunate enough to have the financial means and the appropriate education to adapt to new professional demands can often even benefit from rapid economic change. However, not everybody is able to keep up. As changes are ever greater and faster, more and more families may find themselves unable to follow. The greater the rift between those who seem to have everything and those who do not, the higher the risk becomes that subjective insecurity and anti-foreigner sentiments increase and that political voices become polarised in the competition for public support.

## The European context

The process of democratisation in Central and Eastern Europe and the globalisation of trade and industrial competition has set in motion a wave of integration in many parts of Europe. It is to a great extent encouraged by the European Union's own integration. Many, if not most former communist countries in Central and Eastern Europe wish to join the EU as soon as possible. For them, political and economic reforms have not only led to more freedom for individual citizens. It has also made people aware that security is no longer provided by a fixed political regime and a planned economy.

European countries in the East and the West are becoming part of a world-wide web of trade, politics and values. Societies become more interdependent – hence also more sensitive to change happening elsewhere and challenges coming from neighbouring countries. Such growing together affects patterns of production, consumption and life-style from which shared concerns about internal security cannot be separated. One country's security is, in a way, a function of another's behaviour – not merely behaviour that reaches beyond its national border, but also that which is purely domestic. Included in this study are therefore all European countries which share the following general characteristics:[24]

24 In part from: KREVERT, Peter, "Europäische Einigung und Organisierte Kriminalität: Konzequenzen für Polizei und Nachrichtendienste, Wirtschaft und Gesellschaft", in *Europäische Beiträge zu Kriminalität und Prävention*, Vol. 1, 1998, Münster: Europäisches Zentrum für Kriminalprävention; p. 1; and MOHLER, Markus, "Les expériences de la Suisse en matière de coopération policière...", in BIEBER, Roland, A.-C. LYON and J. MONAR, eds., *Justice et affaires intérieures – L'Union européenne et la Suisse*, Bern: Staempfli Editions SA, 1997; p. 131.

- They realise common commitments to the Universal Declaration of Human Rights of the United Nations and the European Convention on Human Rights.
- They uphold, or are on the way to becoming democracies which permit citizen participation in elections subject to a rule of law defined in a constitution which is guarded by an independent judiciary.
- These same countries profess to guarantee individual privacy, the freedom of speech, of movement and of travel as well as a free press or media.
- These countries have, or are in the process of developing open markets according to capitalist principles.
- The populations within this European region all share a sensitivity to migration and immigration.
- Their national police and crime intelligence agencies increasingly collaborate with each other to pursue suspected offenders. They are all in a process of harmonising their criminal laws and the management of their criminal intelligence.
- These same countries have entered into or are developing agreements either bilaterally with member countries of the EU or directly with the European Union that specifically refer to the need for closer collaboration in matters of police competence along with cross-border facilities for criminal investigations and pursuit.
- This region also shares specific characteristics of public insecurity as a consequence to developments in crime, violence and clandestine migration.
- Finally, because of the similarities and shared political, economic and social changes in the region, these countries also recognise the need to promote public confidence in the police and in respective national as well as EU-wide security agencies. This requires a greater harmonisation of crime prevention initiatives, police training facilities and the development of a common understanding of the causes of crime and violence among their populations.

All this means that the Western, Central and Eastern European states form a distinct group of countries characterised by a liberal, democratic and free-market system. To the extent that their borders are opened and obstructions to trade are reduced, chances for law-breaking may also rise. As a result,

Europe is increasingly becoming an integrated region subject to many shared and often linked criminalistic characteristics. These include local developments of juvenile delinquency and violence in society as well as international organised crime and trafficking. The transnational aspect of these developments increasingly links this European region to Russia and other Republics of the former Soviet Union, China, Asia, the Middle East, Africa and Latin America.[25] In reaction to these developments, these same European countries all make great efforts to reform their national police forces. They realise a need to develop crime prevention methods that focus not merely on fighting crime, but bring the police closer to the public to help people feel more secure.

A development which should also be mentioned here are the political, economic and social developments brought about by the gradual integration of European Union institutions. Political and economic incentives for the creation of several Agreements, including the Union itself, the Schengen Agreement or the Treaty of Amsterdam, require that appropriate security institutions and migration policies are added. The four freedoms provided within the EU (free movement of persons, services, goods and capital) facilitate mobility, but they also make is easier for economic migrants and offenders to travel across borders.[26] The Treaty of Amsterdam, is meant to coordinate EU-wide security provisions such as border-controls, asylum regulations, policing and judicial co-operation.


## Why look at Switzerland?

Switzerland is considered in more detail in this study for several reasons: The country enjoys the same liberal, democratic system and a market economy as its neighbours. Nestled in the centre of Europe, Switzerland is at

---

25 Information taken in part from: KREVERT, Peter, "Europäische Einigung und Organisierte Kriminalität: Konzequenzen für Polizei und Nachrichtendienste, Wirtschaft und Gesellschaft", in *Europäische Beiträge zu Kriminalität und Prävention*, Vol. 1, 1998, Münster: Europäisches Zentrum für Kriminalprävention; p. 1 & 2.

26 PELINKA, Anton and Brigitte HALBMAYR, *EU – Osterweiterung und österreichische Sicherheitspolitik*, Endbericht, Wien, Institut für Konfliktforschung, July 1998; p. 6.

once a full participant (willing or unwilling) in European criminalistic developments while remaining politically and institutionally an "island". It is surrounded by the security, asylum/immigration and crime-prevention mechanisms of the EU and its member countries. This means that it must continuously balance its policing and crime prevention policies between demands by the Swiss population for autonomous security institutions and the obvious need to collaborate more closely with the EU in security matters. How, under such circumstances, Switzerland can develop its crime prevention methods, assess its internal security and adjust to the events in the wider European area is not only interesting for Swiss readers. It is also important for future analyses on the collaboration among security efforts between EU and non-EU Europeans.

Sharing security work requires a degree of integration in political and legal spheres which cannot be carried out effectively through closed political borders or inflexible institutional barriers. The EU plays an increasingly significant role in the development of regional crime prevention and law enforcement. Its Schengen Agreement, the Dublin Convention and Europol are among its principal institutional developments which advance the Union's crime prevention not only within its borders, but also beyond it. The EU's neighbouring countries are under the influence of the Union's constant policy changes that concern internal security as well as all other spheres where regulations are imposed, such as in business, health care and social services. Sometimes neighbours are asked to adapt their domestic policies (criminal and taxation laws, banking regulations, etc.) to those which the EU recommends – Switzerland is no exception. It cannot afford to remain isolated with regard to security-related policies even if its citizens refuse to fully join the European Union.

# Chapter 2
# Sources of Insecurity

The following chapter attempts to show how subjective our understanding of security is. It begins with a discussion on our assessment of security and how it is influenced by the socio-economic environment specific to European society.

The confidence of Europeans in the internal security of their country and in their personal safety has become more fragile in recent years. The following example may illustrate this: crime in Europe rose gradually ever since the 1960's, but the general fear which the public feels has increased sharply only since the end of the Cold War.[27] The "fear of crime is increasing [...], even in a time of (almost) stable official crime rates."[28] Taking the example of Germany, this change of perception was such that in 1992, 42% of the public were dissatisfied with the police's fight against crime.[29] The fear of becoming a victim of crime rose steadily and so did the concomitant subjective insecurity. By 1995, about 50% of citizens believed that they could not fully trust the police to fight crime as it should.[30] In other words,

---

27  JASCHKE, Hans-Gerd, "Eine verunsicherte Institution: Die Polizei in der Auseinandersetzung mit Rechtsextremismus und Fremdenfeindlichkeit", in HEITMEYER, Wilhelm, *Das Gewalt-Dilemma*, Frankfurt am Main: Suhrkamp Verlag, No. es1905, 1994; p. 305.

28  FELTES, Thomas, "Pro-active Prevention: An Efficient Police Tool?", in KÜHNE, Hans-Heiner and Koichi MIYAZAWA, eds., *Internal security in modern industrialized societies*, Baden-Baden: Nomos Verlagsgesellschaft; p. 182.

29  JASCHKE, Hans-Gerd, 1994, Op. cit.; pp. 305 & 344. See also, for example: SCHLOTH, Stephanie, "Irgend etwas nimmt immer mehr zu: Kriminalitätsfurcht und Kriminalität", in *Vorgänge*, No. 124, 32. Jahrgang, Dezember 1993, Heft 4; pp. 87–89, and 95.

30  According to the "Allensbacher Umfrage" quoted in: WASSERMANN, Rudolf, "Kriminalität und Sicherheitsbedürfnis: Zur Bedrohung durch Gewalt und Kriminalität in Deutschland", in *Aus Politik und Zeitgeschichte*, No.B23, 2 June 1995; p. 5. A majority of those Germans questioned in another recent study furthermore believed that most types of crime will increase and that the risk of becoming a victim will be greater in five to ten years than it is today. See: WITTKÄMPER, Gerhard W., P. KREVET and A. KOHL, *Europa und die Innere Sicherheit*, Wiesbaden: Bundeskriminalamt (BKA) Forschungsreihe Nr. 35, 1996.

public perceptions of security and actual objective security conditions diverge ever more.

A reason for this divergence is no doubt the change which the notion of security has undergone in the public mind. What Europeans understand by security relates most generally to the confidence which they have in their national governments. The notion of security, in particular as it concerns the expression "internal security", has also become increasingly diversified in the sense of both the overall security that the state offers to society and the feeling of personal safety of the citizen. In the combination of these two, the debate is much more complex. It contrasts with what used to be major security concerns of both state and citizen, namely external aggression by a foreign power. As mentioned in the previous chapter, internal security is now considered to encompass such diverse issues as economic security, the prevention of all forms of crime and violence as well as social security.

## Perceptions of insecurity

One of the principal sources of public discomfort and insecurity is disorder in open spaces such as streets, city parks or inner cities. This is especially so when disorderly behaviour by some individuals is easily observed and commented on by onlookers, the media and the majority of ordinary citizens. Garbage left in public places, graffiti, loitering youth in streets or in shops, vandalism visible by smashed windows, spoiled flower beds in city parks or broken public telephones as well as excessive noise from partying or aggressive begging: these manifestations of a seemingly growing disorder trigger increasing resentment among the general public. It may gradually consider such disorder or disorderly behaviour as a threat to the quality of life and to security. One consequence is public disappointment with government services, especially those responsible for law and order.

The police can become the object of public disapproval when it is perceived as being incapable of coping with new or more intensified forms of disorder and crime. In fact, the public in Europe increasingly asks for more safety. Once it begins to see crime as a potentially unmanageable problem for society, some political parties may play on this source of anxiety and demand rapid action. Such calls can be for more police officers in the streets, "zero tolerance" towards small offenders, a drastic reduction of immigration, fewer resident foreigners or harsher punishments for convicted offenders (regardless of their age).

However, slogans that propose simple measures against perceived threats to public safety do little to actually improve security. Rather, arguments in favour of quick measures tend to heighten expectations for better government/police services (such as more crime fighting capacities). They may cause greater disillusionment, especially when the media report on new waves of crime and immigrants. Deep differences in opinion about why public safety is an issue and how to improve it can indicate that long-running security issues have not been resolved by the existing political institutions. Such is the case in several European countries; political discourse risks becoming polarised.

Security-related problems (whether imagined or real) that directly affect the citizen's feelings of safety are liable to be exploited by special interest groups or individual politicians. A heightened fear that society may become less safe incites the public to demand stronger leadership and tougher measures to fight crime or eliminate disorderly behaviour. In a mutually reinforcing manner, the more political leaders call for greater security, the more the public feels insecure and demands more rapid action. A spiral of declining confidence in internal security may ensue and can be seen as a "continuum of threats".[31] It points to three things: First, public confidence in national security institutions or the local police is fragile. Second, the public's feelings about security depend directly on how these institutions deal with visible and acute problems. And third, the government's failure to act quickly to alleviate the most visible problems as perceived by the public can have long-lasting consequences. One consequence is that continued denunciations by some politicians of the government's failure to provide adequate safety increases public distrust in security institutions. Another consequence is that in an increasingly polarised debate about how to address security complaints, the underlying causes of offensive and criminal behaviour which should be addressed are forgotten. Instead, simple and sometimes radical solutions come to dominate political debate about how to provide public security.

Quick solutions for complex social and behavioural problems are difficult to come by. Instead, approaches to solving security problems, whether

31 BIGO, Didier, *Police en réseaux*, Paris: Presses de Sciences Po, 1996; pp. 258–267.

objective or subjective, require time to develop and to show results. The development of any such problem-solving approach demands that both security and sources of insecurity are understood in the first place. The discussion below is meant to contribute to such understanding.

## The context of security and insecurity

The concept of security contains many different expectations and needs. We want reliable and predictable government services and we expect them to prevent our society from becoming disorderly, chaotic or violent. We want to be confident in the predictability of our own personal future, the stability of our society or, more ambitiously, the future of mankind. We also want security in an objective sense; i.e., the absence of thieves, rowdy teenagers or international mafiosi traffickers. In daily life this means: no burglar should enter our house even when we leave the door wide open, the bicycle or the car will not be stolen when left unlocked and our children will never meet dubious characters who sell marijuana or ecstasy. Is such an expectation realistic, however?

The notion of security is based on the feeling that there is something which endures all through the days and changes in life. We work to ensure the continuity and safety of our health, our families, homes and our society. Fear is the result of the unpredictable or the unknown. We never know objectively whether our society, the family or our health is secure. There are elements in our society which we consider to cause more insecurity than others. That is true for political instability, high unemployment, economic crises or high rates of crime. The reason why crime causes the immediate sensations of danger is because it is frightfully unpredictable. It is tangible and many of us have personal experiences of theft, seeing the consequences of aggression among teenagers or violence between criminal gangs. The fear of crime will always have a much higher emotive resonance than, say, the fear of nation-wide economic instability.

The way in which the word "security" is used here applies either to things or to persons. The security of things is most often that of our financial savings or property. For the security of these, certain steps can be undertaken to minimise risk and dangers such as robbery, losing the house to a fire or being dispossessed of all savings due to hyper inflation. To prevent

44

theft, we can lock the door, to stop a fire, we can install automatic extinguishers, and to keep our savings, we invest in various currencies, precious commodities or land.

Security for people, however, is different. We may guard against illness by living healthily, but whether we feel safe depends primarily on our subjective assessment. One person may suffer from a disease, but otherwise be content and feel safe, while another person with the same disease may feel terribly insecure. Security or insecurity is the result of an evaluation of preferences or expectations (health, comfort, freedom, professional stability, respect in society, safety from crime, etc.) and how we obtain these in relation to the context in which they are available. When our individual preferences (but also those of the state or of society as a whole) are in conflict with what is available and we find no ready solutions, a sense of bewilderment, apprehension or insecurity sets in.

There are no easy ways to reconcile our personal feelings of fear with the objective difficulties of crime prevention. We expect personal freedom and privacy, but we also want the police to identify and control the activities of suspected criminals. There is no easy solution either for overcoming the contradiction between what we know confidently to be a security risk and what we feel to be a risk. Is a risk or a danger merely imagined or is it real? Is it necessary to install a burglar alarm in the apartment or to carry a gun for self-defence? Thus, security may be objective (avoiding a known danger – "don't let the children accept candies from strangers") just as it may be subjective (feeling safe in a busy train station). Moreover, we can never be entirely free of doubt – "do I have the confidence that I understand the risks and will not overstep my freedom?".

A risk is seen or felt according to the social environment in which security is assessed. There are four sources of risks to our security: (1) the risk to health and physical integrity, such as illness, injury and death; (2) the risk of losing personal integrity and freedom because of imprisonment or a denial of civil liberties; (3) economic risks, such as the loss of employment, of property or the destruction of industrial assets; and (4), the risk of losing position or status in society or self-esteem.[32] This last one is perhaps the

---

32 In part from: Buzan, Barry, *People, States and Fear*, Hertfordshire, UK: Harvester Wheatsheaf, 2nd edition, 1991; p. 37.

most difficult to identify as each person evaluates his or her own position according to a personal degree of confidence. Confidence in security is variously defined by the social, cultural and historical context in which people live. The context is the environment, so to speak, in which recent historical developments (a), socio-economic conditions (b) and the consumer society (c) influence the manner in which people assess risks and personal security. These three contextual influences are discussed below:

First (a), recent historical events affects the degree to which the general public may feel secure or insecure. For example, the opening of international borders to Central and Eastern Europe after 1989 represented a significant development. It produced unforeseen consequences from which the West was shielded when the Iron Curtain still existed. Perhaps most unsettling to many Europeans is the impression that with the greater mobility of migrants from the East who search for employment, crime now also comes to the West. Other related historical developments are the political and legal transformations which former communist countries initiate today. These are often undertaken in very difficult conditions and much economic instability. Many former state industries have closed, unemployment has risen and government budgets are forever too small for the political and security reforms needed. The difficulty to adapt quickly enough to new criminalistic conditions has led to the rapid growth of corruption and organised crime in some of the transition economies.

Second, (b) socio-economic conditions produce insecurity where people are confronted with stark differences of life-style and living conditions. The gap between rich and poor within European societies as well as between Western states and populations in the former communist East or in developing countries is significant. The temptation for quick wealth is enormous where people in economically dire straits suddenly find themselves faced with the material riches of the wealthy. This divide between the "have's" and the "have not's" is an important source of insecurity for both. Economically privileged communities feel insecure because they fear losing their wealth to crime while the disadvantaged in both, the West and the East, are insecure because they fear losing their jobs or never finding one at all, or they worry about their social welfare benefits.

The greatest threat to economically least fortunate is economic and social exclusion. This form of physical and often mental marginalisation increases today as the discrepancy in wealth grows. During the economically

46

prosperous 1960's to 1980's, Europeans became accustomed to an extensive welfare system. Now, these same people and their children must grapple with large national deficits that are, to some extent, the consequence of social services too generous for the economies of the 1980's and 1990's.[33] Similarly, Central and East Europeans must often live with reduced government services since the end of the communist state. Many welfare provisions have been reduced and citizens find themselves thrown out of a context which, while politically rigid, was socially secure.

Third, (c) consumerism provides the context in which violence, in its various manifestations and thanks to the ever-present media, has become almost daily fare.[34] With a mixture of both fear and fascination, observance and obsession, it is part of daily life in wide circles of modern societies – both in the industrialised and in the other parts of the world. It is reputed to happen always everywhere to the extent that television and movies have made delinquencies commonplace. The underlying, often complex, origins and causes of violent or offending behaviour are easily lost. Whether reported as existing in poorer urban suburbs, marginalised city quarters, in local schools, and whether perpetrated by drug addicts, mafia-gangs or suspected "Islamic fundamentalists", the images violence and crime continuously nourish the public's insecurity and fascination.[35] It appears, then, that insecurity can be a by-product of a particular life-style.

But how is "feeling safe and confident" to be interpreted when we speak of internal security? Threats and risks will always remain vague to some extent because we never know whether we understand them well enough. "The subjective feeling of safety or confidence has no necessary connec-

---

33  MIEGEL, Meinhard, "Wachsender Wohlstand, zunehmende Enttäuschung", in *Merkur*, Deutsche Zeitschrift für europäisches Denken, Vol. 52 (Jahrgang), No. 5, May 1998; p. 434.

34  For a debate on the effect violence in the media has on society, see: SANDER, Uwe, "Beschleunigen Massenmedien durch Gewaltdarstellungen einen gesellschaftlichen Zivilisationsverlust?" in HEITMEYER, Wilhelm, *Das Gewalt-Dilemma*, Frankfurt am Main: Suhrkamp Verlag, No. es1905, 1994; pp. 273–293. Also, see: SCHUBARTH, Wilfred, "Jugendprobleme in den Medien", in *Aus Politik und Zeitgeschichte*, (Beilage zur Wochenzeitung *Das Parlament*, B31/98, 24 July, 1998; pp. 29–36.

35  WIEVIORKA, Michel, "Le nouveau paradigme de la violence", in *Cultures & Conflits*, No. 29–30, Printemps/été 1998; p. 16.

tion with actually being safe or right."[36] For the individual or for society, to understand where *objective* (actual) security has its limits and where *subjective in*security takes over is not merely impossible to comprehend; it is a real dilemma for individuals as well as for the police. Since it is impossible to know for sure whether the security services provided by a government are adequate, and since people can never know for a fact whether their feelings of insecurity correspond to objective risks and dangers, both, state and individual, are left guessing.

Government efforts to provide internal security are usually limited to the objective aim of establishing law and order. A development of subjective security is not often seen as part of a state's responsibility. The fight against crime – whether it is against small delinquency or high-level international organised crime – represents a constant effort on the part of the state. It requires increasingly thorough investigations using ever more sophisticated technological tools. But whether policing efforts actually reassure the public about security is a matter of individual assessment.

Like our assessment of security, our understanding of violence is also individually and often culturally determined. We are taught to regard violence as either something that is by definition bad, or as something that occasionally may be justified. When people use violence to try to resolve a dispute or conflict, it is an expression of personal dissatisfaction and exasperation when other possibilities for communication seem to be unavailable.[37] A parent hitting his or her child as part of a punishment is a fairly common occurrence – physical force here is justified in terms of "teaching a lesson that will not be forgotten". However, most of us disapprove with this practice today, but that would not have been the case a couple of generations ago. This indicates that our view of the use of physical force has changed over time. Only recently, physical punishment was still accepted

36 BUZAN, Barry, *People, states and Fear*, Hertfordshire, UK: Harvester Wheatsheaf, 2nd edition, 1991; p. 36.
37 SCHWIND, Hans-Dieter, J. BAUMANN, U. SCHNEIDER and M. WINTER, *Ursachen, Prävention und Kontrolle von Gewalt* (Gewaltkommission), *Summary of the Final Report of the Independent Governmental Commission the Prevention and Control of Violence*, Berlin: Duncker & Humblot, 1990; p. 464.

in most schools. The death sentence – the ultimate form of officially sanctioned violence – is still accepted in most countries around the world.[38]

While notions change over time of the kinds of physical force or violence that can be justified, modern commercial culture has produced a new kind of societal contradiction. We are (justly) intolerant towards violence and crime in real life, but both are adored in virtual life. Violence on television, in movies and other forms of entertainment and commercial advertising constitutes an affront to the values which we claim to espouse in our daily behaviour. We are increasingly calling "violent" all those abrasive acts which hurt other people (or animals) physically or mentally and which we consider unjustified or unfair. Some experts in the matter go further and define violence as "anything avoidable that impedes human self-realization".[39] How self-realisation is defined remains up to each individual. Governments are merely expected to establish criminal laws, control their observance and assure that each person can enjoy the greatest possible freedom in a safe environment.

## Contradiction in searching for security

There seems to be a contradiction between the expectations we have from our government for security – i.e. to control the behaviour of potential offenders – and the life-style we choose. We desire to be perfectly safe while asking for maximum freedom. Control implies that the very nature of behaviour remain constant and that unpredictable changes are eliminated. The contradiction lies still deeper, though, than the mere conflict between the *desire* for security and the *fact* of change. To be secure means not only to halt change, but also to isolate (fences around private property or around countries) and fortify oneself, one's society and one's country.

---

38  SCHNEIDER, Hans Joachim, "La violence en milieu scolaire", in *Interpol: Revue internationale de police criminelle*, No. 456, 1996; pp. 26–27.

39  This definition could even include the pollution of the natural environment as this will invariably impede the future of human well-being. This expression is from Johan Galtung, quoted in: RUPESINGHE, Kumar, "Forms of Violence and its Transformation", in *The Culture of Violence*, RUPESINGHE, K, and M. RUBIO C., eds., Tokyo, New York: United Nations University Press, 1994; p. 23.

High security walls around luxury residential "gated" communities, or the attempt to render the outer EU border impenetrable for unwanted individuals (clandestine migrants and criminals) is a form of self-isolation. Such isolation may in fact inrease fear of the "other", the neighbour, the stranger or the foreigner. The more security we want in our society, the more we might be afraid of those who come from outside and hence, we may desire still more security.

> To put it more plainly: the desire for security and the feeling of insecurity are the same thing. To hold your breath is to lose your breath. A society based on the quest for security is nothing but a breath-retention contest [...]. We look for this security by fortifying and enclosing ourselves in innumerable ways. We want the protection of being 'exclusive' and 'special', seeking to belong to the safest church, the best nation, the highest class, the right set, and the 'nice people'. These defences lead to divisions between us, and so to more insecurity demanding more defences.[40]

The effort to achieve greater security can, in other words, become self-defeating. A greater police presence or tightened controls at the country's border may be objectively successful (more criminals get caught). However, they risk raising awareness "to such a pitch that felt insecurity is greater than before the measures were undertaken. [...] Paranoia is the logical endpoint of obsession with security"[41]

Those public authorities and security agencies which are expected to "offer" security, find themselves under constant pressure to improve their "product" or their service. In the private security sector, it is not difficult to imagine that competition drives specialised firms to promote their services by finding gaps in the "security market". As in the market place for other services, customers can be found where the service offered appears convincing and necessary.

---

40  Watts, Alan, *The Wisdom of Insecurity*, London: Rider, Ebury Press, Random House, 1993; p. 71–72.
41  Buzan, Barry, *People, states and Fear*, Hertfordshire, UK: Harvester Wheatsheaf, 2nd edition, 1991; p. 37. Also, see: Schubarth, Wilfred, "Jugendprobleme in den Medien", in *Aus Politik und Zeitgeschichte*, (Beilage zur Wochenzeitung *Das Parlament*, B31/98, 24 July, 1998; pp. 29–36.

While government agencies are not subject to competition for market share, they appear increasingly under pressure for approval from the public. When government agencies (police, border guards, criminal investigation offices, the military) can constantly show their ability to improve their services, then the reward is not to be confronted with critical media reports that accuse them of laxity. The news media represent a formidable force of opinion when they tell stories that relate safety problems. For example, spectacular seizures of narcotics or traffickers, criminals who committed horrible acts, gangs of hooligans who terrorise the public at sports stadiums, etc. Public reaction to most reporting on crime and police work tends to be negative; i.e., there will always be too much crime, too little policing and insufficiently hard punishment for convicted offenders.

## Conclusion

The desire for more security is endless; one never knows whether the present condition is the best that can be obtained. Essentially then, security as perceived by the public is to be understood as a subjective assessment of the absence of known threats and of contradictions between preferences (desires and expectations). At the root of this assessment lies the comparison between what is desired and what is perceived as being reality; i.e., how each person evaluates their situation in the context of their personal life, recent historical events and socio-economic changes. We can thus summarise that "the greater the rift becomes between the world as it is and the world as we imagine and want it to be, the more heightened becomes our sense of basic insecurity".[42] Here lies the fear of the unpredictable and uncontrollable. Crime or "floods" of asylum seekers are commonly seen as unpredictable phenomena. They instil in us a sense of helplessness at best and paranoia at worst.

---

42 BATCHELOR, Stephen, *Alone with Others*, New York: Grove Press, Inc., 1983; p. 100.

Chapter 3

# Challenges to Internal Security

This chapter presents various challenges to internal security in Europe to-day. They include: juvenile delinquency, group violence, hooliganism, transnational and organised crime, terrorism and public confidence in the police. While many other challenges to security could be added to the list, such as environmental pollution, computer hacking or the spread of flu viruses, only those are addressed below which figure most prominently in public debate. They are considered as "challenging" because they are likely to influence public feelings about security in society.

After discussing particular challenges, we briefly attempt to assess whether and how problems for internal security might arise. We do this by asking "who is affected" by perceived or actual security problems. We begin with the more visible and perhaps most fear-inducing challenges to security perceptions, namely those forms of deviance which are most frequently mentioned in the commercial media.

## Deviant, un-civil and aggressive behaviour in public

Many will agree with the complaint that social discipline, law and order are not what they used to be. Incidences of small deviant and uncivil forms of behaviour, especially by juveniles and children, are debated far more often today in the news media, in television talk-shows and in newspapers than a generation ago. The effects and consequences of delinquency are visible almost everywhere, particularly in big cities. We are familiar with graffiti on public buildings, excessive noise at large parties or rowdy and threatening behaviour by groups of youngsters in public transportation. Society's tolerance towards un-civil behaviour is often felt to be too great. Only when a number of people become the victims of deviant behaviour and once the media begin to report more frequently about it, then the general public begins to take notice.

53

The spraying of graffiti by children on public walls is an example. All too long, politicians, the public and the police paid little or no attention. Only in communities where complaints became too numerous for local governments to ignore, have counter-measures been taken. The situation is similar with other forms of deviant behaviour. Juvenile delinquency and violence by children and young adults has always existed. However, wider public attention has, since the mid-1980's, consistently risen in most European countries.[43] The search for solutions began with various counter-measures that often include the dispatch of more police officers, zero tolerance policing, evening curfews for youth, metal detectors in schools or harsher punishments for convicted juvenile offenders. Such measures, however, merely touch the surface of far deeper and often socially and economically determined causes.

Whether in Europe or elsewhere, the motives of behaviour for each person are usually a result of a shared cultural heritage, traditions and customs. Everybody is expected to abide by social or civil norms in his or her behaviour so as not to negatively affect the family's and the society's general well-being. These norms include a degree of tolerance by which all members can accept one another as part of a common social order. However, with seemingly greater permissiveness in society, youngsters are tempted to see forbidden activities as a kind of sport or entertainment. A lack of family, social and educational structures may partially be the cause of such behaviour.

Groups of teenagers who linger in streets or shopping centres are not an unfamiliar sight. We may even feel a sensation of fear when encountering youngsters who seem to look for excitement by engaging in delinquent activities. Some of them are indeed bored and find little to do to fill their days and evenings. It is in this context that teenagers may run the risk of becoming involved in impulsive offending or gang-like behaviour that bor-

---

43 The rise of juvenile offences was studies by Ch. Pfeiffer in: Austria, Denmark, France, Germany, Italy, Poland and the Netherlands. The united States is also included in the same study where juvenile crime and violence, as measured by the police and the judiciary, have also increased. See: PFEIFFER, Christian, "Jugendkriminalität und Jugendgewalt in europäischen Ländern", Hannover: Kriminologisches Forschungsinstitut Niedersachsen, 1997. (Summary in English by the National Institute of Justice, U. S. Dept. of Justice, under the title "Trends in Juvenile Violence in European Countries", May 1998).

ders on the criminal. In many inner cities, suburbs, *"Stadtviertel"* and *"banlieues"*, juvenile offences and youth violence have become a serious problem. Local residents, school teachers and social workers as well as the police are all affected.[44]

For many teenagers, especially those from socially or economically marginalised communities, disregarding social or traditional barriers of civil behaviour is precisely the "fun" aspect which promises excitement. Among groups of kids who have a tendency to value rule breaking, running the risk of punishment by committing a crime is considered praiseworthy. Peer pressure adds for many youngsters a sense of belonging to a group by daring to rebel against what seems a boring "normal" society and thus becoming its outcasts.

Three characteristics are common among juveniles that have been convicted for an offence. First, they come mostly from families who have a lower than average socio-economic living standard. Second, they mostly live in urban neighbourhoods and inner cities where living conditions are less favourable. Third, they often come from families in which they experienced violence. "They were beaten, their siblings were beaten, or one of the parents was beaten".[45] Besides these three characteristics, delinquent youngsters from immigrant families often have one added difficulty. They must integrate in the host society of their peers while maintaining the link with their parents' traditional society and customs.

The higher the density of the residents in suburban blocks, the greater becomes their exposure to stress and social tensions. Their risk of involvment in crime either as victims of aggressive behaviour or as offenders themselves is also higher.[46] This causes insecurity for a large proportion of

44  See for example: DUBET, François and Didier LAPEYRONNIE, *Les Quartiers d'Exil*, Paris: Éditions du Seuil, 1992.
45  Quoted from the Summary of: PFEIFFER, Christian, "Trends in Juvenile Violence in European Countries" (Hannover: Kriminologisches Forschungsinstitut Niedersachsen 1997), as published by the National Institute of Justice, U. S. Dept. of Justice, May 1998; p. 2.
46  This is discussed on the basis of a victimisation study published by: ROBERT, P., R. ZAUBERMAN, M. L. POTTIER and H. LAGRANGE, "Mesurer le crime, entre statistique de police et enquêtes de victimation (1985–1995)" in *Revue Française de sociologie*, Vol. 40:2, April/June, 1999; pp. 255–294. See also confirmation of this in: PFEIFFER, Christian, "Jugendkriminalität und Jugendgewalt in europäischen Ländern", Hannover: Kriminologisches Forschungsinstitut Niedersachsen, 1997; pp. 43–46.

the public, especially for those who live and work in urban regions where socio-economic conditions and living standards are lower than average. What is more, the greatest risk that children and teenagers learn to engage in impulsive offending or in periodic crime exists in just these communities. This must be taken seriously. It is there that economic conditions are not only poor, but that the families concerned are also to varying degrees marginalised from society. Being marginalised means feeling ignored or even discriminated against by the majority of local residents or by the national population. This may be due, for example, to unemployment (of one or both parents), the inability to afford holidays and sports activities which other children and adults enjoy or because of an ethnic or linguistic "difference".

Among youth from marginalised families, criminalisation (as different from mere impulsive delinquency) begins often among the groups of semi-bored teenagers. At first, teenagers and young adults (who are perhaps addicted to drugs, do not attend school or are unemployed) act on impulse to sell or steal something. But with experience and contacts (buyers of stolen goods or suppliers of drugs), they risk becoming, what one may call "episodic" offenders; that is, they commit offences at fairly regular intervals. They may do so because they find no other means of earning pocket money, because they have become addicted to drugs and need to steal to support the habit, or because they were not given educational and vocational training opportunities to find interesting jobs. Through contacts with "adult" criminal organisations, these young offenders may then find their "street jobs", i.e., selling illegal goods (most often drugs) or stealing (electronic equipment or cars).

> The "level of crime is determined by the joint influence of motivational factors such as the prevalence of socio-economic strain among the population and of the here-and-now presence of criminal opportunities. Relevant indicators of strain are the employment rate and, more directly, the proportion of young males who are dissatisfied with their financial situation."[47]

47 Van DIJK, Jan J. M. and John van KERSTEREN, "Criminal victimization in European cities", in *European Journal on Criminal Policy and Research*, Vol. 4, No. 1, 1996; p. 16.

The conditions for entry into criminal activities are particularly promising in areas of Europe where major industries have suffered a large decline and where employment and training prospects for teenagers and young adults are insufficient. This is the case in many former industrial towns of Central and Eastern Europe, in former East Germany, but is also the case in some parts of Western Europe as well.[48] Looting, crime and small delinquency are on the rise. An illustrative example, but by far not an isolated case, is the rioting and youth violence that erupted following the beating to death of a boy by police in the town of Slupsk, Poland, in January 1998. This region, like so many others, suffers from 25% unemployment. Salaries of workers are far below that of employees in the economically more prosperous cities where private entrepreneurship is creating new jobs. "The old social nets of communism, dependable if minimal, are no longer free. After-school programs are for those who can afford them. Bored youths, more often than not, are left to their own devices".[49]

This tells us that wherever economic pressures are high and the population cannot have access to certain needs, such as vocational training that is suited to new industries, employment opportunities as well as interesting leisure-time activities, there exists a greater risk of criminalisation. This is true for all European countries. All have areas in cities and older or stagnant industrial towns in which lower economic development characterises a particular community. The chance that youngsters and adults from these areas become involved in small delinquencies or in serious crime is always higher than for persons in middle and upper socio-economic segments of society.

48 PFEIFFER, Christian, "Guppendrill und Fremdenhass: ..." in *Schweizer Monatshefte*, Vol. 79/80, No. 21/1 December/January 1999/2000; pp. 61–65; and by the same author: "Jugendkriminalität und Jugendgewalt in europäischen Ländern", Hannover: Kriminologisches Forschungsinstitut Niedersachsen, 1997; pp. 18–19 & 42.

49 SPOLAR, Ch., "Crime and Unrest in Post-Communist Society", *International Herald Tribune*, 9 February 1998. See also, for example, the study on Central and Eastern European developments in crime by: ULRICH, Christopher J., "The Price of Freedom: The Criminal Threat in Russia, Eastern Europe and the Baltic Region", in *Conflict Studies*, London: The Research Institute for the Study of Conflict and Terrorism, No. 275, 1994.

## Assessment

Deviant behaviour, especially when aggressive, criminal or violent, is one of the greatest challenges to internal security. Among the general public, violence and crime by youth cause perhaps the greatest fear and thereby raises some critical questions. Seeing children and teenagers involved in violence or offending leaves us grappling for answers. Why are there no clear and quick solutions to these problems? One reason is that solutions will most likely have to be found at the very root of our society – most notably in the cohesion of families and the socio-economic environment in which they either prosper or fall apart. Most difficult of all is to find solutions for the lack of social support which many families – indigenous and immigrants alike – seem to need. This is especially so where a sense of marginalisation highlights the gulf that separates the wealthy from the less fortunate. In particular children and teenagers in socio-economic areas of lower living standards are at a high risk to suffer from multiple social and economic stress factors. In the areas where they live, impulsive juvenile offences, small crime and violence are a serious challenge for society.

At the same time, we must ask to what extent small crime and juvenile delinquency present a challenge to political institutions and governments. Is the state as a whole threatened by such challenges? We can question whether crime by children and youth affects the normal functioning of government. To what extent is public administration affected by various forms of crime? Do small crime and juvenile delinquency present equal challenges as, say, corruption and financial fraud? Or can we safely assume that, under normal circumstances, delinquency and small crime do not undermine democratic governance or of the rule of law?

The majority of small offences are local phenomena even if their perpetrators come from afar. This is perhaps one reason why so little attention – except from the commercial media and some politicians seeking votes – has been given to finding practical solutions. These would have to be comprehensive enough to address causes that lie at the base of our society. At the same time, they should tackle the consequences of deviant behaviour in families, residential communities and schools. Comprehensive solutions would need to be address actual delinquencies and crime as well as the public's subjective feelings of insecurity.

# Group violence

Another very visible challenge to public security is deviant and aggressive behaviour by groups of mostly young men. The example, mentioned above, of violence in a Polish town is typical. In a large crowd, a mixture of emotions based on economic or political frustration, on boredom and an inadequate surveillance can become explosive. When emotionally charged, each member in a group contributes to a sensation of heightened excitement. Under such conditions, each individual member behaves differently than he or she would when alone. Each member of a group also assesses risks and opportunities differently than if he or she were alone. The threshold of violence which each member is willing to tolerate also rises. The result is that rules are more easily broken and individuals give less consideration to likely consequences when they engage in delinquencies as a collectivity.

The anonymity afforded by the group allows each member to imagine that he or she can get away with otherwise unimaginable behaviour. This can be observed with *casseurs* at demonstrations, vandalism as a form of thrill-seeking behaviour by groups of juveniles or during sports games when hooligans and fans become embroiled in fights. Young people are all the more willing to exploit emotions in a group where they find a sense of social cohesion – something which is often the case where members share a dissatisfaction with their normal daily routine.[50] This is a well-known behavioural characteristic of group psychology. Among the public, it can instil an impression of lawlessness and a lack of police vigilance.

Cases of group aggression are always well covered by the media. This is particularly true for what we may call football hooliganism. The word "hooligan" probably originated in the 19th century. It came to mean a "poor follow", a "tramp" who had nothing better to do than to steal and cause trouble. An article in the London Times of 1890 declared that hooligans were systematically terrorising areas of the city.[51] Today, hooligans are also

---

50 In part from: Branger, Katja and Fraziska Liechti, "Jugendgewalt und Freizeit", in Eisner, Manuel and Patrik Manzoni, eds., *Gewalt in der Schweiz: Studien zu Entwicklung, Wahrnehmung und staatlicher Reaktion*, Zürich: Verlag Rüegg, 1998; pp. 96–91; and Eisner, Manuel, "Jugendkriminalität und immigrierte Minderheiten im Kanton Zürich", in *Jugend und Strafrecht*, Zürich: Verlag Rüegg, 1998; pp. 129 & 131. Also: "Bungee-Springen ohne Seil", *Der Spiegel*, No. 27, 1998; pp. 86–87.
51 Quoted in: "Bungee-Springen ohne Seil", *Der Spiegel*, No. 27, 1998; p. 74.

feared by the public. The largest "football war" in Europe occurred at the Heysel stadium in Brussels in 1985. There, 39 people died either directly because of the fighting among fans or because they were unable to extricate themselves from a barrage of panicking spectators all trying to escape.[52] Other notable fights were organised on numerous occasions in England, the Netherlands, Spain, Italy and more recently in Denmark. Thus, in 1997, some 350 "extremist" followers of two rival Dutch football clubs met for a "war". One person died and many were seriously wounded. Perhaps the most highly publicised act of violence by hooligans in recent years was the beating into unconsciousness of a French police officer on 25 April 1998 during the Football World-Cup in the French town of Lens.

But not only hooligans and bored teenagers search for "adrenaline-kicking-excitement". Many people in Western countries with plenty of leisure time engage in activities where they push themselves to experience extraordinary sensations. Extreme sports, such as bungee jumping, white water rafting or canyoning, are examples which provide the thrilling excitement not offered in "normal" life. Many of these extreme sports are expensive, however. They can usually be pursued only with the appropriate equipment. This restricts access to those people who can afford such sports. In other words, a proportion of the general public does not have access to these activities. Those who cannot, like many teenagers with a lot of energy to burn, will seek thrills that are less expensive or even free of charge. The entertainment and beverage industries tap into this market with consumer goods such as video games, movies, music or "energy drinks". But for some people, that is not exciting enough. They seek still greater thrills by consuming illegal narcotic substances or engaging in delinquent activities such as burning motorbikes, setting off burglar alarms or joy-riding in stolen cars.

Finally, a form of excitement for many young people consists in participating in violent activities during large public demonstrations and political rallies (vandalism, looting, fighting the riot police). When such behaviour becomes part of demonstrations, public security is instantaneously lost. At such times, governments must be seen to use adequate force in order to control potentially violent demonstrators or *casseurs*. At the same time, a

---

52 "Gewalt ist im Fußball zu einer alltäglichen Erscheinung geworden", in *Frankfurter Allgemeine Zeitung*, 17 May 1999; p. 3.

government's need to use force (police at demonstrations) must not be seen to be an abuse of power at the cost of innocent demonstrators. Such restraint is not without its difficulties.[53] Government force and capacities to carry out surveillance must be balanced with the public's expectation for maximum freedom and privacy.

## Assessment

The most perplexing question is perhaps why deviant group behaviour is possible at all. Why do governments seem unable to prevent or control violent behaviour by groups? Images of riots or hooligan fights challenge the public's confidence in state authorities. They also raise demands for a greater government engagement to provide security.

The visual coverage of violent groups by the media for its commercial value risks heightening public frustrations about what seems a "decline of civil society". However, given that such events and media reports about them are mostly periodic and do not appear in the news media as frequently as stories about juvenile delinquency and small crime, they do not constantly undermine the public's confidence in security. The fact that hooligans can and do meet or travel from one country to another is nonetheless a serious challenge for governments and their police forces. The same can be said with regard to political extremists and protesters. As long as demonstrations and crowd violence remain a relatively rare occurrence, the stability of the state and its legal and democratic institutions are not directly questioned. However, the stability of a state is seriously tested if protests against an incumbent government involve a very large part of the population over a long period of time. A related example are protests against international negotiations such as in the World Trade Organisation. Finally, an excessively heavy-handed use of anti-riot forces against demonstrators causes deep public grievances.

53 GREGORY, Frank, "Policing the Democratic state: How much force?", *Conflict Studies*, No. 194, London: The Centre for Security and Conflict Studies, 1986; p. 1.

# Transnational crime, organised crime and corruption

Transnational crime implies offending behaviour perpetrated by individuals who, either on their own or as members of a group, commit crimes in more than one country. Their activities are "organised" when a group has "a corporate structure whose primary objective is to obtain money through illegal activities, often surviving on fear and corruption".[54] Organised crime is also considered as transnational when it reaches across a single border or acquires an international dimension.

However, not all organised criminal groups have "a corporate structure". Some cities are at times assailed by small *ad hoc* gangs of thieves. After the event, their members disband again and go their own way. That is, for example, the case of some Romanian robber gangs who organise overnight burglary expeditions into foreign cities. They maintain little group cohesion once their activities are over. Similarly, African "investment brokers" work in teams to collect capital funds in Europe only to disappear as soon as a sufficient number of people have been cheated off their money. In other words, organised crime is not necessarily and always conducted by well-structured or hierarchically organised groups. Instead, they can consist exclusively of temporary criminal conspiracies. This makes it a particularly confusing issue in public debate.

An element that characterises transnational organised crime is that the leading members are often of a same linguistic, national or ethnic group. Such groups may be relatively small when compared to multinational syndicates or mafia-style organisations. Among criminal groups in the majority of EU member states, co-operation at the national and international level is most frequently found between fellow nationals or individuals with the same ethnic background. "Relationships are established with criminal elements in source- transit- and target areas to facilitate the trafficking of illegal commodities and to safely hide or invest the proceeds of illegal activities."[55] The leadership of such groups is mostly composed of professional "white-collar" offenders. They have learned their trade within their com-

---

54  This is a very general definition as provided by Interpol.
55  Van der HEIJDEN, Toon, *Assessing Nature and Extent of Organised Crime in the European Union*, Driebergen: National Police Agency of the Netherlands, 20 March 1998; p. 9.

munities and, when they consider it profitable, expand their activities beyond the limited membership of their kin or ethnic group.

A simple illustration of a small and ethnically homogenous group is that of three Chileans who were apprehended by police on 25 July 1996 in Zurich. They were found to have stolen over Frs.90'000 in a period of seven weeks up to the time of their capture. Furthermore, they had stolen and falsified Swiss postal cheques with a combined value of Frs. 74'000 which they were about to mail to Chile. The three men, in their forties, were later accused of 94 thefts representing a value of over Frs. 160'000. They admitted to the police that they had come to Switzerland expressly to steal and send money back to their home country.[56]

Larger and more influential forms of transnational crime have developed in the former Communist countries of Central and Eastern Europe. The Russian Government estimated in June 1997 that there are over 9000 organised criminal gangs in the former Soviet Union (FSU). They are thought to control more than 40'000 state and private enterprises and more than half of all economic entities within the FSU. Of these, according to the American Federal Bureau of Investigation (FBI), 24 are active internationally. Their interests lie in money laundering and fraud, narcotics, prostitution and the trade in arms and technology. More than 30% of Russia's GNP is believed to be derived from such criminal activities. These groups are frequently based on networks of former communist informers around the world and maintain links with the security and intelligence apparatus of the Russian state. This has permitted the Russian mafia to spread their illegal activities throughout industrialised countries in Europe, North America and Asia.[57]

Besides the opportunities for criminal activities that developed in former Communist countries through the 1990's, a large proportion of profits is earned by international criminal organisations coming from sales to West-

---

56 "Kriminaltouristen", in *Info Ch: Informationsdienst zur sicherheitspolitischen Lage*, Zürich: Presdok AG., No. 4, 25 July, 1997; p. 16.
57 The above information from: O'BRIEN, Kevin and Jason RALPH, "Using the Internet for intelligence", in *Jane's Intelligence Review*, November 1997; p. 526. See also the following study: ULRICH, Christopher J., "The Price of Freedom: The Criminal Threat in Russia, Eastern Europe, and the Baltic Region", in *Conflict Studies*, Research Institute for the Study of Conflict and Terrorism, No. 275, October 1994.

ern consumers (narcotics, cigarettes, clandestine migrant workers, prostitutes, etc.). To varying degrees, consumers condone or are willing contributors to the commercial ventures of transnational crime.

> The purchase and market demand for 'grey-market bargains' are not major crimes in themselves, but represent a profit-seeking consumer addiction by West Europeans who claim innocence while participating in the maintenance of brutal criminal networks.[58]

Crime, even in its organised form, has always existed. What is new, however, is that criminal enterprises today work along the same principles as do legal multinational companies. It is not so much the kind of crime that is different than the growing number of criminal groups, their methods of operation and the speed with which they develop their activities.[59] In contrast to multinational firms, however, drug-traders, traffickers and smugglers need not bother with official procedures or national laws. Illegal activities are not slowed down by commercial legislation, bureaucratic regulations and requirements such as licences, investment or joint-venture agreements, accounting procedures and labour laws. At the same time, organised crime can take advantage, like any legal business, of communication technologies and the services of lawyers, investment brokers and asset managers. It uses for its own benefits the most convenient legal loopholes or tax havens in Europe.

A further characteristic of organised crime is its ready use of bribery and corruption. Both are important "means" to enter a new market sector or to obtain "help" from civil servants, politicians and business leaders.[60] With the use of corruption, profits from alliances between members of organised crime and administrative personnel in industry and government can be

---

58  The quote and information in the preceding paragraph translated by the author from: HEFTY, Georg Paul, "Konsumenten in der Verbrechenskette: Organisierte Kriminalität kommt nicht nur aus dem Osten", in *Frankfurter Allgemeine Zeitung*, 21 May 1999; p. 12.

59  BESOZZI, Claudio, *Organisierte Kriminalität und empirische Forschung*, Chur, Zürich: Verlag Rüegg, 1997; p. 25.

60  STAHEL, Albert A., "Organisierte Kriminalität: Eine Herausforderung", in *Organisierte Kriminalität und Sicherheit: Ein Zwischenbericht*, Bern: Verlag Paul Haupt, 1999; p. 5.

maximised while risks can be reduced. Hence, it is important to look at corruption as a particular challenge to internal security, not so much for the sake of subjective public security feeling, but for the stability and reliability of governments.

The term corruption implies a general departure from accepted norms of behaviour (e.g., corruption of the language, moral corruption). Today, it is more often used as meaning the misuse of public office, authority and/ or public money. Simply put, the root of corruption in government is due to a failure to separate decision-making power held by certain individuals in authority from the control of financial transactions. Many politicians and upper-level government administrators are in a position where they can grant licenses or permits for the development of industries or infrastructure works. The temptation to channel some of the profits for themselves may be great.[61]

However, not only persons employed in government can be tempted to earn extra profits. A business manager is also guilty of the same offence if he or she sells private property to the business for an inflated price. Common forms of corruption in both private and public are: (a) bribery (providing favours to a person for a service which is not permitted or does not conform to regulations), (b) extortion (the unauthorised extraction of money by officials from members of the public), and (c) misuse of official information.

In countries where legal regulations on free enterprise and public-private business relations remain poorly defined, opportunities for crime and corruption are readily exploited. This is the case in several post-communist countries of Eastern and Central Europe. Privileged government technocrats in some of the transition economies have managed to amass wealth often through dubious accounting manoeuvres. What is known in Central Europe as "under-tunnelling", "hollowing out" or "asset stripping" refers to emptying an enterprise of its assets. The privatization of many former public enterprises implies exploiting legal loop-holes through accounting procedures to place financial assets into foreign private bank accounts or into questionable off-shore firms and leaving the unrecoverable debts to

---

61 HASSAL, Mark and Ken MURPHY, *Stealing the state, and Everything Else: A Survey of Corruption in the Postcommunist World*, TI Working Paper, Berlin, Transparency International, 1999; p. 2.

the name of the enterprise which then goes bankrupt.[62] The Hungarian-American financier, George Soros, once noted that first "the assets of the state were stolen, and then when the state itself became valuable as a source of legitimacy, it too was stolen".

In fact, corruption, bribery and cronyism are widely believed to be among the root causes of the Russian as well as the Asian financial crises in the late 1990's.[63] Many Russian leaders in the military, the police and the former secret services as well as in economic sectors made use of their former communist networks to expand profit-earning ventures across the globe. With little risk to themselves, they established criminal partnerships with organised crime groups in Western Europe, North America and Southeast Asia. "By 1997, this web of transnational links has been recognised by Western governments to be one of them most serious threats to national and international security".[64] Also, alleged money which Western industries invested in Russia or which the International Monetary Fund provided to support that country's economy partially ended up in Western tax shelters and banks.[65]

While organised crime and corruption present serious problems in many less industrialised countries and former communist states, highly industrialised countries are not exempt from similar challenges. Profits from "under the table" cartels or bribery may not always be considered a crime. However, they always undermine business ethics and fair competition among industries. Grey-zones of business activities as well as illegal corrupt practices have expanded almost everywhere over the last ten years. In Europe as a whole, the "shadow economy" has grown three times more rapidly since 1960 than the official open economy. In countries with high taxation, such as in Sweden, the black market and shadow economy is high (18% of gross national product/year), while in countries where the tax on industry

62 In part from: "Der Pager Finanzminister unter Betrugsverdacht", in *Neue Zürcher Zeitung*, 17/18 June 1999; p. 5. See also the March, 1998, issue of *Transitions* (vol. 5 No. 3).

63 "Corruption in the spotlight", in *Outlook 99 – Business, Politics, Security*, London: Control Risks Group Ltd., 1999; p. 11.

64 Information for the above paragraph from: O'BRIEN, Kevin and Jason RALPH, "Using the Internet for intelligence", in *Jane's Intelligence Review*, November 1997; p. 526.

65 "Vertrauen is gut, Kontrolle ist besser", in *Neue Zürcher Zeitung*, 17./18. July 1999; p. 3.

and employment is comparatively lower, such as in the USA (10% of GNP), Austria (8%) and in Switzerland (7.5% of GNP), tax evasion is lower. In Italy where taxes are low as well, however, the shadow economy corresponds to more than 25% of GNP while in Russia, where taxes are higher but not exceedingly so, the unofficial economy is nevertheless estimated to be as large as the official one.[66]

As for the international links of organised crime, we can refer to police statistics in Germany. They reveal that in over 70% of all criminal investigation proceedings in 1996, indigenous offenders had collaborated with persons in other countries.[67] The high degree of international connections is in part due to the lowering of physical border controls among the former Warsaw Pact countries following the end of the Cold War and the elimination of internal borders among the EU's Schengen member countries. This has facilitated Illegal trafficking.[68] This form of criminal activity is helped still further in those countries where the administrative and security (police intelligence) capacities are as yet insufficient or where there seem to exist connections between political party leaders, government fiscal policies, the police and the judiciary.[69]

"Global illicit production of different drugs has increased greatly over the last decade".[70] Their trafficking is among the most profitable transna-

---

66 "Schattenwirtschaft schädigt Schweiz", in *Info Ch: Informationsdienst zur sicherheitspolitischen Lage*, Zürich: Presdok AG., No. 4, 25 July, 1997; p. 12.

67 *Bulletin*, Presse und Informationsdienst der Bundesregierung, Bonn, Nr. 48, 12 June 1997; p. 543. And: SCHELTER, Kurt, "Organisierte Kriminalität und Terrorismus: Die Beurteilung aus Deutscher Sicht", in *Organisierte Kriminalität und Sicherheit: Ein Zwischenbericht*, Bern: Verlag Paul Haupt, 1999; p. 30–31.

68 In part from: SCHELTER, Kurt, "Innere Sicherheit in einem Europa ohne Grenzen", in MEIER-WALSER, Reinhard C., Gerhard HIRSCHER, Klaus LANGE and Enrico PALUMBO, eds., *Organisierte Kriminalität: Bestandsaufnahme, Transnationale Dimension, Wege der Bekämpfung*, Munich: Hanns-Seidel-Stiftung, Akademie für Politik und Zeitgeschehen, 1999; pp. 15–35.

69 In part from: SCHELTER, Kurt, "Organisierte Kriminalität und Terrorismus: Die Beurteilung aus Deutscher Sicht", in STAHEL, Albert A., ed., *Organisierte Kriminalität und Sicherheit: Ein Zwischenbericht*, Bern: Verlag Paul Haupt, 1999; p. 29. And: STAHEL, A., "Organisierte Kriminalität: Eine Herausforderung", in STAHEL, Albert A., ed., *Organisierte Kriminalität und ...* ibid., 1999; pp. 4–5.

70 NEWMAN, Graeme, ed., *Global Report on Crime and Justice*, United Nations Office for Drug Control and Crime Prevention, Oxford: Oxford University Press, 1999; p. 173.

tional forms of crime, followed by the smuggling of clandestine migrants, car theft as well as money and document falsification. Other forms of highly profitable illegal trafficking are related to military hardware and women for prostitution. Furthermore, the extortion of protection-money (a traditional mafia activity) and using corruption to obtain favours from union leaders, politicians, police officers, high-level state bureaucrats and judges are common in organised crime circles. The cycle of these "industries" always ends with the laundering of profits in financial institutions and their eventual re-investment in either legal or illegal industries.[71]

Before the end of the Cold War, narcotic drugs came to Europe mostly from Latin America, Turkey, South and South-East Asia. Today, these traditional sources must compete with sometimes more ruthless traffickers from countries of the former Soviet Union and the Balkans. Competition among traffickers for markets in Europe has also facilitated an expansion of the number of consumers. More and more people consume an increasing range of organic and synthetic drugs. The latter are produced in large quantities in Central and Western Europe, while organic drugs, for reasons of climatic and political conditions, are mostly cultivated in Latin America and in Central and South-East Asia.[72]

Closely behind drug trafficking in terms of profitability is the smuggling of clandestine migrants and of automobile theft. Traffickers find a ready supply of expensive cars in the West and a huge market for stolen ones in the East. In 1993, some 250'000 passenger cars were stolen in Western Europe and the number has increased since. In 1996, 110'000 cars were stolen in Germany, 279'000 in France, 509'000 in the United Kingdom and 405'000 in Italy. Furthermore, the countries most at risk of high car theft are those that lack sophisticated registration and controls of new

---

71 In part from: STAHEL, Albert A., "Organisierte Kriminalität: Eine Herausforderung", in *Organisierte Kriminalität und Sicherheit: Ein Zwischenbericht*, Bern: Verlag Paul Haupt, 1999; p. 4.

72 In part from: NEWMAN, Graeme, ed., *Global Report on Crime and Justice*, United Nations Office for Drug Control and Crime Prevention, Oxford: Oxford University Press, 1999; p. 173; and DEL PONTE, Carla, "Organisierte Kriminalität und die Schweiz", in STAHEL, Albert A., *Organisierte Kriminalität und Sicherheit*, Bern: Verlag Paul Haupt, 1999; p. 14.

automobiles and which are closest to the markets for stolen motor vehicles; i.e., Central Europe, Southern France and Italy.[73]

Over the last decade, there has been an exponential growth of trafficking organisations which operate along sea, air and land routes.[74] With political and economic crises as catalysts for emigration from the Balkans, Eastern Europe and some parts of Africa, the trafficking of clandestine migrants has become highly profitable in the 1990's. What we mean by "clandestine migrants" with the help of "trafficker" or "smugglers" is defined as follows: The "smuggling" of migrants implies facilitating the crossing of borders for persons who do not have valid visas and travel documents. In this sense, "trafficking" implies the transportation of something not permitted by law. Both "trafficking" and "smuggling" of persons is organised by criminal groups for a given cost, mostly paid in cash and sometimes in the form of labour provided by the migrants themselves (transporting illegal goods or working as labourers in illegal factories and sweat shops). Furthermore, the organisations engaged in the trafficking of migrants are often involved in other types of organised criminality. This for the simple reason that since, with already established cross-border networks of contacts, they can make use of these for other profitable activities. In other words, migrant trafficking and smuggling is not merely a migration-related crime issue. Most of the time it is linked to other types of transnational criminal activities.

Besides the smuggling and trafficking of migrants, a related (and often connected) form of trafficking is that of women for prostitution. It is very lucrative and a "much less risky activity for criminals than other forms of crime, such as drug smuggling or the smuggling of stolen cars."[75] Approximately half of all prostitutes in Western Europe come from outside the region. Somewhere between 200'000 and half a million women averaging 21 years old work illegally in the European Union.[76] These young women

73 Ovchinskii, Vladimir, "Russian Interpol", in *International Affairs*, Vol. 44, No. 6, 1998; p. 189.
74 Savona, Ernesto, "European Money Trails", in *Transnational Organized Crime*, Vol. 2:4, 1996; p. 3.
75 International Organization for Migration, Migration Information Programme, *Trafficking and Prostitution: The growing exploitation of migrant women from Central and Eastern Europe*, Budapest, May 1995; p. 13.
76 Newman, Graeme, ed., *Global Report on Crime and Justice*, United Nations Office for Drug Control and Crime Prevention, Oxford: Oxford University Press, 1999; pp. 225–226.

are also vulnerable to becoming involved in crime. While the prostitution market by itself is not a direct threat to internal security, the smuggling of women, not unlike that of migrants, is often carried out in parallel with other forms of transnational crime.

## Assessment

Do the challenges posed by transnational organised crime, corruption and trafficking of humans pose a danger to European internal security? Who is affected and who is not? In general terms, we have seen that organised crime does not affect the public sense of security to the same degree as do small crime and juvenile delinquency. However, organised crime and corruption come to public attention once they "spill over" into the streets and into public life. When organised criminal groups begin to commit murders or engage in terrorizing activities (perhaps because different groups compete for market share and control of political offices), then the population will obviously get frightened.

It is not uncommon that criminal gangs perpetrate violent attacks against rivals, civil servants or politicians. In the process, they may kill or wound civilians. This kind of violence resembles terrorism. In Russia and other CIS states it occurs more frequently than elsewhere. Closer to Western Europe, however, one example – and by far not the only one – of violence in public conducted by organised crime was the explosion of an 11 pound bomb on July 2, 1998 on a street in Budapest. The explosion obliterated not only a Hungarian mobster, but also killed his body guard and two bystanders.[77]

The extent to which the public feels safe about these forms of crime depends on whether and how it is informed about them. Each member of the public assesses personal safety in relation to how he or she feels directly affected by what appear problems of law and order at the level of government and industry. As long as crime and corruption remain hidden in a restricted black market or in "high" white-collar circles in industry and government, the general public will know little about them.

---

77 FINN, Peter, "Crime Wave in Hungary Sets Off Alarm in U. S.", *International Herald Tribune*, 23 December 1998; p. 2.

Nevertheless, society as a whole, the state as well as national or local governments can be seriously challenged by organised crime. This is so in at least two aspects: First, organised crime profits from the discrepancy between wealthy and poor countries. This is particularly obvious where economic migrants travelling to the West are rapidly exploited by criminal trafficking groups. Trafficking and smuggling encourages not only emigration from poorer countries, but also leads many clandestine migrants into criminal activities once they are in the West.[78] This is bound to affect the degree to which small crime is carried out by clandestine migrants or so-called "tourist offenders". Second, organised crime can undermine democratic governance and judicial institutions. The manner in which organised criminal groups become the brokers of political power and office in some regions in Europe tells us of what could occur in countries where politicians and state authorities become enmeshed in criminal interests. This is the case, for example, in Sicily, where the Mafia controls large sectors of the economy and much of the local government's allocation of public funds:

> [...] another chapter in the old story of politicians and the Mafia conspiring to spirit away public money in Sicily. [...] the current capo di tutti i capi (boss of all bosses), a fugitive from justice since 1963, [...] has about 3000 soldiers under his command in Palermo alone, three times as many as the list compiled by Judge Falcone before his assassination. [...] The island's 19 Roman Catholic bishops, meanwhile, in their five-yearly report to the Pope, blamed the Mafia for the island's chronic state of economic underdevelopment. Public investments [for infrastructure and city planning...] remain uncomplete or come in way over budget because the Mafia controls the construction companies.[79]

Indeed, political offices or economic sectors in Italy as well as in some former communist countries could come under ever greater influence of criminal groups if nothing to prevent this is done. What must be avoided is that large syndicates with enormous financial resources manipulate the nor-

---

78  In part from: SCHELTER, Kurt, "Innere Sicherheit in einem Europa ohne Grenzen", in MEIER-WALSER, Reinhard C., Gerhard HIRSCHER, Klaus LANGE and Enrico PALUMBO, eds., *Organisierte Kriminalität: Bestandsaufnahme, Transnationale Dimension, Wege der Bekämpfung*, Munich: Hanns-Seidel-Stiftung, Akademie für Politik und Zeitgeschehen; pp. 16–17.

79  *International Herald Tribune*, 13 May 1999; p. 7.

mal and legally controlled operations of a society. The challenge posed by organised crime and corruption is thus a complex one. It can cause serious problems in the following areas:

(A) Economically, the open markets, business practices and government revenues are undermined by illegal practices that obscure regular financial accounting.
(B) Legally, business and taxation laws are circumvented. Organised crime and corruption reduce the efficiency of national laws and penal systems.
(C) Politically, corruption and bribery weaken the integrity of civil servants in all branches of administration. They destroy the institutional checks and balances upon which stability and political accountability rest.
(D) Institutionally, modernisation and reforms of security agencies, such as the police, are hampered if criminal and corrupt officials profit from ineffective security regulations.
(E) Politicians who do not remain accountable to their electors make themselves and the government vulnerable to popular cynicism and frustration. Permissiveness that allows corruption in government administration can generate widespread dissatisfaction.
(F) Socially, welfare and health services are abused or undermined where corrupt practices favour those who can pay bribes.
(G) Finally, the employees rights to health and safety are violated when labour, business and environmental laws can be circumvented by corrupt or criminal industrialists.

## Terrorism as a challenge to security

Terrorism is violence committed in such a manner as to frighten people (the "target audience") into acts they would otherwise not do. The intention is to spread fear – "kill one, frighten a thousand" – through violence directed at a small proportion of a target audience. This distinguishes terrorism from other forms of violence.[80] In Europe, the 1990's saw such terrorist acts in France, including Corsica, Ireland, Spain and Turkey.

---

80 In part taken from: STONE, Martin, "Terrorism: Higher impact, lower risk", in *Outlook 99 – Business, Politics, Security*, London: Control Risks Group Ltd., 1999; p. 7.

Generally, most terrorism is carried out in countries where heightened political tensions create deep divisions among the public. But extremist groups commit violent acts also in other countries where they believe they can influence political events through the use of force. Thus, in the night of February 15 to 16, 1999, the Kurdish diaspora communities terrorized personnel in Greek embassies in several West European countries. They took hostages and occupied buildings in protest against the capture of their leader Abdullah Öcalan. Other examples are the explosion of the Pan-Am flight over Lockerbie, Scotland, in 1989, or the bombings in the Paris metro in 1995. Each time members of politically disenfranchised groups acted outside their homeland, but their motives were closely linked to political tension in their own countries.

Other forms of terrorism are targeted against persons or communities in response to extreme ideological conflicts (racism, religious fundamentalism, xenophobia). These acts are often committed for societal reasons: to voice a protest or frighten a target population into changing their ways. Examples are the anonymous letter bombs in Austria (following the model of the "Unabomber" in the USA) or the bombing of London pubs frequented by the homosexual community in the spring of 1999.[81]

If we accept the above definition of terrorism, then the following acts could also fall in this category: arson fires set at asylum centres in Switzerland and Germany, the petrol bombs thrown at residential homes of Turkish families in Germany, as well as the arson fires set to fast food restaurants in Belgium, the Netherlands, France and England by hard-line animal rights groups or persons protesting against globalisation. The aim of such acts was clearly to scare a larger target community in the hope of producing a change in its activities – be they business managers, government asylum/refugee administrators or ethnically distinct residents and immigrants.

Finally, terrorism has also been used to extort money in the form of kidnapping tourists, international civil servants or humanitarian workers

---

81  The author of the Austrian letter bombs was apprehended by police in the Autumn of 1997 after he had sent out some nine packages, one of which destroyed the left hand of the former Mayor of Vienna, Helmut Zilk. The Austrian police spent close to ATS 700 million and mobilized over one hundred investigators in Austria and at the American FBI. ("L'arrestation de l'auteur des lettres piégées en Autriche...", in *Journal de Genève*, 13 October 1997; p. 4.).

and industrialists. Financial terrorism also includes the bombing of stores or the assassination of business managers by mafia groups who try to intimidate other businesses into paying "protection money". This kind of terrorism is most often linked to illegal profits and competition for criminal markets. The link between terrorism and organised crime can thus be close even where political motives play a part. This is the case of some of the Corsican groups. Mafia clans there have a history of rivalries and enmities in the *Union Corse* as well as among them and younger movements such as the National Front for the liberation of Corsica (FLNC). In the past few decades, and in connection with a large emigration of young people, the Corsican groups developed world-wide networks of mafia activities with centres in Marseille, on the Côte d'Azur, in Italy, Sicily and Turkey. The Corsican mafia is suspected to maintain links with the Italian Cosa Nostra, the Turkish and Kurdish drug traffickers, Chinese Triads as well as with Lebanese and Bulgarian organised crime groups. Thus, while speaking up for political objectives (greater autonomy or independence for Corsica), some of the members are also active in the drug trade, smuggling of weapons, corruption and subsidy fraud in EU agricultural and infrastructure financing.[82]

## Assessment

The descriptions of terrorism above may give the impression that this form of violence in society has become more frequent and is thus a growing challenge to internal security. In some parts of the world this is so indeed. In Europe, however, the opposite has actually been the case. Terrorism declined in frequency of attacks. The risk for a person to get caught in terrorist violence in Europe is lower today than it was ten years ago.[83] An example is airline hijacking. This form of terrorism has become rare in Europe today compared with twenty years ago. Worldwide, the 1970's saw an av-

---

82 KREVERT, Peter, "Europäische Einigung und Organisierte Kriminalität: Konsequenzen für Polizei und Nachrichtendienste, Wirtschaft und Gesellschaft", in *Europäische Beiträge zu Kriminalität und Prävention*, Vol. 1, 1998; p. 11.

83 STONE, Martin, "Terrorism: Higher impact, lower risk", in *Outlook 99 – Business, Politics, Security*, London: Control Risks Group Ltd., 1999; p. 7.

erage of 30 to 40 hijacks per year while in the 90's there has been a yearly average of 13 with most taking place in Asia.[84] One reason for the decrease is the improved supervision at airports. Another is the relative low political benefit which terrorists with political or religious motives can reap for themselves. For this reason, the most lethal terrorism has been religious extremism aimed at populations in the country or region where the terrorists wish to influence change. Most of the time, such acts occur outside Europe (for example, the killings of citizens in Algeria, of tourists in Egypt and in other African countries, or the hostage-taking of foreigners in South East Asia).

On European soil, the potential of attacks in the future should never be underestimated, however. Extremist attacks from religious or political groups may not figure as a high risk for internal security, but the fact that they can happen should not be dismissed. This is especially the case if organised crime infiltrates political parties and government administration. For where crime syndicates become powerful, terrorism, like corruption, is likely to follow where illegal markets and profits can be secured.

Finally, increasing dependency on information technology in support of economic growth renders industrialised society vulnerable to new forms of terrorist attacks. Computer hackers have already managed to enter national intelligence services in several Western countries. Computer viruses have caused havoc in many financial trading and industrial centres and a hacker-terrorist could potentially destroy computer systems that regulate anything from electricity supplies to a city, railway networks or airport. In this respect, state action to maintain internal security takes on a new dimension. It becomes one of developing ever more sophisticated protection mechanisms. Because these are usually remote and often so highly specialised, the general public and the media learn about them only when a terrorist attack occurs. In other words, so long as terrorist acts remain a mere probability, the public will see no serious challenge to its security. This does not mean, however, that when the public does not complain, governments do not need to take preventive measures seriously.

---

84 STONE, Martin, "Terrorism: Higher impact, lower risk", in *Outlook 99 – Business, Politics, Security*, London: Control Risks Group Ltd., 1999; p. 9.

## Public confidence in the police and the government

Before concluding this chapter, another challenge to internal security needs mentioning. This one is not simply a consequence of crime. Rather, this challenge concerns the perception of the public towards its national and local security agencies such as the police, border guards, criminal police and civil protection forces. Public confidence especially in the police is crucial for the maintenance of internal security. The level of this confidence affects how people assess their personal safety. It belongs in the category of subjective security feelings based on both, how the police and the criminal justice system are seen by the public and what the public expects from them. We rely on the state not only to prevent violence, but also to discourage it through education and the help of social, political, and legal institutions. The public expects to be provided with a "safe" environment in which crime, violence and public disorder are, if not completely eradicated, then at least kept to a minimum.

The confidence in and support for local or national police forces on the part of the general public can indicate how government security provisions are perceived. A citizen evaluation of police performance conducted over the past ten years reveals that there are large differences between public perceptions of how well their national police forces do their job. These evaluations are based on the percentage of respondents who were satisfied with how their reports to the police were dealt with, their satisfaction with the way the police control crime in their area, and the percentage of victims of contact crimes who reported their injury to the police. From the lowest ranking to the highest, these countries are: the Russian Federation, Latvia, Romania, Estonia, Belarus, Lithuania, Ukraine, Poland Croatia, Yugoslavia, Bulgaria, Czech Republic, Hungary, Malta, Slovenia, Austria, Italy, Albania, Norway, Slovakia, Spain, Germany, Finland, Belgium, France, Netherlands, Northern Ireland, England, Sweden, Scotland, Switzerland.[85]

---

85 For the sake of comparison, the USA followed by Canada figure in between Sweden and Scotland. Adapted from the table of "Categorization of Countries, According to Citizen Evaluation of Police Performance Index" (CEPPI) in: KANGASPUNTA, K., M. JOUTSEN and N. OLLUS, *Crime and Criminal Justice Systems in Europe and North America 1990–1994*, Helsinki: European Institute for Crime Prevention and Control (HEUNI), 1998; P. 186.

Such public evaluations are inevitably subjective. To a large extent, they relate what people want from the police and do not necessarily reflect what a police force is capable of. In other words, a Russian police officer has far fewer resources to do what people expect from him than his West European counterpart. Furthermore, this type of evaluation does not tell us whether the police is actually able to control crime. The general public is more aware of small crime, civil disorder and aggressive behaviour and therefore expects the police to rectify these instead of dealing with the less visible forms of international trafficking, corruption or industrial and financial crime.

This tells us that not only criminals must be caught to maintain or improve public confidence in the police. Nor does the police need only to provide better services to victims. Rather, the public must come to see that law, social order and civil behaviour prevail in society. To fulfil this need and satisfy public expectations for security, far more is required than merely "better" police or harsher criminal justice procedures. Rather, contributions from cultural, social, public welfare, education and citizen-community initiatives are needed. Only through closer collaboration between social institutions and authorities responsible for public security can a sense of safety and confidence be developed. The police and other public or private security agencies have an important role to play. However, they must not be seen as sole guarantors of internal security. Such a view would mislead not only the public, but also some politicians and the media. The public must not be led to believe that when crime rises or when juveniles behave violently, that it is only because the police is not doing its job. Other factors, such as social dislocation, economic disparities or international migration affect levels of crime. Today's dilemma can be illustrated in the following manner:

> Public opinion and informal social control have the central role, not only in defining what is crime, but also in maintaining social order. Many police agencies and local governments have reached a critical point in their response to social unrest, disorder, and crime. They can no longer adhere to traditional forms of police work because the world is changing rapidly and quite often is in an upheaval. Large-scale migrations are bringing people of different races, cultures and languages into closer contact with each other, making enormous demands on their tolerance. Increasing numbers of immigrants are moving to cities in affluent Western countries that already harbor the majority of that country's population along with most of its problems. At the same time many of these countries are faced with uncertain

economies, overburdened social and public services, and declining educational standards. There are widening class divisions, more broken families, home- and hopelessness, growing anger among the disadvantaged, and a rise in violent crime.[86]

## Conclusion

In response to the complex causes and consequences of what appears increasing lawlessness, some politicians and journalists appeal to the police for rapid solutions. Calling for "more security" or "less crime", however, may actually create the impression among the public that the government and the police are not doing their job. Political opinion-leaders may question security conditions and government services with the best of intentions. Nevertheless, if they do so merely with criticism and without offering constructive and comprehensive suggestions for improvements, they risk being counterproductive. They may actually worsen the way security is perceived by the public.

Preventing disorder and lawlessness is more difficult today than it was twenty or thirty years ago. This is not only because the causes and consequences of deviance are deeply linked with socio-economic factors not directly related to crime (high density in residential areas, heightened competition on the labour market, socio-economic stress, greater international mobility for travellers of all kinds or an increasingly multi-cultural and heterogeneous population in most European cities). Preventing criminal behaviour is increasingly difficult because the context in which professional and juvenile offenders can exploit opportunities for impulsive or carefully planned illicit activities is not easily controlled. The freedom of individual people cannot simply be restricted.

We must recognise that the more liberal and open a country and a society become, the more opportunities appear in which behavioural norms can change. The traditional social order is no longer accepted by members of

---

86 FELTES, Thomas, "Improving the training system of police officials – Problems of creating an international standard for police officers in a democratic society", Unpublished paper prepared at the University of Applied Police Sciences, Villingen-Schwenningen, Germany, August 1998; p. 2.

the younger generation who search for new ways to realise an identity of their own in work and play. Western Europe, like all liberal and highly industrialised societies, offers countless possibilities for people to chose their life-styles, their employment, their movement (travel) and their circle of friends. The broad personal freedom which we all enjoy implies that public safety measures must provide security in times of great change and of expanded personal freedom. This is no easy task. It is especially difficult because just during such times of great change, the public focuses more readily on the instability which change produces. Internal security and the confidence which citizens have in their government security services have therefore taken on greater importance today for the public, for politicians and for the police.

Chapter 4

# Crime statistics, Victimization and Perceptions of Insecurity

The purpose of this chapter is to show that, contrary to popular assumptions, police and media reports about crime do not tell how safe Europeans are. Internal security is as much a subjective concept as it is a product of the objective numbers and types of challenges to it. But crime statistics cannot show how much crime there really is in society. Neither can they clarify why the various kinds of offenders and their activities change over time. Rather, data on crime in a given country provide an overview of crime trends as recorded by the police and assembled by national statistics offices. In other words, crime statistics by themselves do not say much about how "safe" a given population actually is.

We learn about crime in two ways. Either we experience it first-hand, or we read and hear about it. It is similar with security. We may feel secure or not depending on personal experiences and on what we learn from others. Furthermore, we all have certain expectations for security. These are essentially based on information from three sources:

The first source is governmental. Depending on how the administrative distribution of responsibilities is organised, information about crime or security is provided through local, national and international channels. We obtain information from the police (types and numbers of reported crimes, suspects or arrests), the judiciary (court cases, arrest warrants issued, etc.) and prison authorities (conditions of incarceration, numbers of persons in jails or enduring other kinds of restrictions on their freedom). Also from border guards can we obtain information regarding offending behaviour such as the number of persons caught for smuggling or for not having valid travel documents. Moreover, national ministries and government departments, such as those responsible for interior affairs, health or public safety also supply us with security-related information. Moreover, we can learn about crime rates from other countries (bi-lateral police, civil security and military collaboration) as well as from multi-lateral organisations such as the United Nations. Their reports may raise our awareness of certain kinds of crimes. However, most often, we are reminded of criminal cases when security authorities report about a major event such as large drug seizures at a border or the conviction of a known international gangster.

The second source of information on security comes from offices that collect and analyse information, such as academic institutes of criminology and national statistical offices. In many cases, however, the information which these latter two bodies publish are based on the official data which the government or its security agencies (the police) provide. Only a small amount of data is garnered through independent surveys carried out periodically by academics or polling agencies. Such data may, for example, consist of victimization surveys or random public polls on how safe Europeans think they are or which security concerns are most important for them.

The third source of information, finally, are the commercial news media. Here information is often reduced to palatable bites for readers and television viewers. While usually not false, information in the media is reported in isolation from its real-life context and is thus apt to interpretations which distort the issue. In general we can assume that only those crimes and statistical figures are reported which attract the attention of an audience. This means that the media provides us with a limited or partial understanding of the criminological landscape.

The media's emphasis on specific types of crimes for their emotive value has also been found in several studies. These revealed that the frequency and size of newspaper articles on violent crimes grossly over-report the incidence of actual violent crimes. At the same time, thefts of property (small theft, break-ins in homes and thefts of automobiles) are mentioned far less frequently in newspapers. It means that while official statistics in most countries show that violent crimes are relatively rare when compared to property crime, the media, however, provides the opposite picture.[87] This is an obvious reason for why media reporting on crime and police figures says little about the actual objective security of a country's residents.

87 Information taken from various studies as summarised in: *Global Report on Crime and Justice*, edited by Graeme NEWMAN, United Nations Office for Drug Control and Crime Prevention, Oxford: Oxford University Press, 1999; p. 14.

Thus when stories on crimes are represented, based on a narrow selection of police statistics or on partial results from criminological research, the context of criminal behaviour is left out. Such hand-picked reporting is especially noticeable in articles or television stories which use witness testimonies or random public interviews to focus on the suffering of the victim(s) and the opinions of spectators. By highlighting the emotive aspects of a crime, a story is brought closer to the public – the consumer. However, the background of offending behaviour or the context in which such behaviour is likely to develop are left out. To discuss why young men in lower socio-economic living conditions, for example, are more likely to be involved in violence and crime requires more in-depth analysis. In contrast, spelling out the latest crime figures or merely naming the nationality of offenders caught by police is not only easy to do, it also attracts attention because it triggers an underlying fear of insecurity among the public.

## Reporting on crime

Police data tell us that throughout history we have always lived with a certain amount of crime. On the average, Western countries have today between 5000 and 8000 recorded crimes for every 100'000 inhabitants.[88] The differences among the countries are due in part to (1) the varying definitions of "crime" as applied by police agencies; (2) the willingness of victims to report offences to the police; (3) the ability of the police to uncover and record ("white-collar") crimes for which there may be no obvious victims (such as in cases of fraud, corruption or money-laundering); and (4), legal procedures which place different sanctions on offenders (the youngest age of criminal responsibility differs even among West European countries).

88 *Eurostat Yearbook 1997*, "Crimes per 100'000 people, 1994", Luxembourg: Office for Official Publications, Statistical Office of the European Communities, 1997.

*Table:*

Number of offences recorded by national statistics per 100'000 inhabitants.[89]

|                 | 1990            | 1998    |
|-----------------|-----------------|---------|
| Austria:        | 6'002           | 5'939   |
| Belgium:        | 3'337           | 8'478   |
| Canada:         | 10'200 (1994)   |         |
| Denmark:        | 10'270          | 9'427   |
| Finland:        | 16'984          | 14'505  |
| France:         | 6'169           | 6'095   |
| Germany:        | 7'108[90]       | 7'868   |
| Greece:         | 3'306           | 3'759   |
| Hungary:        | 3'287           | 5'926   |
| Italy:          | 4'358           | 4'214   |
| Japan:          | 1'100 (1994)    |         |
| Luxembourg:     | 6'628           | 6'409   |
| Netherlands:    | 7'613           | 7'807   |
| Norway:         | 5'562           | 10'048  |
| Switzerland:    | 5'275           | 5'405   |
| Spain:          | 2'635           | 2'312   |
| United Kingdom: | 18'796          | 8'428   |
| USA:            | 5'500 (1994)    |         |

The figures above represent only the numbers recorded and not the real quantity of offences committed. Furthermore, they represent only those crimes which could be termed as such under the various national police and judicial definitions.

It is important to keep in mind that the crimes mentioned above are not only recorded following very different methods, but they are also qualitatively different. One example to show this may be illustrated by comparing the USA with Switzerland. Both have similar proportionate numbers of recorded crimes, but they are qualitatively very different. Americans live

89  INTERPOL, International Crime Statistics, Statistiques Criminelles Internationales des pays européens de 1990 à nos jours; Lyon, 1998. The figures for Canada, Japan and the United States are added for comparison. They are approximate numbers for the year 1994 taken from the *Eurostat Yearbook 1997*, "Crimes per 100'000 people".
90  Figure for 1990 is from West Germany only.

with more violent crime which is most likely due to the high rate of gun ownership in the USA.[91] Apparently, nearly half of all gun deaths reported in all Western industrialised countries for 1994 took place in the United States.[92]

Furthermore, the proportion of crime to population generally does not consider the demography of the country. Here again, we may come to believe that crime has risen when actually it remained in constant proportion to a growing population. For example, the total European population continues to grow meaning that we must also accept that crime figures continue to rise.[93] This rise will most likely be in proportion to the population's development. The proportion of those individuals who knowingly break the law corresponds to about 5% of the adult population in Western countries. This percentage excludes the far more common offences such as breaking traffic laws while driving a car, exceeding the permitted amount of goods when cross-border shopping (alcohol, meat or cigarettes without paying duties), or fare-dodging on public transportation.

Most types of offences and crimes have increased in recent years according to police statistics in Europe. Notable among them are burglaries and thefts, violence among young people as well as so-called "white-collar" crimes (money laundering, fraud and the trafficking/smuggling of illegal goods and services).[94]

---

91 From: "Summary: The Fifth United Nations Survey", in KANGASPUNTA, K., M. JOUT-SEN and N. OLLUS, *Crime and Criminal Justice Systems in Europe and North America 1990–1994*, Helsinki: European Institute for Crime Prevention and Control (HEUNI), 1998; p.xv. Also: Van DIJK, Jan J. M. and John van KERSTEREN, "Criminal victimization in European cities: some results of the International Crime Victims Survey", in *European Journal on Criminal Policy and Research*, Vol. 4:1, 1996; p. 11.

92 The U. S. rate for gun deaths in 1994 was 14.24 per 100'000 people. Taken from: *The International Herald Tribune*, 19 April 1998; p. 3

93 Most national statistical institutes expect their populations to continue growing for the next 10 years at least. From: Population Projections, *Eurostat Yearbook, 1997*, see charts "Total population at 1 January 1997" and "Population projections by different organisations".

94 While most offences are recorded as having increased in Europe since the end of the Cold-War, some crimes and forms of violence have also come down again. Murder rates, for example, rose up to the early 1990's and then decreased again. An example of the difficulty to find out exactly whether a type of crime has increased over time is discussed by Manuel EISNER in "Die Zunahme von Jugendgewalt – Fakt oder

*Table:*
Rise or fall of number of court cases for violent offences recorded in percent during the period 1993 to 1996.[95]

| | |
|---|---|
| Finland: | 8.6 |
| Belgium (1994–96): | 8.5 |
| Norway: | 7.5 |
| France: | 7.3 |
| Ireland: | 6.7 |
| England and Wales: | 5.5 |
| Portugal: | 3.9 |
| Germany (includes threats of violence): | 3.9 |
| Switzerland: | 2.1 |
| Netherlands: | 1.9 |
| Italy: | 1.5 |
| Sweden: | 1.0 |
| Greece (1993–1995): | 0.1 |
| Austria: | - 0.3 |
| Denmark: | - 2.5 |

## Statistics and security

A mistake which many people, the media as well as some politicians make when speaking about crime statistics is to assume that they say something

Artefakt?" and by Oliver Bieri "Unterschiedliche Verlaufsmuster von Homizidraten im Zeitraum 1877 bis 1995", in Eisner, Manuel and Patrik Manzoni, eds., *Gewalt in der Schweiz: Studien zu Entwicklung, Wahrnehmung und staatlicher Reaktion*, Chur/ Zürich: Rüegg Verlag, 1998. Statistical comparisons are difficult to establish; this study refers to the following: Kangaspunta, K., M. Joutsen and N. Ollus, *Crime and Criminal Justice Systems in Europe and North America 1990–1994*, Helsinki: European Institute for Crime Prevention and Control (HEUNI), 1998. And: the *Global Report on Crime and Justice*, United Nations Office for Drug Control and Crime Prevention, Oxford: Oxford University Press, 1999.

95  Taken from: Waard, J. de, M. Schreuders, and R. Meijer, "Geweldscriminaliteit in 15 Europese landen", in *SEC*, Tijdschrift over samenleving en criminaliteitspreventie, Netherlands Ministry of Justice, Vol. 12, No. 2, April 1998; p. 7.

about the state of internal security. As complete as any police agency may try to present its statistics, the figures tell us little or nothing about security conditions in society. This is apparent from the following: numbers of criminal offences or police arrests may tell us whether the offences where murders, car thefts or thefts with the use of violence. However, if not differentiated by the police, we will not know whether these crimes where committed within a certain amount of time (over a given number of weeks or months), at certain times of the day, or whether they were geographically specific (in urban areas where socio-economic living conditions are lower, higher or where the population is particularly dense). Not only these considerations play role in providing safety and security for the public. Other issues may also be important, but are rarely considered when reading crime statistics. For example:

- the level of schooling and education of an offender,
- the socio-economic conditions and/or
- the permissiveness which exists in the family and in the educational background from which an offender comes from,
- the ease with which potential offenders can find opportunities for crime, and
- the characteristics of the social peer group with whom the offender spends his or her leisure time (the number of violent incidents among the groups' members, the gang-like or party-type behaviour it engages in).

Moreover, crime statistics from the police or the judiciary cannot help us understand the context in which an offence was committed. Was, for example, a murder committed during a brawl among semi-drunken customers in a night-club or in a shoot-out among drug-trafficking gangs? Was a car stolen from an unlit and lonely parking lot at night or from a busy street during the day? Was the robbery in the food store committed by a gang of intimidating young men or by a couple of older persons dressed in rags? Statistics provide no indication of the motives that lead people to commit an offence. An analysis of motives requires a study of the causes of deviant behaviour which are, to a large extent, the result of the context in which the offenders live, work or travel. In this context, opportunities, motivations, risks and stress factors affect each individual differently just as they also influence the character of a community. As no two rural or urban communities or two countries experience the same kinds of crime, an overview of crime would have to include, besides police statistics, information on the socio-economic living conditions and possibly the ethnic composition of a community. Without such differentiation, it remains very difficult to know why a specific residential or business area may be sheltered from crime and why another is more strongly affected.

When comparing crime data, another set of problems arises. These are rarely mentioned in the popular media. First, the police may have become more effective in catching offenders and so can record more crimes. We must remember, however, that a police force can only record those offences which are reported by victims or which it discovers through its investigations. This means that a police agency can never know about each and every crime that is committed in a community or a country.

Second, crime figures may rise not because there is actually more crime, but because the public may have a growing confidence in the police. Victims become, then, less reluctant to report a crime. This applies especially to victims of sexual crimes and to victims in immigrant and ethnically distinct communities. These groups often prefer to resolve their disputes among themselves or cover-up a crime if they cannot speak to a police officer who is not a member of their gender or ethnic background. Thus, the closer the police can collaborate with the public, the more statistics of recorded crimes will increase. This would hold true even where the real number of crimes (recorded and unrecorded) actually remains the same.

Police effectiveness may indeed influence statistics considerably. Police forces use increasingly more sophisticated electronic means to find suspected criminals and many have access to international information intelligence services to exchange data on offenders and crimes. They also develop new preventive strategies for which many police officers undergo considerable training. Such strategies may include community policing and security-building methods that facilitate greater confidence between them and the public. The result is often that following such new developments, crime figures increase before they decrease over a certain number of years.

Another lacunae of crime statistics is the ability to learn about the details of a specific type of offence. For example, did an offender, who was reported to have stolen something, steal a small suitcase or an industrial shipping container? Some stolen items are identified by the police (e.g. automobiles, fine art objects or endangered tropical birds). However, most stolen items are not identified. Hence a stolen suitcase may look the same as a shipping container on the statistical report. Clearly, these two thefts represent very different kinds of crimes. The first requires impulsive, rapid action by an individual offender at a train station or in an airport, while the other implies an organised manoeuvre with the use of heavy lifting equipment and/or the falsification of shipping and identification records.

In addition, this brief introduction to reading crime data tells us that because of different definitions, police registration methods and criminal legal procedures in each country (and even among regions in some countries), the number of recorded offences will always vary. Methods of police work and record-keeping differentiate to such an extent across Western Europe that even if each country had an identical number of crimes per year, the statistically recorded figures would still vary. Hence, one must always use caution when using crime statistics to interpret internal security conditions in a country.

So what use do crime statistics have? They can provide an idea of the work which the police and criminal courts do over a given period of time. They can also inform on the number and types of offences which are reported to the police. Most importantly, statistics can be used to establish guidelines for planning crime prevention strategies and targeting law enforcement efforts. For example, if the number of minor offences among juveniles in a specific area has risen over a given number of years, it may be useful to find out what other factors have also changed in that same area. If in that same period and within roughly the same community the number of drug abuse victims is also reported to have increased (hospital and medical records), then we can perhaps assume that the rise of crime figures is related to the consumption of drugs. Any prevention strategy therefore, must focus on both: public education (for children and parents) on addiction-related problems as well as enforcing international criminal investigations of drug smuggling rings and their local contacts. The best crime prevention project will have little effect if it focuses only on one aspect of a larger criminalistic and sociological issue. In other words, if only repression of the possession of drugs is enforced but education is ignored, or if local drug-abuse is treated, but international criminal investigations are neglected, then the fight against crime remains incomplete. This implies that crime statistics cannot be considered independently from other information on public health, family living conditions, crime victim surveys or public education.

## Differentiated reporting and victimization studies

In comparing police statistics in conjunction with victim reports, it becomes clear that, on the one hand, not all populations live with the same amount of crime, and on the other hand, not all the same offences are reported or recorded equally across different communities. Cultural factors, public confidence in the police as well as confidence in judicial authorities play a role in the preparedness of the public to report crimes. In general, West Europeans who have always lived in a liberal democratic country have far greater confidence in their public authority than populations in countries undergoing political and economic transition. Central and East Europeans are less likely to report crimes to the police (even when these are serious) and the police appear also less likely to record a reported offence than is the case in Western Europe.[96] Similarly, foreigners who reside in Western Europe and who are not familiar with the criminal justice system and have difficulty with the local language are also less likely to communicate a crime to the police.

To obtain a better picture of crime and security, police statistics can be complemented with independent polls and surveys. In this way, it becomes possible to obtain an idea of how the general public perceives its security in light of crime and small offences as well as how the public feels about the police and its performance. Victim surveys conducted in recent years generally confirm that public security in Europe has not worsened in the last twenty years when all socio-economic classes in the population are considered. However, great differences exist when residents in rural areas, villages, small towns and larger cities are looked at separately. Still greater discrepancies become evident when socio-economic classes are studied in isolation.

First, residents in towns and cities with a population of more than 20'000 are exposed to the greatest risk of victimization.[97] This is the case in all

---

96 "Summary: The Fifth United Nations Survey", in Kangaspunta, K., M. Joutsen and N. Ollus, *Crime and Criminal Justice Systems in Europe and North America 1990–1994*, Helsinki: European Institute for Crime Prevention and Control (HEUNI), 1998; p. xvi. Also: Zvekic, Ugljesa, *Criminal Victimisation in Countries in Transition*, Rome: United Nations Interregional Crime and Justice Research Institute (UNICRI), Publication No. 61, 1998: p. 97.

97 Van Dijk, Jan J. M. and John van Kersteren, "Criminal victimization in European cities: some results of the International Crime Victims Survey", in *European Journal on Criminal Policy and Research*, Vol. 4:1, 1996; and Robert, P., R. Zauber-

societies. It is largely due to the higher density of the population and the greater exposure to both opportunities for offending and a commercial cultivation of desirables. By far the most frequently reported offences in urban areas are property crimes and not violence. Second, thefts, minor aggressions and crime are mostly concentrated in specific urban regions which are generally inner cities where commerce is concentrated and in lower socio-economic residential areas. Here, residents, workers and evening entertainment seekers – especially younger men – are exposed to a higher risk of involvement in minor aggressions and crime than are people who live in wealthier neighbourhoods and work in "white-collar" professions. The only exception to the concentration of offences in inner cities are thefts that target property of the wealthier communities; i.e. automobiles or break-ins in private residences.

Regardless of socio-economic class, young men between the ages of 15 and 25 figure at the top in statistics on offences of all sorts (including traffic violations) as well as in violence and victimization. They commit the most violent crimes and are also the most frequent victims of violence. They are recorded by police in increasing numbers for small offences, violence, theft and mugging.[98] This conclusion is the result of criminological studies and

MAN, M. L. POTTIER and H. LAGRANGE, "Mesurer le crime: Entre statistique de police et enquêtes de victimation (1985–1995)" in *Revue française de sociologie*, Vol. 40:2, April/June, 1999; p. 263.

98 See for example: PFEIFFER, Christian, "Trends in Juvenile Violence in European Countries", (Hannover: Kriminologisches Forschungsinstitut Niedersachsen, 1997) as summarised by the National Institute of Justice, U. S. Department of Justice, May 1998. Also: ROBERT, P., R. ZAUBERMAN, M. L. POTTIER and H. LAGRANGE, "Mesurer le crime: Entre statistique de police et enquêtes de victimation (1985–1995)" in *Revue française de sociologie*, Vol. 40:2, April/June, 1999; p. 263. In the case of Switzerland, see: "Warum die Jugendkriminalität stark zunimmt", *Neue Zürcher Zeitung*, 7/8 March 1998, p. 81, and his chapter "Die Zunahme von Jugendgewalt – Fakt oder Artefakt?" in EISNER and MANZONI, eds., *Gewalt in der Schweiz*, Chur/Zürich: Rüegg Verlag, 1998; pp. 13–40; and EISNER, Manuel, "Jugendkriminalität und immigrierte Minderheiten im Kanton Zürich", in *Jugend und Strafrecht*, Zürich: Verlag Rüegg, 1998; pp. 128–129. The Dutch example is also typical for most West European rises of offences by young adults and teenagers, see: HAKKERT, Alfred, "Geweld in Nederlandse gemeenten", and ROBERS, Ben, "Het wel en wee van de happy 80 %", in *SEC*, Tijdschrift over samenleving en criminaliteitspreventie, Den Haag: Ministerie van justitie, Vol. 12, No. 3, June 1998; pp. 22–24 and pp. 25–26.

victim surveys. Young men are increasingly willing to tolerate violence and use it as a means to resolve disputes. Oddly enough, however, the majority of young men worry the least about their security. This contrasts sharply with elderly people of 60 years or more, who are at the lowest risk of victimization, but worry the most about crime. Finally, in contrast to young women, young men are more likely to contact social groups that engage in violence. They are more likely to carry a weapon (a knife or a gun) for "self-defence". The consequence is that they have the greatest tendency to engage in violence and live a lifestyle where they are at a greater risk of becoming a victim of violence.[99]

A distinction needs to be made, however, between those teenagers and young adults who have money to spend for entertainment and expensive leisure or sports activities and those who do not. The wealthier ones spend their time in relatively safe night-clubs. They engage in sports activities that provide them with satisfying thrills without necessarily engaging in excessive risks. The economically less fortunate who also seek entertainment and excitement, however, do so more frequently in areas that are exposed to higher rates of delinquency. The consequence is that these young men are also exposed to a greater risk of becoming involved in small aggressions, drug consumption and crime.[100]

---

99 Von FELTEN, Mirjam, "Geschlechtsspezifische Perzeption von Gewalt im Jugendalter", in EISNER, Manuel and Patrik MANZONI, eds., *Gewalt in der Schweiz: Studien zu Entwicklung, Wahrnehmung und staatlicher Reaktion*, Zürich: Verlag Rüegg, 1998; pp. 94–119. Also, KILLIAS, Martin and Juan RABSA, "Weapons and Athletic Constitution as Factors linked to Violence among Male Juveniles: findings from the Swiss Self-reporting Delinquency Project", in *British Journal of Criminology*, Vol. 37, No. 3, Summer 1997. Also: ROBERS, Ben, "Het wel en wee van de happy 80 %", in *SEC*, Tijdschrift over samenleving en criminaliteitspreventie, Den Haag: Ministerie van justitie, Vol. 12, No. 3, June 1998; p. 26.

100 KILLIAS, Martin and Juan RABASA, "Weapons and Athletic Constitution as Factors linked to Violence among Male Juveniles", in *British Journal of Criminology*, Vol. 37:3, Summer 1997. ROBERT, P., R. ZAUBERMAN, M. L. POTTIER and H. LAGRANGE, "Mesurer le crime: Entre statistique de police et enquêtes de victimation (1985–1995)" in *Revue française de sociologie*, Vol. 40:2, April/June, 1999; pp. 259–264.

# Security as seen through crime statistics and victim surveys

From the combined victim and police data, we learn that the most significant sources of insecurity about which victims complain are small aggressions and inconsiderate or reckless behaviour. These can be of the following kinds: First those which may be called nuisances not aimed at any person or object in particular such as noise at night in or around apartment buildings. Second, aggressions that are not physically violent such as angry verbal abuse or threats of violence. Third, there are the minor aggressions such as physical shoves and hits, small fights and throwing objects at a person. Finally, aggressions aimed towards private and public property such as breaking a window, damaging public property or reckless vandalism. All these forms of small aggressions cause the greatest nuisances and insecurity for people – especially for those who live in lower-end socio-economic urban areas.

However, police statistics record these minor aggressions far less frequently than crimes which victims willingly report. Often, such small problems are therefore not seen as important in national statistics. The reason is quite simple: on the one hand, for the victim to call the police is often considered too great of a counter-action which may even lead to unwanted embarrassment for the victim. On the other hand, broken windows, damaged public property or vandalism are not reported unless the damage is financially significant. For many residents, nuisances and minor aggressions (neighbours threatening each other) are often considered as "part of life in an economically less favoured neighbourhood".

Another factor that influences the preparedness of victims to report a small crime or aggression to the police is whether they have sufficient insurance to cover eventual claims for reparation or a visit to the doctor for an injury. For minor aggressions, insurance policies do not provide refunds unless the victim has a higher insurance premium with a low franchise limit or none at all. This implies that many minor cases of violence, vandalism or small thefts remain largely unreported. In contrast, large thefts, such as a stolen automobile or a break-in in a private home, will almost always be reported because the victim wants a reimbursement from the insurance company. According to a French study, only about 5% of all victims of minor and serious aggressions actually suffered physical injuries that were critical enough for repeated visits to a doctor, a stay in a hospital or an absence from work or school.[101] Confidence may be very high, but if insurance premiums are considered expensive by the victims, then reporting will still remain low. It follows that reports of crimes and aggressions, as they appear in crime statistics, depend heavily on whether the victim actually decides to mention the grievance to the police. In fact, it is estimated that half of all victims of minor offences as well as of more serious crimes and violence do not report to the police. We must therefore keep in mind a very large "dark" area of unknown offences.

Victims of less serious offences often do not want a police investigation or a medical examination. These may disrupt an otherwise tolerable living condition (perhaps in a tense family or urban environment). The more a physical aggression or violence is an internal family matter or represents an embarrassment to the victim (such as sexual violence), the less likely that the police will ever know about it. "Willingness to report *contact* crimes to the police [...] reflects the willingness of victims to confide and trust in the police."[102] An indicator of public confidence in the police and the criminal justice system of a country can be estimated by the number of victim reports. This is especially true for crimes that require greater personal courage on the part of the victim to report the offence.

Many offences or even physical aggressions are not reported because in the communities in which these happen most frequently – in the lower socio-economic urban areas – the police is also least trusted by their residents. This is even more noticeable among two groups. First, foreign residents and immigrants who have not fully integrated in the host society and second, teenagers. Communities and families who consider themselves already marginalised (unemployed or poor) or who have settled recently and remain unsure about how the police treats them are more reluctant to establish contacts with state authorities. In the same vein, immigrants and foreign workers may also try to keep a low profile so as not to attract attention or criticism from their neighbours.

---

101 In part from: ROBERT, P., R. ZAUBERMAN, M. L. POTTIER and H. LAGRANGE, "Mesurer le crime: Entre statistique de police et enquêtes de victimation (1985–1995)" in *Revue française de sociologie*, Vol. 40:2, April/June, 1999; pp. 261 & 264.
102 KANGASPUNTA, K., M. JOUTSEN and N. OLLUS, *Crime and Criminal Justice Systems in Europe and North America 1990–1994*, Helsinki: European Institute for Crime Prevention and Control (HEUNI), 1998; p. 106.

The second group are teenagers. Many do not respect state officials such as the police or social workers. They have no desire to be seen by their peers as "softies" who ask for help. Regardless of whether they are of foreign, immigrant origin or whether they are indigenous. Few teenagers want to report their victimization unless they are seriously injured. In contrast, established middle and upper-class adult communities, whether they are indigenous citizens or well-integrated immigrants, generally have greater confidence in the police and in the criminal justice system of the country. This indicates that crime statistics are perhaps most reliable where they record the number of offences reported by well established middle-class populations.

We can summarise, then, that the more marginalised a community is, be they youth, foreigners or economically less fortunate indigenous families, the less reliable police records of delinquency, violence and crime become. A similar bias in criminal records also exists at the opposite "upper end", so to speak, of marginalisation. Statistics on so-called "white-collar" crime committed by professional offenders are generally far more difficult to uncover and record than the more obvious crimes committed in public. Organised crime groups and individuals who evade taxes, use bribery and corruption or commit financial fraud will, by the nature of their offences, conceal their activities. Moreover, as there are rarely identifiable victims who would call the police or visit a doctor for injuries in many of these types of crimes, the data can be based mostly on criminal investigations and judicial procedures. Their effectiveness depends less on the confidence which the public has in the police than on the quality of criminal police intelligence information technology, its geographical mobility and its good collaboration with police agencies and legal authorities in different regions and countries.

## Conclusion

Contrary to the impression which crime statistics, media articles and stories on yearly crime figures may provide, numbers and types of offences or numbers of certain kinds of offenders do not help us to understand how safe we are in society. As regards our concern here for internal security, the information from crime statistics and victim surveys tells us the following:

- First, police records principally show us those thefts which are relatively serious and important for the victim financially or health-wise and which he or she was willing to reveal publicly.
- Second, information on crime and victimization surveys reveals that there exists a correlation between deviant and offending behaviour and economic and social factors (economic stress, life in high-density urban settings, greater opportunities for crimes as well as greater exposure to communities who are already involved in crime or violence).
- Third, most minor aggressions remain part of the "dark" area not recorded in official statistics. The same goes for white-collar crime which is kept hidden from police and public scrutiny.
- Fourth, victim surveys tell us that is it precisely the small offences (reckless impulsive or offending behaviour, vandalism or minor aggressions) which make people feel insecure. In other words, if (subjective) security among the population is to be improved, more attention must be given to the vulnerable and marginalised population groups. Regardless of nationality or ethnic origin. This applies particularly to young men between the age of 15 to 25 who live in or come from lower socio-economic urban areas and who have experienced violence either in their own families or in countries where war, poverty and crime may have influenced their behaviour.
- Finally, where statistics are only of very limited use is in obtaining an understanding of the context in which offences are committed. Without such an understanding, it remains difficult to design appropriate crime prevention strategies or improve public security.

In conclusion, then, comprehensive preventive strategies can be developed only when crime data is interpreted within the context in which specific communities experience a greater risk of crime.

Chapter 5

# Migration, Immigration and Internal Security

The following chapter examines whether migrants and immigrants represent a challenge to internal security in Europe today. The challenges considered here are of both kinds, objective and subjective. The former include problems with regard to the numbers of migrants or asylum seekers and the capacity of individual countries and the European Union to deal with these. The latter subjective challenges concern the public perception of safety in society. Unexpected changes which large numbers of refugees or ongoing immigration can introduce to a host country may be a cause for anxiety or feelings of insecurity. However, such feelings are not predestined. Insecurity can be prevented by adapting migration (visa, asylum, immigration and integration) policies to new domestic and international needs as well as to shifting public perceptions.

To come to terms with these two approaches, the following subjects will be discussed in the pages that follow:
- Migration and asylum trends;
- The momentum of migration and recent developments;
- Pressures and incentives that lead to emigration;
- Immigration in a multi-cultural Europe; and
- The potential challenges to internal security.

A migrant is defined here as a person who has left his or her home country and who does not have a residency permit in any other country. This person may be enrolled in an asylum procedure (by claiming to be a refugee) in a host country and must be distinguished from migrant labourers who travel to a predefined place of temporary employment and residency.[103] A mi-

---

103 For the purpose of clarity, immigrants are defined as persons who are legally or illegally (clandestinely) in the host country of their choice and have the intention to settle, if not permanently, then at least for an undefined period. This usually implies

grant may thus be a refugee, an economic migrant, a clandestine migrant or a clandestine immigrant.[104]

The capacity of European society to accommodate more and more new settlers was rarely a topic of debate until about twenty years ago. At the time, the integration of immigrants and of temporary foreign workers was simply not addressed – foreign labour was seen as a short-term economic measure that would disappear without a trace as soon as it would not be needed any longer. Even the accommodation of migrant labourers and their families seemed un-problematic. This was because economic growth, scientific progress, the strength of the welfare state and the corporatist collaboration between government and industry were able to moderate tensions between different interest groups within society. Phenomena, such as unemployment, shortages of housing, poverty, crime as well as crime by foreigners were then simply regarded as normal side-effects of a modern liberal society.[105]

Since the 1980's, however, migration, foreign labour and immigration have become topics of debate, especially when they are linked to economic and social security or public safety. Furthermore, many Europeans do not wish to see their continent become one of immigration in the image of North America. They have the impression that social stability and internal security will be threatened – national and personal identity becoming unrecognisable as Europe becomes "less" European. A significant cause of subjective insecurity is the fear that foreigners will take away jobs, exploit social welfare programmes and perhaps commit more crimes than any in-

a time-span in which they can try to acquire a long-term residency permit and/or citizenship (naturalisation). In contrast, foreign labourers are persons who come to a host country to find temporary employment and do not intend to settle for longer than the duration of their employment. With respect to European statistics on immigration, however, several countries include foreign workers once these live and work for a given amount of time in the country.

104 A clandestine migrant is a person who crosses international borders in such a manner as not to be seen or controlled by border guards. He or she has no appropriate travel visa or personal identification for the journey. A clandestine immigrant is one who lives in the host country with the intention to remain without appropriate residency permits or personal identification.

105 In part from: HEITMEYER, Wilhelm, "Einleitung: Sind individualisierte und ethnickulturell vielfältige Gesellschaften noch integrierbar?" in HEITMEYER, W., ed., *Was hält die Gesellschaft zusammen?* Frankfurt a. Main: Edition Suhrkamp, 1997: p. 9.

digenous European would. Such perceptions represent a challenge to internal security which can be as serious or even more so than objective data measured in statistics.

## Population pressures, poverty and wealth

Migrants come to Western Europe because of the prospects ("pull factor") of employment, better wages, material comforts or family reunification. Or, people may leave their homes because of pressures ("push factor") such as abject poverty and a lack of income-earning opportunities. One such pressure in the home country is high population density. For example: while the indigenous European population is not growing with the average family having less than 2 children, some migrant-exporting countries are experiencing the opposite trend. The vast majority of the population in the Maghreb countries of North Africa is under the age of thirty and fertility levels are three to four times higher than in Europe.[106] The young segment of these countries' populations constitute by far the largest group that try to come as migrant workers or settle as long-term immigrants in Europe.

Furthermore, while the indigenous European population is shrinking, the new immigrant population in Europe is growing due the gradual increase of new residents and higher fertility.[107] Most national statistical institutes therefore expect the total population in Europe to continue growing for the next 10 years at least – a development which inevitably will make European society become increasingly heterogeneous.[108] So long population demographics and living conditions remain as they are, a momentum of emigration will persist in African and other less industrialised countries.

Migration will slow down in only two instances: either a great majority of new settlers are unsuccessful in the host country and return home, or the

---

106 WAXMAN, Dov, *Immigration and Identity: A New Security Perspective in Euro-Magreb Relations*, London: Research Institute for the Study of Conflict and Terrorism, September 1997; pp. 5–7.

107 *Eurostat Yearbook, 1997*, Tables "Natural population increase per 1000 inhabitants" and "Net migration including corrections per 1000 people" for the years 1986–1996.

108 Population projections, *Eurostat Yearbook, 1997*, see charts "Total population at 1 January 1997" and "Population projections by different organisations".

home country's economy improves to such an extent that fewer and fewer young men and women want to leave. Today, however, the standard of living in Balkan or Maghreb countries is three to ten times lower than in Western Europe. The discrepancy of living standards makes the West attractive to potential migrants.

## Changes and Trends

In order to shed some light on why security and public safety are so often linked to migration, asylum and immigration, it is useful to look at the dynamics that appear to turn Europe into an immigration society. An estimated 20 million people are permanently on the move around the world today. The reason for this enormous migration is, on the one hand, disparities in wealth, and on the other hand, advances in communications and transportation technology. The world's wealthy travel for business and pleasure while the poor travel in search of employment or survival. Over the next fifteen years, the world's population will have grown to seven billion from six in 1999. During that same time-span, air travel will have doubled for the rich, and clandestine migration will have tripled for the poor.

Western Europe as well as the present and future Central European candidates for membership in the European Union form an attractive region of destination for many young men and women from less industrialised countries.[109] Not counting tourists and short-term professional travellers, about 1 million people enter the EU legally each year to stay for longer periods of time. This corresponds to the approximate number of immigrants that arrive in the USA and Canada. Some come for determined periods as foreign workers, others come to join families and settle as immigrants. Still others

109 Western Europe includes all the countries that were part of the "West" during the Cold War. For the purpose of this text, Central Europe includes, from North to South, the three Baltic states, Poland, the Czech and Slovak Republics, Hungary, Romania, Bulgaria and Albania as well as all the regions that belonged to the former Yugoslavia. While the countries and territories immediately eastwards (Belarus, Ukraine, Moldova and the Russian territory of Kalinigrad) could also be included in the term Central Europe they are – their geographic proximity to "Central" Europe notwithstanding – left out here because they are generally not considered as likely members of the EU in the near to medium future.

100

remain clandestine until they obtain an amnesty and legal residency. An approximate average of 200'000 additional migrants come each year as asylum seekers.[110] Thus Europe is what many refuse to recognise: a land of immigration.

In 1982, there were about 14.6 Million foreign residents in Western Europe (not including East Germany).[111] In 1996 there were some 19.8 Mill. persons with foreign nationality registered in Western Europe.[112] With regard to Central Europe, an estimated 5 to 8 million foreigners live in these former communist countries.[113] Their proportion to the indigenous population in both Central and Western Europe is between 4% and 6%. This proportion is similar when compare to other immigration regions in the world.[114]

---

110 *The Economist*, April 4, 1998; p. 29.
111 Among registered foreigners in most West European countries are also those who were born of foreign parents in the host country, but have not been naturalised. "Foreigners" implies all persons with a foreign citizenship.
112 MÜNZ, Rainer, "Demographische Vergangenheit und Zukunft der Industrie Gesellschaft Europas", in *Schweizer Monatshefte*, Vol. 78., No. 11, November 1998; p. 23.
113 These numbers include foreigners from one Western or Central European country who live in another European country. The figures of foreign residents for Central Europe can be but a rough estimates as thousands of migrants travel through these countries every day.
114 This includes all indigenous EU and non-EU citizens who live in another EU country. ANGENENDT, Steffen, ed., *Asylum and Migration Policies in the European Union*, Berlin: Research Institute of the German Society for Foreign Affairs (DGAP), 1999; p. 6. (In 1995, the EU had a population of 371 Million – 15 member states. In 1996, 18'134 million people in the EU had a nationality other than the one of the country in which they live.) In comparison, the United States has a population of 274 million, (265 million in 1996). 1.8 million persons in 1991, 720'500 in 1995 and some 915'900 people in 1996 were given a permanent immigrant status. The proportion of persons who reside in the USA but were born outside of the country is over 4 % of the citizen population. (Of the number of new immigrants each year, some are admitted as refugees. This number is approximately 200'000 per year). As for Canada, it has a population of about 29 million. In the 1990's, an average of about 220'000 persons per year were registered as new immigrants. The proportion of persons who reside in Canada but were born outside the country is over 16 % of the citizen population. (Of the number of new immigrants each year, some are admitted as refugees. For example, in 1997, some 48'800 refugees were admitted). Family reunification is the most important reason for immigration in both, Canada and the USA and corresponds to about 60 % percent of all immigrants.

*Table:*

Number of foreign residents in selected countries for the years 1989 and 1996 and their proportion in percentage to citizens. These figures include West Europeans who live in another European country.[115]

|  | 1989 |  | 1996 |  |
|---|---|---|---|---|
| Austria | 456'000 | 5.9% | 728'200 | 9.0% |
| Belgium | 904'500 | 9.1% | 911'900 | 9.0% |
| Germany | 5'342'000 | 8.4% | 7'314'000 | 8.9% |
| France | 3'596'000 | 6.3% | 4'000'000 | 6.8% |
| Italy | 781'100 | 1.4% | 1'095'600 | 2.0% |
| Netherlands | 692'400 | 4.6% | 679'900 | 4.4% |
| United Kingdom | 1'723'000 | 3.2% | 1'972'000 | 3.4% |
| Switzerland[116] | 1'100'300 | 16.3% | 1'371'000 | 19.3% |
| West. Europe[117] | 16'085'000 | 4.5% | 19'853'000 | 5.2% |
| Czech Republic | ——— |  | 198'600 | 1.9% |
| Hungary | ——— |  | 142'500 | 1.4% |
| United States[118] | 11'770'300 | 4.7% | ——— | 4.0%[119] |

Meanwhile, the number of naturalisations has grown in Europe just as it has in the USA and Canada: For example, in 1988, the fifteen countries now part of the EU gave 186'788 new citizenships while in 1994 they handed out 330'117. The USA and Canada gave new citizenships for the same two years: 242'100 and 58'800 (1988) and 407'400 and 217'300 (1994) re-

115 Taken from two sources: MÜNZ, Rainer, "Demographische Vergangenheit und Zukunft der Industrie Gesellschaft Europas", in *Schweizer Monatshefte*, Vol. 78., No. 11, November 1998; p. 23; and OECD/OCDE Organisation de Coopération et de développement économiques, *Tendances des Migrations Internationales*, SOPEMI Rapport annuel 1998; p. 244.

116 Figures for Switzerland do not include seasonal foreign workers nor civil servants in international organisations.

117 For Western Europe, 18 countries are added up. Source: MÜNZ, Rainer, "Demographische Vergangenheit und Zukunft der Industrie Gesellschaft Europas", in *Schweizer Monatshefte*, Vol. 78., No. 11, November 1998; p. 23.

118 Foreigners in the USA, as in the other immigration countries, are persons who were born in another country and have not yet acquired citizenship.

119 For the USA, the percentage of foreign-born residents is the author's estimate.

spectively.[120] For the 15 EU countries, the number of new citizenships per year in the late 1990's has reached about 350'000 (1997).[121] It is important to note that the rise of naturalisations does not necessarily mean that there is a corresponding rise of new immigrant settlers in Europe. Rather, it may indicate a gradual change in naturalisation policy towards favouring a speedier acquisition of citizenship for immigrants.

*Table:*
Acquisition of citizenship (naturalisation).[122]

|  | 1990 | 1996 |
|---|---|---|
| Austria | 9'200 | 16'200 |
| Belgium | 8'500 (1991) | 24'600 |
| Germany | 101'377 | 302'830 |
| France | 88'500 | 109'800 |
| Hungary | 3'200 | 12'100 |
| Italy | 4'500 (1991) | 7'000 |
| Netherlands | 12'800 | 82'700 |
| United Kingdom | 57'300 | 43'100 |
| Switzerland | 8'700 | 19'400 |
| Canada | 104'300 | 227'700 (1995)[123] |
| United States | 270'100 | 1'044'700 |

The figures indicate that European countries are immigration countries for all the hundreds of thousands of new settlers. However, "rare is the politician brave enough to call his country a land of immigration."[124] Every time the news media report about the arrival of large numbers of migrants and

---

120 *Eurostat Yearbook* 1998/99, "Acquisition of citizenship"; p. 106; and OECD/OCDE Organisation de Coopération et de développement économiques, *Tendances des Migrations Internationales*, SOPEMI Rapport annuel 1998; p. 245.

121 MÜNZ, Rainer, "Demographische Vergangenheit und Zukunft der Industrie Gesellschaft Europas", in *Schweizer Monatshefte*, Vol. 78., No. 11, November 1998; p. 23.

122 OECD/OCDE Organisation de Coopération et de développement économiques, *Tendances des Migrations Internationales*, "Acquisitions de la nationalité dans certains pays de l'OCDE", SOPEMI Rapport annuel 1998; p. 245.

123 In proportion to the size of its population of some 28 million, Canada allows the greatest number of persons to become citizens.

124 *The Economist*, April 4, 1998; p. 29.

asylum seekers in Western Europe, concerns are heard that social stability and public safety may be compromised. An underlying current of anxiety becomes especially palpable when interest groups or nationalist political parties call for restrictive isolationist measures. For example: a halt to immigration and naturalisation, tougher controls at national borders to stop migrants from coming or to impose stricter limitations on the number of foreigners who can reside in the country.

## Asylum seekers and clandestine arrivals and departures

Since the end of the Cold War and the opening of the formerly guarded "iron curtain", Western and Central European countries have all experienced strong fluctuations in the numbers of migrants and asylum applicants. Temporary steep increases of asylum seekers and resident foreigners in various West European countries reflect the political and economic instability around the world. However, as the next table shows, the number of asylum seekers has been declining since the all-time high was recorded in 1992. Then, about 693'000 persons applied for asylum in Western Europe.[125] This decline of applications is mainly a consequence of the more restrictive asylum policies in the EU. Even the temporary high numbers of applicants due to the war in Kosovo have not reversed this overall decreasing trend of asylum applications.[126]

125 MÜNZ, Rainer, "Phasen und Formen der europäischen Migration", in ANGENENDT, Steffen, ed., *Migration und Flucht*, München: Verlag R. Oldenbourg, Bundeszentrale für politische Bildung, (Schriftenreihe Band 342) 1997; p. 42.
126 ANGENENDT, Steffen, ed., *Asylum and Migration Policies in the European Union*, Berlin: Research Institute of the German Society for Foreign Affairs (DGAP), 1999; p. 19.

*Table:*
Asylum applications in selected countries 1989–1997.[127]

|  | 1989 | 1991 | 1993 | 1995 | 1997 |
|---|---|---|---|---|---|
| Belgium | 8'000 | 15'000 | 27'000 | 11'000 | 12'000 |
| Germany | 121'000 | 256'000 | 323'000 | 128'000 | 104'000 |
| France | 61'000 | 47'000 | 28'000 | 20'000 | 21'000 |
| Netherlands | 14'000 | 22'000 | 35'000 | 29'000 | 34'000 |
| Austria | 22'000 | 27'000 | 5'000 | 6'000 | 7'000 |
| United Kingdom | 17'000 | 73'000 | 29'000 | 44'000 | 33'000 |
| Switzerland | 24'000 | 42'000 | 25'000 | 17'000 | 24'000 |

Political and economic crises during the 1990's produced large numbers of economic migrants. Besides the collapse of the communist planned economy, drastic reforms unsettled many industries and workers in Central and Eastern Europe. Thousands of people either fled from violence or departed westwards and northwards in search of a safe haven and jobs. Particularly the wars in Bosnia and Kosovo brought the experience home to Europeans of how quickly refugees and migrants can appear at their doorstep asking for help, a new home or a job. All through the 1990's, thousands of Bosnians, Serbs, Croatians, Kosovars and other populations from the former Yugoslavia including the Roma (Gypsies) travelled to Western Europe. Kurds from eastern Turkey came as well to the West along with significant numbers of North Africans and, in smaller numbers, economic migrants from Western Africa and Asia.

The political and economic instability in Albania, for example, caused a massive emigration of young men which began in the Spring of 1997. It followed the collapse of pyramid investment schemes into which many Albanians had placed their savings. The ensuing financial chaos led to a

127 Source: *Eurostat Yearbook 1998/99 and 2000*, Table "Asylum applicants in the asylum countries". Note: as the definition and determination process of asylum seekers varies in most countries, these figures are not strictly comparable. Furthermore, some countries have left out some asylum applicants such as children (Belgium and France) or those who qualified for an exceptional status (Austria with regard to refugees from the Former Yugoslavia) or who were rejected at the border upon entry because they did not have identity papers (Switzerland). In contrast to Belgium and France, Germany includes all children.

security crisis in the south which the government in Tirana could not control. As a consequence, Italy was confronted with a wave of Albanian "boat people" as well as with the need to intervene militarily in Albania in 1997 to help the local authorities control the movement of potential migrants. Nevertheless, Albanians in Italy represented the largest group of asylum seekers in the years since 1997. But other nationalities were also significant among new arrivals. Among them large numbers from North Africa, Iraq, Turkey and the province of Kosovo. As Italy is not able to control all arriving migrants at its borders nor keep large numbers of them in reception centres until they are either offered asylum or repatriated, many manage to leave on their own and travel northwards. Finally, the number of asylum seekers accounted for are not the only migrants on Italian soil. An estimated 250'000 to 300'000 clandestine migrants (for 1998) must be added to the numbers of asylum seekers.[128]

Like Italy, all of Europe is becoming home to an increasingly diverse population of foreign residents and immigrants. Legal and clandestine migrants do not only come from the Balkans, Eastern Europe or North Africa. Iraqi Kurds, West Africans and Asians from as far away as Sri Lanka and China also contribute a large proportion of the total numbers of migrants in Western and Central Europe. Each year, anywhere between 150'000 to 300'000 clandestine migrants come to Western Europe. Many tens-of-thousands receive amnesties after they have lived in a country for a certain amount of time. For example, Belgium, Britain, France, Greece, Italy, Portugal and Spain have all offered legal residency status for so-called "*sans papiers*".[129] But such restricted generosity never seems enough. The resident clandestine population in Western Europe today is estimated at 2.5

128 For Italy, some figures are given in: *Migration und Bevölkerung* Newsletter of the Lehrstuhl Bevölkerungswissenschaft, Humboldt-Universität, Berlin, issues No. 7, September 1998; pp. 3–4; and No. 3, March 1999; p. 3.

129 *The Economist*, April 4, 1998; p. 29. Also: "Frankreichs '*sans-papiers*' nach der Teilregularisierung…80 000 Antragsteller", in *Neue Zürcher Zeitung*, 21. January 1999, p. 9; ANGENENDT, Steffen, ed., *Asylum and Migration Policies in the European Union*, Berlin: Research Institute of the German Society for Foreign Affairs (DGAP), 1999; pp. 45–46. Also: "Belgique", *Le Temps*, 11 January 2000; p. 5; and for Switzerland: "De l'occupation […] de Saint-François à Lausanne", in *Le Temps*, 25 February 2000; p. 15.

million persons.[130] In comparison, more than 5 million clandestine immigrants live in the United States, giving that country a higher per capita number of "illegal aliens".[131]

A problem with all the numbers of asylum seekers and clandestine migrants is that, statistically, the records of new settlers is not counter-balanced with numbers of departures. This renders estimates of clandestine residents very difficult and can lead to an over-estimations of their numbers. The number of clandestine immigrants who leave a West European country can range anywhere between 100% and 50% of the number of new arrivals in any given year. However, little is known about those who leave and the direction in which they go. Still, this is important to note because discussions on asylum seekers and clandestine migrants often give the impression that everybody comes to the West, but nobody leaves. Clearly, this is wrong. The difficulty is that departures are almost always "clandestine" while a majority of arrivals are eventually registered through the issuing of permits either for asylum or residency.

One principal reason for the constant arrival of clandestine migration flows into Western Europe is that migrants face increasing difficulties in entering legally. Few opportunities remain to apply as foreign labourers, and the option of family re-unification has also been restricted. As a consequence, asylum requests and clandestine immigration are replacing the former legal and foreign-labour-needs-oriented immigration options.[132] In other words, the asylum system has become the "overflow container" to the extent that legal channels for entry have been restricted.[133]

130 Estimate of clandestine immigrants by Jonas Widgren of the International Centre for Migration Policy Development, Vienna, as mentioned in: *The Economist*, April 4, 1998; p. 29. See also: STRAUBHAAR, Thomas & Achim WOLTER (1996): "Aktuelle Brennpunkte der europäischen Migrationsdiskussion". *Wirtschaftsdienst*, 1996/IX; p. 482.
131 *Migration und Bevölkerung* Newsletter of the Lehrstuhl Bevölkerungswissenschaft, Humboldt-Universität, Berlin, issues No. 7, September 1998; No. 3, March 1999; p. 4.
132 TRAUBHAAR, Thomas & Achim WOLTER: "Aktuelle Brennpunkte der europäischen Migrationsdiskussion". *Wirtschaftsdienst*, 1996/IX: p. 482.
133 OBERNDÖRFER, Dieter and Uwe BERNDT, "Möglichkeiten der Einwanderungsbegrenzung", in WEBER, Albrecht, ed., *Einwanderungsland Bundesrepublik Deutschland in der Europäischen Union: Gestaltung und Regelungsmöglichkeiten*, Osnabrück: Universitätsverlag Rasch, 1997; p. 186.

The "old continent" is obviously a "new world" for many young migrants. How do all these people manage to enter Europe? Most migrants that come to Western Europe, be it first to Italy, Britain or any other country, are transported by migrant smugglers. These operate in all the countries where migrants come from and have networks of middle-men along the major routes northwards and westwards. More than 80% of all migrants coming to Western Europe are smuggled across borders by these criminal groups. This is revolting when we realise that traffickers exploit the economically deprived migrants who are most often unemployed or even politically persecuted; it is "as scandalous as it is global".[134]

In 1993 and 1994, an estimated 500'000 clandestine migrants were smuggled into the EU. They each paid "anywhere between 250.00 and 25'000.00 US dollars depending on the distance and the services provided by the trafficking organisation".[135] A specific example of this migrant smuggling business is the United Kingdom. Some 20 groups compete in the smuggling "market". Migrants who want to reach England pay anywhere between £250.00 and £15'000.00 to be "brought" to their destination. Some 2'000 to 4'000 such migrants arrive in the U.K. each month.[136]

The dynamics that drive migration are not about to diminish. In fact, several trends can be discerned which developed over the last few years. They are likely to determine the future character of migration and immigration in Europe: (1) The total number of resident foreigners has increased along with (2) their ethnic diversity. (3) Western European countries have shown a gradual tendency to facilitate the naturalisation of foreigners who have lived in Europe for a given number of years (legally or illegally). Finally, (4) the numbers of asylum applications have decreased through the second half of the 1990's and will most likely do so in the years to come. This is in large part because asylum regulations have been restricted since 1993 in all West European countries.

134 GASTEYGER, Curt, "Migration: the 'Crisis of our Age'? in The Japan Foundation Centre for Global Partnership, *The End of the Century: The Future in the Past*, Tokyo: Kodansha International, 1995; p. 200.
135 ANGENENDT, Steffen, ed., *Asylum and Migration Policies in the European Union*, Berlin: Research Institute of the German Society for Foreign Affairs (DGAP), 1999; p. 34.
136 GREGORY, Frank, "Migrants and Transnational Crime", Paper prepared for a conference at Chatham House, *Policy Challenges of the New Migrant Diasporas*, London, April 22–23, 1999; P. 6; unpublished.

## The migration momentum

Most migrants arriving in Western Europe choose to do so for their own economic betterment and/or to meet up with their family. To a large extent, migration is determined by periodic rises and declines of economic opportunities and the development of family and friendship networks. First, a so-called "culture of emigration" develops in communities that collectively learn about the benefits of having their young men and women work in industrialised countries.[137] Gradually, as the benefits become significant enough, a momentum develops which motivates not only more young people to emigrate to the West, but induces entire families to follow. The demand in Western markets for goods, labour and services from less industrialised countries stimulate the creation of these networks. They, then, become the links or bridges over which migrants find their new employment or new homes in Western Europe or other immigration countries.

"Cultures of emigration" also existed among Europeans. Up to the middle of the twentieth century, several West European countries experienced a large emigration of their citizens. Germany did so after the First and the Second World Wars while Ireland, Italy, Spain and Portugal experienced significant emigrations for over a hundred and fifty years. Most recently, some 2.7 million Europeans emigrated between 1950 and 1959.[138] Only by the late 1960's were more asylum seekers recorded in Western Europe than indigenous Europeans who emigrated. European emigration reached its peak when poverty and despair in the home/"old country" was most strongly felt while the destination countries provided hope for prosperity. In other words, a "culture of emigration" affects any given population at a specific period in their history. This occurs when economic development does not provide the quality of life expected while at the same time, emigrants are successful in finding better lives in a new host country.

It is not absolute poverty that drives emigration. The poorest populations groups are not often able to emigrate. Rather, it is the intensity with which migrants and industry form links of communication and commerce

---

137 The term "culture of emigration" was suggested by Mr. Werner Blatter, Regional Representative, UNHCR, Vienna, 22 March 1999.
138 Münz, Rainer, "Phasen und Formen der europäischen Migration", in Angenendt, Steffen, ed., *Migration und Flucht*, München: Verlag R. Oldenbourg, Bundeszentrale für politische Bildung, (Schriftenreihe Band 342) 1997; p. 43.

between the home and the immigration country which drives migration. Sustained exchanges of information and material benefits produce the "bridges" across which potential migrants learn of opportunities and then travel to the destination country.[139] Such bridges were first built by Europeans during the colonial period. Its heritage left many profitable commercial trade networks alive. It is on the basis of these that long-established exchanges of goods and services have developed. Colonial history has also left a linguistic legacy linking the metropolitan states to regions in the former "overseas territories". Today, many if not most labourers and immigrants come from these regions. European import and export industries not only benefited from these trade links in the past, they still do so today. The most obvious example of how influential former colonial ties are can be seen from the nationality of migrants who travel to Europe. The U.K. is, for example, home to most immigrants from its former colonies in South Asia, especially India and Pakistan. France receives asylum seekers mostly from North and West African countries which at one time belonged to the Francophone zone of colonial influence while the Netherlands is the country of choice for immigrants from Indonesia.

As was the case in Europe up to the 1950's, many less industrialised countries now experience a "culture of emigration". In many families, the older generation of parents help their sons or daughters to emigrate to a Western county. The success which the younger migrants then have in finding a job in the new host country helps to motivate more family members and friends to try the same. The continuous employment of foreign workers in Western Europe contributes to developing the migration momentum. Today, Germany and Switzerland are among the most popular destination countries for asylum seekers and migrants from the Balkans. This is so particularly for emigrants from Turkey and the former Yugoslavia. Germany employed large numbers of citizens from these countries from the 1950's to the 1970's while Switzerland is home to a large number of Albanian-speaking Kosovars who came as Yugoslav workers in the 1970's and 1980's.

---

139 In part from: OBERNDÖRFER, Dieter and Uwe BERNDT, "Möglichkeiten der Einwanderungsbegrenzung", in WEBER, Albrecht, ed., *Einwanderungsland Bundesrepublik Deutschland in der Europäischen Union: Gestaltung und Regelungsmöglichkeiten*, Osnabrück: Universitätsverlag Rasch, 1997; p. 185.

But not all potential emigration dynamics develop as expected. For example, no tradition of departure manifested itself in Russia following the opening of the Iron Curtain. The same is true among other Eastern or Central Europeans except for communities in the Balkans where outright war forced many to flee. One principal reason is that Russian or Polish immigrant and foreign labourer communities in Western Europe are very small. They have not established the intense communication and commercial links with families and friends in the home country as Turks and Yugoslavs have done. The news of successes which earlier emigrants convey to their families and communities in the home country is perhaps the strongest factor that contributes to emigration. As long as positive signals (employment, savings sent back to the family, reunification with family members) find their way to the "old" home, then the migration momentum will persist.

Nevertheless, most people around the world prefer to live and prosper in their home communities and societies. To emigrate is to abandon a part of one's identity and culture. This is almost always a difficult undertaking for it implies adapting to a new cultural, social and professional environment. The few communities who still want to leave their homes permanently include highly educated professionals (business entrepreneurs, scientists) who cannot pursue their careers in the home country. They therefore move to a place where this is possible (often the United States). This is worth remembering because the vast majority of people who migrate to Western Europe (legally or illegally) each year leave their homes reluctantly and mostly because "making a living" at home has become more difficult and frustrating than expected.

## Immigration and the "multi-culturalisation" of Europe

Problems of integrating new settlers, be they temporary asylum seekers, temporary foreign labourers or permanent immigrants, have become a headache for those trying to promote multi-cultural harmony in European cities. One cause of the problem is that the integration of new settlers in indigenous communities becomes very difficult when the latter are unwilling to accept immigrants and the changes they bring. This difficulty is not new. It has existed in all cultures in the past and is also very visible in so-called immigration countries.

Immigration, when it is large and long-lasting, changes the character and way of life of the region where the migrants settle. This was the case of North America where European immigrants changed the continent into colonies first and then into two new countries. The North American natives could not halt this massive immigration of Europeans and had to accept the inevitable.

Almost no population or indigenous community in the world happily welcomes and accommodates new immigrants. Each society is protective of its social, economic and cultural wealth. Even the USA and Canada have their social problems due to immigration. At different periods in their history both countries tried to reduce the number of new immigrants with forceful means and restrictive policies. Nevertheless, large numbers of Latin Americans and Asians continue to settle in the United States today. Frictions and occasional violence between different older and newer immigrant communities or between these and descendants of White Europeans appear in the news media at an almost predictable regularity. Racism and so-called hate crimes catch public attention and create an impression that life in the USA must be unbearable for descendants from African slaves or immigrant minorities. Interestingly, however, most members of these minority groups would disagree. Almost none of them, regardless of their ethnic background, choose to emigrate to Europe, Australia or elsewhere today. Rather, the continuous arrival of new immigrants from Africa, Latin America and Asia, as well as the continuous "brain-fill" of foreign, highly trained professionals, attest to the attraction which North American society exercises for the rest of the World.

Most countries, including West European ones, welcome new people who can bring desirable professional skills or great financial wealth. The discrepancy between services offered to the fortunate elite and the economically less fortunate masses is telling. It indicates two things: First, migration policies are to a large extent the expression of a country's fear that the world's poorer masses will come to abuse the host's wealth. Anti-foreigner sentiments become all the greater at times of economic insecurity and growing unemployment. Under such conditions, immigrant communities are prone to be seen as undeserving competitors in the market for jobs, housing and welfare benefits. This animosity towards foreigners stems from the basic assumption that citizenship represents a "birth-right" for the indigenous population to the resources and state services of the home country.

These are essentially privileges which most nationals wish to protect. Thus, handing out passports to all immigrants who ask "requires slashing existing privileges ...[which] is precisely why immigration is even more jealously rejected by developed welfare states".[140] Second, poorer migrants are welcomed only when they work to help the host country's industries as low-wage labourers. Today, that the economy grows more slowly in Europe than in did in the 1960's and 1970's, foreign labourers are only wanted in selected industries such as construction and tourism.

*Table:*
Foreign workers legally employed in some European countries and their percentage of the total workforce.[141]

|  | 1990 | 1996 | % in 1996 |
|---|---|---|---|
| Austria | 229'500 | 328'000 | 10.0% |
| Belgium | 196'400 (1989) | ———— | 6.5% (1989) |
| Germany | 2'025'100 | 2'559'300 | 9.1% |
| France | 1'549'500 | 1'604'700 | 6.3% |
| Italy | 285'300 (1991) | 332'200 (1995) | 1.7% (1995) |
| Netherlands | 197'000 | 218'000 | 3.1% |
| United Kingdom | 882'000 | 878'000 | 3.4% |
| Switzerland[142] | 669'800 | 709'100 | 17.9% |
| EU total – 15 member states[143] | | 6'932'300 | |
| Hungary | 31'700 | 18'800 | 0.5% |
| Canada | 2'681'000 (1991) | ———— | 18.5% (1991) |
| United States | 11'564'600 | ———— | 9.4% (1990) |

140 Joppke, Christian, "Immigration Challenges the Nation-state", in Christian Joppke, ed., *Challenge to the Nation-state: Immigration in Western Europe and the United states*, Oxford: Oxford University Press, 1998; p. 7.
141 OECD/OCDE Organisation de Coopération et de développement économiques, *Effectifs de travailleurs étrangers et nés à l'étranger*, SOPEMI Rapport annuel 1998; p. 247.
142 More recent information indicates for Switzerland that the country's economy offers jobs to over 800'000 foreigners. Of this number, almost 700'000 reside in the country on year-permits. Some 27'000 are foreign seasonal workers and a little more than 140'000 are cross-border workers. *Neue Zürcher Zeitung*, 22. October 1999; p. 15.
143 Angenendt, Steffen, ed., *Asylum and Migration Policies in the European Union*, Berlin: Research Institute of the German Society for Foreign Affairs (DGAP), 1999; p. 14.

Many Europeans seem unwilling to recognise that their countries attract immigrants. While clearly not all Europeans are hostile to the idea of becoming members of an immigration society, politicians seem afraid to discuss such a prospect publicly. Immigrants and the migration of people in search of jobs is a political issue as much as it is a practical one. At the political level, accepting the inevitable multicultural and multi-ethnic Europe is a subjective problem. The capacity for politicians to avoid this sensitive issue can be worrying. Merely advocating a politically correct "tolerance" under a banner of official good-will is inadequate. This is also the case if we assume that the *laissez-faire* approach in a liberal democratic society will allow multi-culturalism to develop by itself. Such an attitude may promote just what it is supposed to eliminate: "the ethnic tilt of European nations".[144]

With few concrete and coherent migration and integration policies at hand, Europeans risk to experience a shock each time they realise that the homeland, the *"Heimat"*, is becoming an ethnically diverse society. The result is that members of immigrant communities are at best tolerated and left to become socially, politically and economically marginalised or at worst openly despised.[145]

## Social tensions, insecurity and integration

Perhaps the greatest cause of insecurity among the European public are social tensions related in some way to migration. These are mostly felt where many people must live in narrow spaces such as in crowded apartment blocks and ghetto-like suburbs. It is not uncommon that the wealthy indigenous

144 The quoted passage and argument in part from: JOPPKE, Christian, "Immigration Challenges the Nation-state", in Christian JOPPKE, ed., *Challenge to the Nation-state: Immigration in Western Europe and the United states*, Oxford: Oxford University Press, 1998; p. 37. See also a critique of the concept of multi-culturalism by WIEVIORKA, Michel, "Kritik des Multikulturalismus", in HEITMEYER, Wilhelm, et al., eds., *Die Krise der Städte*, Frankfurt am Main: Suhrkamp Verlag, No. es2036, 1998; pp. 97–122.

145 KEIM, Karl-Dieter, "Vom Zerfall des Urbanen", in HEITMEYER, Wilhelm, ed., *Was treibt die Gesellschaft auseinander?*, Frankfurt am Main: Suhrkamp Verlag, No. es2004, 1997; pp. 271–274.

(and foreign) residents keep to themselves and the middle classes remain largely untouched by these social tensions. The only time when these well-to-do communities hear of social problems is when the media reports, for example, of arson attacks against asylum homes or the desecration of Jewish grave sites. Residents in middle– or upper-middle class neighbourhoods, who can afford to live in more spacious residences, will more often hold liberal attitude towards multi-culturalism and immigration. They are more likely to remain unaware of the frustrations felt by their poorer compatriots.[146]

The danger is that the economically least fortunate indigenous and immigrant communities become marginalised "outsiders", left on one side of an increasingly segregated society.[147] Added to this is also the greater likelihood that subjective insecurity increases among both the indigenous and immigrants population. This is especially the case when social or economic problems (unemployment, lack of education opportunities) come to expression in the form of blunt antagonism towards foreigners. These are usually taken up by the most vulnerable members of society – mostly young and un-employed or under-employed men.

While extremist anti-foreigner or xenophobic political movements may represent only a tiny minority of the European population, it is perhaps true that they say in a direct and sometimes violent manner what many other Europeans might feel but would express differently. One source of the underlying frustrations and anti-foreigner sentiments rests on fears about declining living standards. More immigrants may mean more competition for space and resources. Another cause of frustration is the impression that European governments, their security organs, border guards and authorities responsible for asylum and immigration are unable to cope. A third source of frustration may be the worry that the globalisation of trade and of commerce has made traditionally stable jobs more precarious and that, again, European governments appear unable to exercise sufficient control over these world-wide economic and social changes.

---

146 KAPPELER, Beat, "Wir und die Ausländer: Wohltätig mit dem Geld von andern", in *Die Weltwoche*, 23 July 1998.

147 The study by Jens S. DANGSCHAT entitled "Warum ziehen sich Gegensätze nicht an?" discusses the development of inter-communal/inter-ethnic zones of conflict in cities. In HEITMEYER, Wilhelm, et al., eds., *Die Krise der Städte*, Frankfurt am Main: Suhrkamp Verlag, No. es2036, 1998; pp. 21–96.

The integration of immigrants is often considered as the solution to social tensions. However, it is not a panacea for every migration-related problem in European society. It merely constitutes one vital element in the larger security context which must not be overlooked.[148] Foreigners who receive long-term residency permits can be helped to integrate in society through specific policies. On the one hand, Europeans and long-term immigrants can promote the participation of new immigrants in cultural, educational and leisure activities of the host country. This implies that "integration measures include all activities that would increase the willingness of the native population to accept immigrants" as forming part of the new national population.[149] On the other hand, integration may also include official assistance for immigrant communities to operate their own distinct support groups and associations (cultural, religious, educational or sports centres). Through these, new immigrants can learn from long-established ones how best to live and work in the new host country.

As already alluded to, designing national integration policies requires more than merely the practical means and tools. The (subjective) political and public approach towards immigration also needs changing. Individual countries in Western and Central Europe as well as the EU as a whole must face this challenge. In reality as well as in the imagination, the days of the homogenous national society are over. Western and Central European countries cannot isolate themselves from the human demographic and economic developments around the world. The world's population is growing ever

148 By the term "integration" is meant that different interest groups or ethnic communities within a society enjoy the same rights in law, can participate in the same economic, social, educational and recreational institutions, but may also keep to themselves in all domains which do not adversely affect the interests of other communities. The aim of integration is to promote and maintain a civil society. This implies a society in which all members freely adhere not only to what is legally defined, but also to civil norms of appropriate behaviour with equal respect for all ethnic or linguistic communities and do not infringe on the rights nor disturb the peace of anyone. Thus, a maximum of freedom can be provided for each individual at the same time as a respect for differences among the same people is maintained. Integration must be distinguished from assimilation. The latter implies that all people, regardless of their cultural, religious or social interests, must also participate in the same social, educational and recreational institutions.

149 Quote from: ANGENENDT, Steffen, ed., *Asylum and Migration Policies in the European Union*, Berlin: Research Institute of the German Society for Foreign Affairs (DGAP), 1999; p. 61.

116

larger and countless more migrants will leave their homes in search of better living conditions elsewhere. A multi-cultural future in Europe appears inevitable so long as disparities in wealth and population demographics around the world continue in their present trends.

## The potential challenges to internal security

We come, then, to the question what challenges Europeans face with regard to migration, asylum and immigration. Including the ones already mentioned above, six general areas can be identified. These are:

(1) The mobility of all travellers around the world: This is facilitated primarily by the low costs of travel and the relative ease with which borders can be crossed. Regarding migrants and asylum seekers, another factor plays an important role. This is the large offer of clandestine smuggling "travel services" available inside and outside of Europe.

(2) The discrepancy of wealth and living standards between the West and developing countries: Among the population groups who may envisage to emigrate, the often stark difference in living standards contributes to the "push" and "pull" factors of migration. These are accentuated by technological advances in communication, commerce and entertainment. Together, these factors can contribute to the development of a "culture of emigration" and possibly a sustained migration momentum.

(3) The administration of migration and immigration policies within individual European countries: A major challenge with regard to policy-making is that Europeans are reluctant to admit they live in an increasingly globalised society of which immigration is an undeniable element. So long as the presence of foreign residents and of asylum seekers is seen as a source of problems, then the potential for social tensions and their expression in anti-foreigner sentiments will remain.

(4) The prevention of public insecurity and anti-foreigner sentiments among the indigenous European population: Perhaps the greatest challenge for individual states is to co-ordinate policies that have traditionally been seen as separate issues dealt with by different government departments. Among

these are: travel visas, border control, asylum procedures for refugees, employment and residency regulations for foreign workers, immigration and naturalisation, education for children of foreign residents and immigrants as well as closer collaboration between police forces and immigrant communities. Any effort to prevent public insecurity in a comprehensive manner requires that these different areas of political, economic and social policy are co-ordinated as much as possible.

(5) International European co-operation to develop common migration, asylum and immigration policies: A single country may have the best domestic asylum and immigration provisions, but without an adequate harmonisation of these with policies in neighbouring countries, the importance of international influences will remain overlooked. An isolationist perspective risks adding to the public's insecurity as it promotes the idea that the movement of migrants can be controlled exclusively from within the national territory.

(6) More effective European support for education and economic development in the countries where (potential) migrants come from: This is one of the most concrete methods to reduce migration pressures on both young people in developing countries and European welfare and integration support facilities.

These migration-related challenges affect in some way or other objective security within and among European countries. They also influence the subjective feelings of security among the public. Social tensions blamed on the presence of foreigners often arise because these challenges either remain inadequately addressed by state authorities or because the public is not well informed of what governments do locally, nationally and internationally to provide public security. For members of the public who feel insecure for various reasons, the number of asylum applicants and immigrants will (always) be too high. This is especially the case if the state is seen as not able to prevent insecurity among the population with regard to the presence of immigrants. In such situations, confidence in state institutions risks to erode most rapidly. Anti-foreigner sentiments and violence are to some extent an expression of this lack of confidence.

Governments must take into account the changing social, economic, political and security needs of the general public. This requires that individual governments within the European Union as well as those outside of it collaborate to bridge economic and educational disparities. They must together address the procedures by which foreigners are allowed to settle in a European country; i.e, regulations concerning residency permits, immigration, citizenship acquisition, schooling and employment.

However, procedures regarding the provision of residency permits to potential immigrants as well as the social and educational benefits in support of their integration are still considered essential elements of national state sovereignty. Within and without the European Union, individual states still jealously guard their control over their migration policy, the allocation of residency permits and of citizenships. Nevertheless, a momentum of policy adaptations is already underway today, it is promoted mainly by political movements interested in EU integration.

Due to integration in the EU, a common border control and visa regime exist today. These are regulated through the Schengen Agreement and the Dublin Convention. The latter determines the countries in which asylum applicants must place their requests while the former provides for where and how border controls are carried out. Information for this collaboration effort is managed through the Schengen Information System – a data-base which border guards and criminal police agencies can access. However, the EU states also need to focus on a harmonisation of their immigration and integration policies. Common standards for the assistance of asylum seekers and refugees are needed as well as common regulations on what family-reunification entails. This will not be an easy process as many countries do not wish to surrender control over domestic population and social matters.

When it comes to reforming policies that affect national laws on who can become a citizen and who cannot, or on how citizens of different socio-economic backgrounds are to be supported, each European country resists developing and adopting new EU-wide norms. Nevertheless, the EU member states "must confront the necessity of subsuming their national particularities to the agreed goal of a common European asylum and migration policy."[150] This was first attempted in the Amsterdam Treaty and will un-

---

150 ANGENENDT, Steffen, ed., *Asylum and Migration Policies in the European Union*, Berlin: Research Institute of the German Society for Foreign Affairs (DGAP), 1999; p. 60.

doubtedly be developed further. A harmonisation of migration policies is a logical step if the EU is not to remain a collection of national legal loopholes and regulatory disagreements.

As for countries that remain outside the EU by choice or because they await admission in the future, they have few alternatives but to gradually conform and adapt their policies to those of the EU. Not to do so can mean that they run the risk of becoming the "turntables" where the abuse of asylum regulations or the smuggling of migrants can be carried out or where criminally earned profits can be invested.

One example of the lack of policy harmonisation is heard from time to time when some west European countries complain that their southern or eastern neighbours are not doing enough to control the movements of people. These same countries occasionally also blame each other for their inefficiency in breaking up migrant smuggling organisations or preventing known criminals or terrorists from abusing asylum regulations. The states most often accused of insufficient co-operation are the Balkan countries, Turkey, Greece, as well as Italy and Spain.[151] However, such arguments reflect, on the one hand, a partial vision of the dynamics of migration, and on the other hand, political hesitations in Western Europe to develop coherent immigration and integration policies. Migration will not stop, even if European countries could double the number of police officers and border guards. Migrants would still manage to travel into Europe because at some point, green-, ocean- or river-borders are always penetrable. The passage of migrants through the border on the Rio Grande between Mexico and the USA is an indication of how determined migrants can be.

Given that the world's population is growing and that migration cannot be stopped, European countries must prepare themselves to share their geographic space and wealth with ever more immigrants. This will go on for as long as the emigration countries cannot develop their own economies and provide for their populations the living conditions that are more akin to Western life styles. In other words: "If money does not go to where the people are, then the people will go to where the money is."

This brings us to the last of the challenges. Besides developing more adapted policies of immigration and integration that fulfil security and so-

151 "Die EU und die Flüchtlinge" and "Deutscher Sonderfall?" in *Basler Zeitung*, 9 January 1998; p. 3.

cial needs in Europe, European governments must also contribute to alleviating the causes of migration. West and Central European governments need to recognise the potential for mass emigration in places where instability and a low standard of living are common. This recognition is not only important from a foreign and security policy perspective. It is wholly in the self-interest of Europeans to do everything possible in the neighbouring countries around Western and Central Europe to promote local political stability and economic development. In order to do this, European markets for products and services from these countries should be allowed to open more. Freer and fairer economic exchange can be an effective instrument of economic development in these emigration countries.[152] Western politicians and media can do much to improve the understanding of, and thus increase the importance of, development issues. This is particularly true in the cases of Eastern Europe, the Balkans, North Africa as well as for specific countries in Western Africa and Asia where emigration pressures are felt particularly strongly.


## Conclusion

As mentioned earlier, the principal trends which characterise migration and immigration must be taken seriously. The total number of resident foreigners has increased and will continue to do so well into the future. Furthermore, due to their ethnic diversity, immigrants will continue to influence the cultural character of Europe. This means that international attention both to population movements and national immigration and integration policies must reflect the needs of today.

The most important challenge with regard to migration is to preserve or improve internal security, whereby, not only objective social and economic security is meant. Perhaps more importantly, subjective perceptions of security must not be neglected. The existing opposition among many Europeans against the arrival of new settlers and against a multi-cultural society is a reaction to at least three phenomena. First, traditional European society

152 ANGENENDT, Steffen, ed., *Asylum and Migration Policies in the European Union*, Berlin: Research Institute of the German Society for Foreign Affairs (DGAP), 1999; p. 62.

and its government institutions appear overwhelmed by the large numbers of asylum seekers and some secondary consequences from global mobility such as transnational crime and migrant smuggling. Second, the growing populations in developing countries and the increasing discrepancy of wealth between the West and the South or the East, promotes a momentum of migration. This appears to many Europeans as something which they are unable to change. Finally, the globalisation of markets and of economic values highlights the inability of sovereign states to manage the movement of people across their borders. The global flow of information and the way in which society, the economy and governments are affected by events abroad and markets around the world requires that Europeans work to provide internal security together.

Chapter 6

# Foreign Offenders and Public Insecurity

The topic of foreign offenders is a controversial and politically sensitive one. It is often considered "too hot to touch" let alone to be discussed in the light of how the public perceives its own security. The most prominent feature of this perception is perhaps bewilderment. Nobody seems able to say why or how a society should accept clandestine migrants, asylum seekers or immigrants committing crimes in its midst. Should it make a special effort to understand such foreigners? Should they be considered just like indigenous offenders? Or should they be regarded as doubly guilty: first, for having committed an illegal act and second, in so doing, abusing hospitality? The most bewildering question may, however, be whether foreigners committing crimes represent really the kind of threat to a country's internal security as some politicians and the media sometimes make them appear.

The lack of clear and simple responses means that generalisations about foreigners are apt to polarise opinions among Europeans. Some leaders advocate greater openness and almost an obligation to welcome and accommodate all those who come, be they refugees, tourists, migrants or immigrants. For them, crime is just an inevitable part in any society whatever its political or economic condition. Others disagree. To them, crime is a result of too much liberty and too many opportunities on offer. They call for harsher criminal laws and expect their government to prevent offenders from entering the country. Still others may feel for a variety of reasons outright antipathy towards foreigners and prefer their country to remain as homogenous as possible. However, everybody probably accepts that some foreigners will always manage to cross the border unchecked, be it for tourism, for business or for crime.

In an ideal world, an equilibrium should be found where the number of foreigners travelling through or the number of resident foreigners in the country correspond to the indigenous society's willingness and ability to accept such foreigners. In this ideal situation, the hosts would be able to absorb and integrate new foreign settlers into their society in such a manner that the socio-political balance and thus the host society's stability is not threatened. Such a situation, however, is difficult if not impossible to establish even if restrictions on asylum seekers or quotas for foreign labourers and immigrants are scrupulously observed. This leaves Europeans feeling uneasy and eventually insecure. Three causes of fear may lead Europeans conclude that: already "too many" foreigners are in Europe, therefore social tensions and crimes by foreigners are increasing, and their government is unable to cope with the influx of travellers, migrants and transnational offenders.

Polarised arguments among politicians or in the media on how to tackle crimes by foreigners make the issue look simpler than it is. This is principally because the causes and consequences of crime are artificially detached from many indirectly related factors. These are, for example, relatively open international borders, economic migration from poorer countries to highly industrialised ones, heightened competition on the labour market, high population density in Europe's cities, low socio-economic living conditions in distinct ghetto-like suburbs or inner cities, and an increasingly multicultural and heterogeneous population. All these factors cannot be discussed here in any detail. We therefore concentrate on a few issues and begin by pointing at some misperception and arguments:

- The international mobility of travellers and the migration of people in search of jobs and better living conditions does not by itself "create" crime.
- There is no direct link between citizenship and crime. The former is a legal criteria while crime is a behavioural characteristic. One does not produce or lead to the other.
- One type of ethnicity does not favour or promote criminal behaviour more than any other. There have always been, and there will always be, some individuals in every society who abuse government services or commit crimes no matter to which ethnic group or nationality they belong.
- Crime is not merely something which foreigners learn somewhere else and then bring to Europe.
- Foreigners can also learn to engage in crime while in the West. This is often in result to a demand and supply of low-risk opportunities to earn illegal profits or because legal means to earn an income are unavailable.

124

– Long-term foreign residents who want to live and work in a European country, who want to immigrate and have their family join them, are likely to be as law-abiding as any European indigenous citizen.

## Who is a foreign offender?

Foreigners can be distinguished by the reasons for which they come to Europe. In a simplified manner, these can be listed as follows:

- International diplomatic service officers accompanied by their support and security staff;
- International civil servants and support personnel;
- International trans-border workers with special work permits;
- Seasonal workers who stay for a limited period of time,
- Foreign employees in local industry with time-limited permits that can be renewed;
- Foreigners with temporary residence permits such as students, apprentices or pensioners who are without a regular professional activity;
- Migrants and refugees who request asylum and have permission to move freely while their requests are being processed;
- Applicants for asylum who have not been granted the refugee status or otherwise did not receive permission to remain in the country, but have been allowed to stay for a limited number of days before they are obliged to leave the country;
- Asylum applicants who were refused, but, while waiting for a decision on their appeal, are allowed to stay for a limited number of days while their case is studied again;
- Persons who are not citizens (yet) but are in the process of becoming naturalised (this requires different time-spans in various European countries);
- Foreigners who travel within the permitted tourist period as tourists are generally allowed to stay in a host country for up to 3 months.

Furthermore, there are foreigners who enter and live in a country of their choice as clandestines having never announced their arrival or stay to the country's authorities. These are, for example:

125

- Foreigners who entered the country possibly as tourists or as temporary workers but over-stayed their time-limited visa or other permit;
- Foreigners who entered the country secretly either on their own or by way of a migrant smuggling organisation.

While this list appears clear enough, its application to every-day practice is much more complex and far from easy for any government authority. Is an indigenous German citizen, for example, living in Freiburg in Breisgau and travelling to Mulhouse in France with the intention to rob a bank or sell drugs a foreign offender? Is he to be considered equally foreign as an Albanian clandestine migrant who commits the exact same offence in the same city? Or do we tend to differentiate these two foreigners? A similar question could be asked with respect to juvenile delinquents: if two teenagers were caught by police for the same offence, should the one born in Germany of Yugoslav immigrant parents be considered as *more foreign* than his indigenous German counterpart?

From the strictly legal perspective, the same offence deserves the same punishment. However, subjective public perceptions are not as even handed. They often lead to a differentiation of offenders on the basis of their ethnic or national origin. Once a criminal is identified according to his citizenship, then in the minds of many Europeans, the offenders' compatriots – whether they are legal residents or tourists – can quickly be stigmatised and generally suspected of not being law-abiding. Unfounded assumptions about criminal behaviour by any group of people arise easily. But generalisations are not only disturbing, they can be misleading.[153] Linking crime to legal citizenship is like looking at apples and oranges and deciding that one produced the other. The same is true for national origin, language

153 Manuel Eisner, among others, argues that it is sociologically problematic to use the "foreigner" as a variable when studying criminal actors and crime because this term is based on legal criteria independent of human behaviour. See: "Immigration, Integration und Assimilation", in BAUHOFER, Stefan und Nicolas QUELOZ, eds., *Ausländer, Kriminalität und Strafrechtspflege*, Zürich: Verlag Rüegg, 1993; pp. 289–310. See also: STEFFEN, Wiebke, "Ausländerkriminalität: Notwendige Differenzierungen", in *Brennpunkt Kriminalität*, München: Bayerische Landeszentrale für politische Bildungsarbeit, 1. Auflage, 1996; pp. 68–72; and REBMANN, Matthias, *Ausländerkriminalität in der Bundesrepublik Deutschland*, Freiburg in Breisgau: Kriminologische Forschungsberichte aus dem Max-Planck-Institut für ausländisches und internationales Strafrecht, Band 80, 1998; p. 312.

or ethnic characteristics. None of these cause people to become criminal. Rather, behaviour should be observed that results from personal choices within a context of socio-economic and political conditions in which people live and travel.

Legal citizenship of a person has an influence on criminal behaviour only in so far as a person may be encouraged by the idea that it is easier to hide (himself or his activities) from authorities in a country other than his own. It follows that, in response to some of the misperceptions and arguments mentioned at the beginning of this chapter, persons with criminal intentions can use their citizenship as a means to hide from police investigations; i.e., they attempt to lower the risk of their own criminal behaviour.

Simply to argue that foreigners are more criminal than indigenous Europeans disregards the human behavioural aspect. It cannot be separated from its contextual setting. This setting consists of personal past experiences (life-style, education, violence during childhood, etc.), the socio-economic environment, personally-felt stress factors and the people with whom the individual associates and who influence his or her behaviour. Once we can see that there are different kinds of offenders of foreign nationality, it also becomes possible to avoid generalisations, "stereotyping" or "labelling". As long as foreign offenders are all put in the same category; i.e., offenders because they are foreign, then the link between migration, ethnic origin and citizenship, on the one hand, and criminal behaviour, on the other, become misleading. This is evident in such generalisations as: "black Africans in France are drug pushers", "Kosovo Albanians in Switzerland are arms dealers", "Vietnamese in Germany are cigarette traffickers", "Turks in Austria are migrant traffickers", "Russians in Liechtenstein and Italy are all members of Mafia groups".

Instead, foreign offenders can be differentiated from one another not merely by the nationality they have, but also on the basis of their motives. We could ask, for example, why some people can travel with the intention to commit crimes and use migration and asylum opportunities to do so whereas others, who were previously law-abiding migrants, learned to engage in criminal activities once they arrived in the host country. More specifically, we should ask:

> whether, either, within the migrant group from a particular ethnic background there is a known phenomenon of organised criminality of more than

127

a temporary or *ad hoc* nature. Or, whether for some migrant groups the conditions of the actual migration (e. g. debts incurred, illegal aspects of the migration process) or the conditions of life in the receiving state produce particular levels and forms of criminality that may be either 'generational' in character or of longer duration.[154]

In other words, the question relates to the familiarity which an offenders has with criminal behaviour. If an offence is spontaneous or carried out only for a short period of time, it is quite a different matter than a crime perpetrated by an offender who developed his criminal activities over a long period of time. Distinguishing offenders by their individual motives is useful for two reasons: First, we can come to recognise that offending behaviour is closely linked to the context in which an offender learned his behaviour. Second, when the context of offending behaviour is taken into account, then feelings of insecurity as a result of crime may be better understood. For insecurity perceptions are not the same with regard to all crimes in general. Rather, impulsive delinquency and small crimes are usually more visible in public places than white-collar offences (trafficking, fraud, money-laundering) perpetrated by professional criminals.

Most individual citizens are not directly affected by smuggling, trafficking, corruption or financial crimes. For this reason, public debates about crimes by foreigners tend to focus on small crimes, theft, robbery and juvenile delinquency. Clearly, most members of the public can more easily understand these generally simple types of offences. In contrast, professional crime is generally hidden and difficult to observe for most people including the police. Being hidden from public eyes, white-collar crimes therefore cause fewer feelings of insecurity. Rather, this type of crime potentially poses a greater problem to the state and its legal and democratic institutions.

## International mobility and the context of offending behaviour

The discussion above does not claim that only the behavioural context is of importance and that crime by foreigners is not worth thinking about. In-

---

154 GREGORY, Frank, "Migrants and Transnational Crime", Paper prepared for a conference at Chatham House, *Policy Challenges of the New Migrant Diasporas*, London, April 22–23, 1999; p. 1–2 (unpublished).

deed, as there are many more "foreigners" in all European countries today than fifteen years ago, the proportion of offences committed by them has also risen. In almost all of Europe, police records indicate a rise in the number of foreign offenders. This should not astonish anyone. Migration has increased in the past ten years and new economic markets have been developed between Eastern, Central and Western Europe. A criminal exploitation of the new markets, of the discrepancy in wealth and of differences among penal laws and business regulations among the different countries is in most cases an unavoidable side-effect of large scale migration and increased mobility world-wide.

However, the periodic nature of large population movement and concurrent crime levels is rarely mentioned in debates on transnational crime. One reason is that crime statistics of any given year cannot inform us about this temporary aspect. This can only come to light if statistics are being observed over a longer period of time and if the geographic origin of specific kinds of offenders is taken into account. Thus we can observe an increase in migration as a consequence of either war or economic crisis, or both together. They drive people out of the country searching for security and employment elsewhere. A side-effect of such often massive migration is an increase of both kinds of crimes, the impulsive or temporary offences and the professional crimes.

The temporary nature of most wars and economic crises implies that transnational crime is apt to decline once such conditions improve. The temporary "high" of criminal offences recorded in Western Europe in the first years following the end of the Cold War illustrates this. Criminal activities of both, impulsive and professional kinds followed upon the initial wave of migration and asylum requests.[155] New peaks of migration, asylum and crime in Europe were again recorded in the final two years of the 1990's due mainly to the economic crisis in Albania and the war in Kosovo. Similar situations can be expected with certainty in the future if and when

155 For Western Europe, see: HOVY, Bela, "Asylum in Europe: Arrivals, Stay and Gender from a Data Perspective", paper prepared at the UNHCR, Geneva: the Statistics office of the Programme Coordination Section, UNHCR, 1999. Also, *Eurostat Yearbook* for the European Union and for Switzerland, see: Bundesamt für Statistik/ Bundesamt für Polizeiwesen, Schweizer Polizeiliche Kriminalstatistik 1997; Bundesamt für Statistik, "Verurteilte nach Staatsangehörigkeit, 1984–1996, No. Alzr8418.xls, 1998.

new civil conflicts or deep economic crises engulf communities in the Balkans, in other parts of Europe or in countries south of the Mediterranean Ocean.

Some categories of transnational crime have already begun to decline. They include the illegal shipments of stolen second-hand goods from the West to eastern markets. After a strong rise of thefts in most of Western Europe (especially electronic equipment and automobiles for re-sale) in the early 1990's, some countries are now recording a gradual decline. This is especially the case for those countries furthest away from markets in Central and Eastern Europe. This is to some extent because market demand is approaching an initial saturation point in the East for second-hand household appliances, televisions, car radios or computers.[156] In other words, transnational crime is like any industry determined by consumer demand. In contrast, markets for stolen goods from the West remain high in countries where political and economic instability prevails; i.e., in the Balkans and in some countries of North and West Africa.

With regard to which types of crimes are recorded by police, far more small offences are registered than, say, white-collar professional crimes. As was explained in an earlier chapter, the police can only learn about offences if they are either reported by the victim or uncovered by its own investigations. As a consequence, a large "dark" area of unknown offences and offenders remains. It includes offences committed by both indigenous and foreign offenders who are of the professional kind. They usually know how to hide their activities from police investigations and, if that is not possible, how to bribe public authorities into collaborating with them. This means that when we hear about the number of foreign offenders recorded by police, we must keep the following in mind: statistics contain mostly records of minor offences and of those crimes which are uncovered by the police. Also, the number of offences committed by foreigners and recorded by police is continuously affected by both the rise and fall of political and

---

156 This decline refers to thefts of goods in private homes and offices which were reported to police or insurance companies for reimbursements. Excluded is the theft rate of automobiles which is still growing. ROBERT, P., R. ZAUBERMAN, M. L. POTTIER and H. LAGRANGE, "Mesurer le crime: Entre statistique de police et enquêtes de victimation (1985–1995)" in *Revue française de sociologie*, Vol. 40:2, April/June, 1999; p 281.

economic crises in the countries where the offenders come from and by the demand for Western stolen goods in these countries.

Furthermore, not only the number of recorded offences rise and fall with crises in less industrialised countries. The numbers of transnational offenders are also affected. Most influenced by periodic political and economic changes are those offenders who profit from instability through theft or by working for trafficking networks. Their behaviour is very much shaped by the context in which they are either introduced to criminal activities or choose to profit from trafficking while demand is high. The more migrants take to the road at any given time for political or economic reasons, the more likely it is that persons with criminal inclinations will try to profit from the migrants' plight and from opportunities for asylum in the West to exercise their trade.

In contrast to trafficking and cross-border theft and robbery, impulsive offences by foreigners are also affected by events that cause migration, but less so. In times of healthy economic growth and political stability, tourists, children, teenagers or hooligans engage in occasional impulsive delinquency. They do so not because they have plans to profit from migration or illicit markets, but for the same reasons as any individual may commit small offences: boredom, peer pressure, group behaviour and low-risk opportunities. Hence, when asylum seekers, refugees or immigrants are accused of shoplifting or participating in typically impulsive offences by groups, they should be considered in the same manner as similar indigenous offenders.

Unlike impulsive offending and temporary theft, however, international white-collar crime is far less affected by the ups and downs of political and economic crises. Professionals always seek criminal opportunities wherever profits promise to be high regardless of geographic location. In prosperous as well as in difficult times, international organised crime always manages to supply whatever illegal goods and services earn the greatest profits in markets where demand is high. Thus, while such crime may profit from unstable economic conditions, as in some countries of the former Soviet Union, Asia or in Latin America, it is no less active in healthy economies in Europe and North America.

## Foreign offenders and residency

We come here to another argument listed at the start of this chapter. Simply because some travellers are offenders does not justify linking crime either to tourism, asylum seekers or immigrants. The danger is always present that a mental link is easily made between foreigners and crime – a link which is perpetuated by the notion that "what is evil must come from elsewhere". When we speak of "organised crime" we should not only think of Italians, Colombians or Russians. In fact, "foreign crime groups cannot operate effectively in our midst if their members do not have domestic support".[157] In other words, European offenders readily collaborate with foreign criminals if they can share the profits.

While it may be easy to focus on the foreigners in our midst, it is important to realise that Western countries may also encourage the development of criminal behaviour. This is not merely the case with regard to Western consumers of imported narcotic drugs or other illegal goods and services. Political movements or entertainment ventures can create a setting in which foreigners as well as indigenous citizens may learn to perpetrate offences or engage in violence. At large techno-parades or rock concerts with visitors from several countries, some of the latter may sell or buy illegal drugs. At large sports games, not only docile spectators, but also groups of hooligans from diverse neighbouring countries come to create their kind of excitement. We also know that political demonstrations may attract youthful gangs of *"casseurs"* who profit from the commotion to break windows, loot stores or burn cars. In other words, impulsive offending, trafficking and violence by indigenous Europeans and foreigners can be encouraged or provoked where social or political events attract large crowds.

The above indicates that it is not only the determination of an individual to perpetrate a crime that leads him to engage in illegal activities. Depending on the context, individuals may find encouragement from the group (peer pressure, seeking excitement) to engage in violence or crime. This is something not revealed in crime data and therefore rarely part of any debate on preventing crimes by foreigners. When speaking of foreigners'

---

157 QUELOZ, Nicolas, "International Efforts to tackle Organised Crime: The case of Europe", Paper prepared for the 52nd International Course on Criminology, Univ. of Macao, Faculty of Law, October 1996; p. 4.

crimes, the important question which we should ask is: At what point does a "foreigner's crime" simply become a crime committed by a member of the local population? Or, in different words, does the citizenship of a foreigner in a European country become irrelevant at some point? If an adult has lived for 6 years in a host country before he or she commits a first offence, or if a second generation immigrant child grows up to become a delinquent teenager, can one consider these individuals as foreign offenders? A foreign citizenship may lose its meaning as the foreigner gradually integrates in the host society. This is a question of familiarity of the offender with the society where he engages in crime. All too often, the length of residency is missing in statistics. This can lead to serious mis-evaluations.

When considering the duration of residency, a different picture emerges. In European countries where large numbers of people travel through and where immigrants settle permanently, we find that foreigners who commit crimes have for the most part either no legal residency status or they are staying for only a short period of time.[158] In their vast majority, they are clandestine migrants, tourists and asylum seekers. They are essentially accused of theft, shoplifting, robbery, or involvement in illegal trafficking.[159]

---

158 This is shown in various statistical reports: Switzerland in the year 1991, of a total of 44% of foreign offenders/criminals, only 16% had a place of residence in Switzerland, 7% were asylum seekers, and the remaining 21% were "tourists" and illegal aliens. (See: Storz, Renate, Simone Ronez and Stephan Baumgartner: *Zur Staatszugehörigkeit von Verurteilten: Kriminalistische Befunde*. Bundesamt für Statistik, Bern, 1996; pp. 5 & 13). A more recent German study found that 53 % of suspected foreign offenders recorded by the police of Bavaria are not residents of that *Land*. (See: Steffen, Wiebke, "Ausländerkriminalität: Notwendige Differenzierungen", in *Brennpunkt Kriminalität*, München: Bayerische Landeszentrale für politische Bildungsarbeit, 1. Auflage, 1996; p. 75). Also: Kunz, Karl-Ludwig, *Kriminologie*, 2nd edition, Bern, Stuttgart and Wien: Verlag Paul Haupt, 1998; pp. 273–275.

159 In part from: Killias, Martin, "Immigrants, Crime, and Criminal Justice in Switzerland", in Tonry, Michael, *Ethnicity, Crime and Immigration: Comparative and Cross-National Perspectives*, Chicago: University of Chicago, 1997; p. 386; and Rebmann, Matthias, *Ausländerkriminalität in der Bundesrepublik Deutschland*, Freiburg in Breisgau: Kriminologische Forschungsberichte aus dem Max-Planck-Institut für ausländisches und internationales Strafrecht, Band 80, 1998; pp. 127, 171–174, and 311–312.

Their share in serious crimes, such as violence and murder, is small.[160] In Switzerland, for example, more than half of all foreigners who were convicted in 1997 (24.8% out of 45.4%) were foreigners with no stable residence or employment (tourists, clandestines travellers, workers on the black market and asylum seekers). Thus, as a percentage of the total number of sentences in Switzerland in 1997, the categories were as follows:[161]

- Asylum seekers:                                                  5.9%
- Non-Swiss persons without residency in Switzerland:   18.9%
- Non-Swiss persons with residency in Switzerland:      20.6%
- Swiss citizens:                                                54.6%

In European cities where most crimes are committed, those perpetrated by foreigners are to a great extent determined by the number of regional and international commuters.[162] In other words, it is not so much the number of long-term foreign residents in any given country that increases the proportion of crimes by foreigners. Rather, it is the number of travelling offenders who come to stay in the country or travel through it for only a short period of time who make up the majority of foreign offenders.

From the above, we can infer that crime statistics which mention citizenship can be interpreted as being discriminatory against the vast majority of foreign workers and immigrants who have settled in the host country. The potential of these two groups of foreign residents to engage in crime should be considered as similar if not equal to that of indigenous citizens. Migrants who want to live and work in a Western country and possibly immigrate with their families are as likely to be law-abiding as any European. Given the choice, potential immigrants are usually highly motivated to live honestly and correctly so as not to spoil their chance of

160 ALBRECHT, Hans-Jörg, "Ethnic minorities and crime – the construction of foreigners' crime in the federal republic of Germany", in PALIDDA, Salvatore, ed., Délit d'immigration / Immigrant delinquency, Brussels: European Commission, COST A2, EUR 17472, 1996; p. 91.

161 Bundesamt für Statistik, Switzerland, "Stafrechtliche Verurteilte nach Aufenthaltsstatus, 1997"; Informationsdienst, No. 350–0042, Neuchâtel, May 2000.

162 KILLIAS, Martin, "Immigrants, Crime, and Criminal Justice in Switzerland", in TONRY, Michael, Ethnicity, Crime and Immigration: Comparative and Cross-National Perspectives, Chicago: University of Chicago, 1997; p. 387.

success in building a new life for themselves and their families in the host country.[163]

A clear distinction should be made between resident foreigners (workers and immigrants), on the one hand, and on the other hand, migrating individuals who have few possibilities to obtain legal employment and residency. The latter group of migrants, asylum seekers and travellers should be analysed from the viewpoint of the socio-economic and political context. Here, pull- and push-factors motivate people to leave their homes in search of legal employment or illegal profits. In other words, care should be taken to distinguish migrants and immigrants who are involved in crime from offenders who are engaged in crime in a professional and systematic manner. What is more, migrants of all kinds, whether legal travellers or clandestines, must not be placed in the same category as criminals. In doing so, travellers in Europe who appear to be economic migrants are then unjustifiably suspected to be criminals.[164]

## Crime data and public perceptions

One aspect of crime statistics which easily lends itself to accusations against foreigners is data which shows an over-representation of foreign offend-

---

163 This is the main argument in support of the creation of a proper immigration system for Western Europe in the same manner as we find in the United states or Canada. Given that approximately the same number of migrants come to Europe each year as to North America, it makes political and economic sense to do away with a confusing asylum regime through which many migrants (who come for economic reasons) are bureaucratically rejected. This process may furthermore push many migrants, who wish to become immigrants, into a clandestine life more conducive to crime.

164 To quote Didier BIGO: "à travers le terme d'immigré clandestin ou d'immigré en situation illégale on crée une association entre immigration et crime. Cette extension permet d'inclure aussi les demandeurs d'asile dans les pratiques d'illégalisme et d'incivilité". In *Polices en réseaux*, Paris: Presses de Science Po, 1996; pp. 318. See also: ALBRECHT, Hans-Jörg, "Ethnic minorities and crime – the construction of foreigners' crime in the federal republic of Germany", in PALIDDA, Salvatore, ed., *Délit d'immigration / Immigrant delinquency*, Brussels: European Commission, COST A2, EUR 17472, 1996; p 99.

ers.[165] This can be explained and interpreted in a number of ways. It is important to avoid unfounded arguments about the foreigners' greater tendency to contravene criminal laws. As we have seen above, the motivation to engage in crime is largely dependent on the circumstances in which an individual lives, travels or believes himself to be in. In other words, the context in which behaviour is being shaped plays a significant part in assessing the causes of crime.

Age is a major factor influencing the proportion of foreign offenders in crime statistics. Young men, regardless of their nationality or ethnic group, are most prone to engage in delinquency and crime.[166] They also risk becoming more easily victims of offending behaviour and violence. Since most immigrants and asylum seekers are between the age of 18 and 30, they are, like their European counterparts, more likely to be involved in crime than older people. In other words, their migration to the West in search of better living conditions is one of the principal reasons for why crime figures of foreign offenders have risen in the 1990's.

Another factor that influences the number of foreign offenders is their relative poverty. This is irrespective of whether they are legal foreign labourers, asylum seekers, genuine refugees or clandestine migrants. The relative wealth of their country of destination makes them aware of the economic disparity that separates them from mainstream Western society. The link between crime and poverty is a typical phenomenon in any society. "For as long as social reformers and researchers have studied criminality,

---

165 More comprehensive discussions than the one here on why members of minorities are often over-represented in statistics is offered in the following two texts: PALIDDA, Salvatore, ed., *Délit d'immigration / Immigrant delinquency*, Brussels: European Commission, COST A2, EUR 17472, 1996; 270 p. And: TONRY, Michael, "Ethnicity, Crime, and Immigration", in TONRY, M., ed., *Ethnicity, Crime and Immigration: Comparative and Cross-National Perspectives*, (Crime and Justice series), Chicago: University of Chicago, 1997; 551 p. See also: PFEIFFER, Christian, Jugendkriminalität und Jugendgewalt in europäischen Ländern", Hannover: Kriminologisches Forschungsinstitut Niedersachsen, 1997.

166 The German government explains this in its yearly crime statistics *Bulletin* as follows: "Die sich in Deutschland aufhaltenden Personen ohne deutsche Staatsangehörigkeit sind im Vergleich zu den Deutschen häufiger männlich, unter 30 Jahre alt und Großstadtbewohner und besitzen somit häufiger Eigenschaften, die auch bei Deutschen zu einem höheren Kriminalitätsrisiko führen." *Bulletin*, Presse und Informationsamt der Bundesregierung, Bonn, 25 May 1999; p. 289.

the correlations between criminality and disadvantage have been clear".[167] Poorer members of any community or national population are more likely than their wealthier compatriots to get involved in crime, particularly in theft. As a result, the vast majority of crimes recorded by police in Western countries concern just such young offenders who come from poorer communities and countries.

A further reason why crime statistics may show high numbers of foreigners is because poorer living conditions produce an accumulation of disadvantages. One such disadvantage becomes apparent where people can find housing only in high-density, poorly maintained apartment blocks in European inner cities or in outlying suburbs. As was mentioned in an earlier chapter, residents in ghetto-like apartment compounds are almost always exposed to a higher risk of victimisation from aggression as well as involvement in crime and violence.[168] This is true for indigenous Europeans as well as for foreign residents. Since immigrants and foreign workers are most often part of the lower-income group, they come to live side-by-side with less well-to-do indigenous citizens. Social tensions become especially serious when employment is precarious and economic insecurity is high. This can lead to "ethnic" or minority-majority tensions that produce security problems (vandalism, aggression, theft or gang wars against the police).

The proportion of foreign offenders in European police statistics can also be explained by the way in which many migrants enter Europe (either as clandestine migrant or as asylum seeker). How they come can greatly influence whether migrants become involved in crime. When an economic migrant, in search of a job, finds that he or she must travel in a clandestine

167 TONRY, Michael, "Ethnicity, Crime and Immigration", in TONRY, Michael, ed., *Ethnicity, Crime and Immigration: Comparative and Cross-National Perspectives*, Chicago: University of Chicago, 1997; p. 13.

168 EISNER, Manuel, *Das Ende der zivilisierten Stadt? Die Auswirkungen von Modernisierung und urbaner Krise auf Gewaltdelinquenz*, Frankfurt: Kampus Verlag; p. 213–214, 1997. See also the study of violence in larger European cities in: PFEIFFER, Christian, *Jugendkriminalität und Jugendgewalt in europäischen Ländern*, Hannover: Kriminologisches Forschungsinstitut Niedersachsen, 1997; and DUBET, François and Didier LAPEYRONNIE, *Les quartiers d'exil*, Paris: Éditions du Seuil, 1992. See also: DANGSCHAT, Jens S., "Warum ziehen sich Gegensätze nicht an?" in HEITMEYER, Wilhelm, et al., eds., *Die Krise der Städte*, Frankfurt am Main: Suhrkamp Verlag, No. es2036, 1998; p. 82.

manner because legal travel is impossible (a tourist visa or legal employment being unavailable), then the risk of becoming involved in the world of black market labour and small crime rises. This risk increases if the same migrants are indebted to criminal smuggling networks who helped them arrive at a destination host country. This explains to a great extent why in Italy, for example, and in other European countries the number of arrests of young male foreigners has increased over the last few years.[169]

Finally, a more subjective reason must be mentioned why crime statistics may show higher figures of foreigners, including foreign workers, tourists and immigrants, than of indigenous Europeans. This reason relates to the frequency with which victims of crime report to the police. When foreign offenders speak the local language poorly and have a skin colour that sets them apart, they are more easily recognised and remembered by their victims and thus reported. In contrast, indigenous offenders can more easily get away unreported because the victims are less easily able to identify them. A related bias can occur with regard to the visibility of foreigners and immigrants. Police or border control personnel may tend to suspect members of a visible minority more easily than members of the majority population. This may be evident in the frequency with which people of darker skin colour are asked to show their identification or have their belongings checked by security personnel. As a consequence, a higher rate in criminal behaviour among these foreigners will then be uncovered and appear in statistics. This is also the case with asylum seekers. Since their movements and whereabouts are controlled, they are also far more likely to be found when committing an offence than, say, an indigenous person who is free to go where he wants and commits the exact same offences. While the frequency with which security personnel ask to check people may be based on sound judgement, a resulting bias in statistical records cannot be excluded. This also implies that offenders who look and behave like the indigenous majority of any European country, even if they come from other countries, are more likely to go unnoticed by the police.

---

169 Transcribed from: PALIDDA, Salvatore, "La construction sociale de la déviance et de la criminalité parmi les immigrés: le cas Italien", in PALIDDA, Salvatore, ed., *Délit d'immigration / Immigrant delinquency*, Brussels: European Commission, COST A2, EUR 17472, 1996; p. 264.

While this final cause of a possible over-representation of foreigners in crime statistics is subjective and based more on human observational tendencies than on facts and figures, the influence which this can have on public perception of safety is considerable. On the one hand, members of visible minorities (foreign workers and immigrants who are easily identifiable by skin colour or language) feel they are more often suspected and discriminated against. On the other hand, members of the majority national population may come to fear that their country's security agencies are not doing enough to arrest all the foreign offenders. Subsequent feelings of insecurity and possibly frustration are a consequence of the failure to differentiate the various kinds of offenders and the contexts in which they act.

## Conclusion

This chapter set out to clarify some common misperceptions and arguments that may cause feelings of insecurity about crimes committed by foreigners. Its purpose was to try to disentangle crime from migration. These issues are better considered separately. As we have seen, linking both immigration and citizenship to offending behaviour can be misleading. Instead, public debate should focus on the type of offenders and the reasons for which they have committed an offence in a country other than their own.

We can conclude that generalisation alone about controversial and complex phenomena should be avoided. The reason for this is simple: since generalisations are conducive to raising feelings of insecurity, the general public ought to be better informed about the context in which people travel across borders and commit offences. Without adequate information, public fears of insecurity come to be based on unverified assumptions. One such assumption claims that foreigners are becoming more criminal than indigenous Europeans. As illustrated above, however, an increase of suspected or incarcerated foreign offenders in crime statistics does not mean that foreigners are more criminally inclined than indigenous persons. Statistics on foreign suspects provide only a partial picture. The data almost entirely hides the context in which crimes are perpetrated and reported.

The context in which offending behaviour is acted out becomes apparent in at least four situations: (1) where impulsive violence or crime can be carried out (small offences such as shoplifting, violence at political demonstrations, at sporting events, or gang-like juvenile delinquency); (2) where periodic theft to finance an addiction or where temporary illegal income-earning opportunities exist through burglary and re-sale of stolen goods; (3) where temporary opportunities exist (due to political or economic crises) for networks of offenders to exploit a market through trafficking and smuggling; and finally (4), where professional crime can make use of financial and legal discrepancies among different countries to operate trafficking networks, launder money and engage in financial fraud or corruption.

Without considering the different kinds of offenders, the forms of crime and their contexts, the public can be misled to believe that criminals are abundant wherever large numbers of migrants and foreign residents are seen. This is not new. Twentieth-century European history has a legacy of political attempts to exclude those who looked and behaved differently. Each time these attempts ended in failure. However, public perceptions of insecurity again and again are quickly affected by the lobbying of some political interests and anti-immigration groups, especially during elections. At such times, the commercial media brings much publicity and thus public attention to the issue of crime. This may then create the impression that Western governments are unable to cope. When, in consequence, harsher policing along with exclusionary or isolationist policies are debated, then the danger arises that economic migrants (legal and clandestine), asylum seekers and immigrants become the target of public frustration and even violence.

Chapter 7

# The Prevention of Insecurity

This chapter and the next present and overview of various efforts aimed at providing public safety and preventing crime. First, we discuss the prevention of insecurity and crime at the local and national levels while the international dimension is presented in the following chapter.

The expression "crime prevention" is often used to describe the influence which criminal justice systems may exercise to discourage would-be offenders from committing crimes. In this text, however, the expression is taken to mean a much broader preventive effort. It not only points at reducing opportunities and rewards for offending behaviour or at increasing its risks and costs. Crime prevention implies all methods that reduce both offending behaviour and insecurity. This can only be accomplished if and when problem-solving activities are based on co-operation between engaged state institutions and citizens. No individual institution, be it the police or a school, is able to prevent crime or insecurity by itself. Many different institutions have to co-operate in partnership with the public to develop both aspects of internal security: objective needs for security and subjective perceptions of safety.[170]

The public most often sees state security agencies as the sole security providers. Internal security is too often considered as the business of the police only. However, providing internal security is best done where both government and citizens can collaborate to build confidence and support the prevention of disorderly behaviour, delinquency, aggression and crime.

In this and the next chapter, several arguments maintain that internal security can be developed only through a comprehensive approach that considers both objective and subjective insecurity. This means that any at-

---

170 The terms "security" and "safety", as used here, mean essentially the same. However, the expression "security" is more often used to mean the security of a collective such as a community, a society or a state while the word "safety" is more often applied to the security of individual people.

tempt to fight crime or bring about law and order in society must be a comprehensive, multi-sectoral and integrated effort. Not only public authorities responsible for security are to be considered. Rather, maintaining law and order in society requires that other state sectors are included such as education, employment, leisure, sports and social welfare services.

Four principal arguments regarding a comprehensive approach to preventing insecurity underline the discussion that follows: The first argument is that the visible forms of crime (by individuals or groups) cause more insecurity in society than less visible ones. These latter include international organised crime, corruption, money laundering, fraud, smuggling or trafficking. The focus in this chapter is on the former, i. e. prevention those types of crime which are often visible and thus perceived as causing the greatest feelings of insecurity. This means that not all types of offences are discussed here nor can all preventive methods used today in Europe to fight crime be mentioned. Taken into consideration are merely those types of behaviour and prevention which figure regularly in public and political debate and appear most frequently in the news media. It is mostly from these information sources that members of the public learn about crime, juvenile delinquency or violence and thus assess the extent of their personal safety.

The second argument taken up here is the following: Any evaluation of safety which looks at objective necessities (police, law and order) only and does not take the public's subjective perceptions into consideration will never reduce insecurity. It is the state's duty to provide safety to its citizens. To do this, it must listen to the public and take its concerns seriously. At the same time, however, not only those safety needs expressed by the public must be attended to. Governments must also address those crime issues which the public does not complain about. These are mostly secretive organised crime, corruption, fraud, money-laundering, trafficking and smuggling. They may not be debated as often in public and the media as small offences and burglary, but they can represent serious challenges to the structure and stability of government, public administration and society at large.

The third argument follows from the first two, namely that both subjective perceptions as well as real objective problems have to be considered simultaneously. In other words, the prevention of crime must address strategies that address real and practical issues as well as subjective feelings and opinions. This will include measures to discourage deviant and criminal

142

behaviour and methods by which to promote confidence in security among the public. These may include education for children, youngsters as well as adults on how to reduce the risk of becoming a victim of crime.

Furthermore, an attempt should always be made to understand why there exists a gap between the fear of crime and the real risk of becoming a victim. This gap varies to the extent that people believe that they live either in a safe or in a dangerous environment. It also varies according to the amount of confidence the public has in government security agencies (the police, border guards, the military or the criminal justice system). Confidence develops where people believe they understand each other and can count on each others' help when needed.

The fourth argument is that to be effective at the subjective level, prevention has to be visible and must be targeted at the communities who feel most threatened. They must be enabled to see, experience, and ideally even participate in prevention programmes. Participation promotes understanding. It builds confidence and therefore gives a greater sense of safety. How to build confidence between government authorities responsible for internal security and the general public is one of the principal issues referred to in the pages below. In fact, some of the preventive policing methods presented here share this common aim: to bring the public and state security agencies closer together so as to promote open communication and understanding.

In conclusion, it is clear that the community for which prevention efforts are made must be well understood by government authorities. We must always keep in mind that it is individual behaviour which leads people to engage in violence or perpetrate crimes. Neither ethnic nor national characteristics of a person cause offending behaviour. To label particular linguistic or ethnic group as "typical" offenders or "likely" criminals is most damaging. Undesirable conduct has to be recognised as deserving remedial attention, it is the result of learning processes and socialisation which can be improved to promote civil and responsible behaviour.

It is obvious that we base our discussion here on the assumption that human behaviour is malleable. It is only partially a product of an individual's in-born character. Personality is to a very large extent shaped by the environment in which an individual lives. This environment consists of a historically-shaped heritage with its shared values as well as a socio-economic context in which the family, the circle of friends and other people live and work. It is in this context, that children and adults develop and adapt their values which influence their behaviour. This can change if a person is subjected to different social environments or education.

## The subjective side of preventing crime and insecurity

We observed earlier that Western countries, with their open economies and liberal societies, offer many opportunities for rule-breaking and crime. Most of those opportunities do not exist in traditionally closed and isolated communities. It is therefore not a simple task to prevent crime in Western societies today. Many more diverging influences (family instability, education, international migration, etc.) play a decisive role in shaping the context in which criminal behaviour becomes possible.

A challenge which prevention strategies must acknowledge from the start is that, in the eyes of the public, they will always remain subjective undertakings. One of the reasons is that neither security nor insecurity can be defined entirely by objective criteria. Both concepts are to varying degrees subjectively understood. A situation of safety or insecurity can always be questioned or criticised. In other words, preventing insecurity or promoting safety must necessarily speak to the subjective perceptions of those who want to feel secure.

We may be aware mostly from police statistics how many offenders are convicted each year, but we will never know how many potential offenders have actually been discouraged from committing a crime. Hence, we cannot be certain that preventive measures are effective to the extent we want them to be. We could argue instead that a growing economy and less unemployment reduce crime far more than any increased number of police officers or better schools will ever do.

The subjective nature of preventing insecurity or promoting public safety becomes more apparent when, as discussed earlier, we consider that crime and victimisation data will never fully inform us about how safe a community or country really is. The police can never know all crimes nor catch all offenders. There are two simple reasons for this: first, some offenders are very good at hiding (at least temporarily); and second, not all victims report to the police.

Furthermore, insecurity which victims report is caused more by small aggressions and disorderly behaviour in urban communities than by "white-collar" offences or international organised crime. The latter are rarely noticed by ordinary citizens and generally do not affect their daily lives. This means that prevention of crime must address both the knowledge (or lack thereof) of white collar crime among the public as well as the sometimes exaggerated awareness and thus fear of delinquencies and small crimes. Nearly everybody is aware of small delinquencies, minor aggressions and general disorderly behaviour in their neighbourhood or city. Most people can recount some personal victimisation (vocal threats, small thefts, vandalism) and much of police work is to help resolve neighbourhood or family problems and deal with small public grievances or disputes.

At the local level, however, the police is not always the best agency to address minor delinquencies and general disorderly behaviour. While the police is often expected to carry out such tasks, it can contribute only one aspect to crime prevention. Enlarging police presence can indeed contribute to three positive developments: first, enforce the feeling that state authority is always near to help; second, that fewer opportunities exist for unseen delinquency; and third, that private businesses and the public can feel safer. We must keep in mind, though, that a greater police presence can also have a counter-productive effect. The public may come to see a greater presence of police officers as a sign that crime is rampant and that conditions of insecurity are real.

Another consideration is that a greater police presence will never change a glaring economic disparity – an existing ghetto, for example – where delinquency may be a most serious problem. An economic disparity lies very often at the root of public insecurity feelings and criminal behaviour. The most common reaction to heightened feelings of insecurity is to call for more police, tougher laws and stiffer jail sentences. The danger, however, is that such measures might "kill" the city which the criminal justice system is supposed to save.[171] Rather, to promote public safety, social and economic causes of insecurity need to be included in crime prevention programmes.

---

171 FELTES, Thomas, "Pro-active Prevention: An Effective Police Tool?" in KÜHNE, Hans-Heiner and Koichi MIYAZAWA, eds., *Internal security in modern industrialized societies*, Baden-Baden: Nomos Verlagsgesellschaft, 1998; p. 180.

Finally, one more reason for why the success of crime prevention depends to a great extent on the public's subjective perception is its confidence in the government's capacity to control both simple disorderly behaviour as well as complex crimes. This is a subjective element of prevention which also concerns us here. Confidence depends to a great extent on how state agencies, such as the police, communicate and collaborate with citizens. As neither the police nor the public can ever know with certainty whether any effort on its own will improve subjective perceptions of security (is it the police, education or more jobs?), we have no choice but to take all relevant spheres of government-public interaction into consideration.

In other words, a very broad approach to preventing insecurity and promoting community safety is necessary. It has to offer school and public education as well as state welfare services (employment, asylum, immigration). This approach could be defined thus: facilitating government-public co-operation at all levels of society where safety or security (however interpreted) can be promoted objectively and subjectively.

> There is [...] potential for pre-empting criminal behaviour by paying greater attention to the prevention of crime. Prevention can and does cover a vast array of activity from environmental design and situationally related measures through pre-school programs, social control, and criminal justice system institutions.[172]

The general aim, then, is not merely to catch offenders and bring them to justice, but to improve the subjective feeling of safety wherever the public feels it is lacking.

## Approaches to preventing insecurity and offending behaviour

There are essentially two sides to preventing crime and insecurity. One addresses the potential offenders and tries to influence their behaviour. The other speaks to the potential victims and attempts to encourage individual

---

172 LAYCOCK, Gloria and Nick TILLEY, "Implementing Crime Prevention" in TONRY, Michael and David P. FARRINGTON, eds., *Building a safer society: strategic approaches to crime prevention*, Chicago: University of Chicago Press 1995; p. 536.

responsibility and more open communication with the police and other related state authorities responsible for public safety. This dual approach is most effectively achieved by promoting greater understanding and, where necessary, collaboration between the public and government agencies. Three general approaches can be illustrated here. They indicate the possible lines of thought which can easily be understood by the public. These can also be used to explain the ideas that underlie methods with which to address public feelings of insecurity. They state a familiar argument and are followed by a list of commonly suggested remedies:[173]

*The law and order approach:*
Argument: Crime and fear of crime result from "too much crime" and insufficiently tough criminal laws.
- More police.
- Tougher laws.
- Stiffer sentencing and more juvenile and adult jails.
- Lowering the age of adult responsibility with regard to punishment.
- "Boot camps" where delinquent youth are "re-educated" under strict supervision.

*The behaviour approach:*
Argument: Crime results from a stress-creating context in which expectations and ambitions clash with reality; i.e. poverty or a lack of access to resources contrasts sharply with the wealth of others; this discrepancy promotes a readiness on the part of potential offenders to use illegal means to obtain personal wealth.
- Developmental approach to preventing crime by addressing anti-social and aggressive behaviour beginning among young children.
- Social, sports and leisure programmes for youth.
- Youth Socialisation.
- Training and education.
- Job creation.
- Economic development especially of poorer suburbs and inner cities.

173 The idea for this schema is borrowed from: FELTES, Thomas, "Pro-active Prevention: An Efficient Police Tool?" in KÜHNE, Hans-Heiner and Koichi MIYAZAWA, eds., *Internal security in modern industrialized societies*, Baden-Baden: Nomos Verlagsgesellschaft, 1998; pp. 181–182.

*The public safety approach:*
Argument: The subjective fear of crime is no less important than objective crime figures.
* Partnership between citizens and police forces.
* Prevention of offending behaviour through environmental design changing physical characteristics to influence behaviour.
* Community-led situational preventive methods in partnership with local business and the police.
* Urban safety programmes promoted through government awareness-raising becomes a catalyst for local social and economic improvements.

On their own, each of these approaches can only be partially effective. In one place, crime may be so rampant that more draconian police force is necessary to bring about an improvement in law and order. Police crackdowns in targeted places are an example of such a need when organised crime networks, hooligans or terrorists must be apprehended. In most instances, however, crime prevention is better served by a combination of socio-economic and educational measures. The prevention of crime and of insecurity rests essentially on linking civil society with state authorities and law enforcement.[174]

At the very heart of this broadly-based effort lies education, especially that which addresses responsibility. There is room for teaching young and old to take more responsibility for their own safety and help others to feel secure as well. This might include awareness-raising efforts about the risks of victimisation in certain situations, anti-violence training for school teachers, vocational training for unemployed persons or the organisation of public participation in community policing (neighbourhood meetings with local police officers and social workers). Such community-oriented efforts do not need to be initiated by the police. They can also be organised by schools, local welfare or employment offices, the private sector, entertainment agencies and resident community associations.

At the level of the individual, there is the responsibility of the potential offender to avoid behaving in an offensive manner as well as the responsibility of each member of the public to guard against becoming a victim of

---

174 DUBET, François and Didier LAPEYRONNIE, *Les Quartiers d'Exil*, Paris: Éditions du Seuil, 1992; p. 214.

crime. At the level of the collective, there is the responsibility of society and of the state. This implies:

> to encourage potential victims of crime to take better security precautions, to remind potential offenders of the consequences of their behaviour, to reinforce and sustain the behaviour of those who normally act in accordance with the advertised recommendations, and to shift attitudes or to create a climate of opinion in which legislation or other action may be introduced by central and local bodies to reduce crime.[175]

All members of a given community can take responsibility to maintain or improve the safety of the environment in which they live and work for the good of society at large. Several types of preventive strategies have been developed in Europe, the United States and other countries that include awareness-raising for responsible action. Furthermore, they touch on spheres where the government interacts with the public. Their aim is not only to enhance responsible civic behaviour by addressing individual, educational and community concerns, but also to promote confidence between the public and government security authorities such as the police.[176]

The crime prevention methods briefly introduced below show that we are not condemned to live with a given feeling of insecurity or level of crime. These methods or strategies involve schooling, public awareness-raising through information campaigns, social welfare and counselling services, youth services, women's affairs, public health, vocational training,

175 LAYCOCK, Gloria and Nick TILLEY, "Implementing Crime Prevention" in TONRY, Michael and David P. FARRINGTON, eds., *Building a safer society: strategic approaches to crime prevention*, Chicago: University of Chicago Press 1995; p. 547.
176 New developments in crimes prevention are analyzed in numerous studies. See for example the chapter on crime prevention in: NEWMAN, Graeme, ed., *Global Report on Crime and Justice*, United Nations Office for Drug Control and Crime Prevention, Oxford: Oxford University Press, 1999. A good overview of new crime prevention methods is provided in: TONRY, Michael and David P. FARRINGTON, eds., *Building a safer society: strategic approaches to crime prevention*, Chicago: University of Chicago Press 1995. A more European focus is provided by: FELTES, Thomas, "Policing a Modern Society: Tougher than the Rest?: Fear of Crime, victimisation, and new policing styles", in *Police Research and Management*, Summer 1998; pp. 13–35; FELTES, Thomas, "Pro-active Prevention: An Effective Police Tool?" in KÜHNE, Hans-Heiner and Koichi MIYAZAWA, eds., *Internal security in modern industrialized societies*, Baden-Baden: Nomos Verlagsgesellschaft, 1998; p. 176–192.

city planning, infrastructure engineering, public transportation, housing, the criminal justice system, law enforcement and, of course, policing. Popular among new methods of crime prevention and building public security are "community policing" or "community crime prevention", "developmental crime prevention" and "situational crime prevention". They all encourage closer co-operation between the public and government agencies and are particularly important in communities that are considered to be at risk of heightened insecurity and crime.

## Developmental crime prevention

"Crime prevention from a developmental perspective is largely based on the idea that criminal activity is determined by behavioural and attitudinal patterns that have been learned during an individual's development".[177] The underlying assumption of this approach is that earlier experiences in a person's life determine later behaviour; i.e., the behavioural approach to crime prevention alluded to above constitutes one important element of developmental prevention. This approach helps to explain how individuals come to live in an environment or context where certain kinds of uncivil or delinquent behaviour develop more easily. A significant reason for variations in patterns of conduct and association can be explained by referring to childhood and family characteristics.

The prevention of crime through a developmental approach, then, addresses the causes of deviance based on how behaviour develops and how it can be guided. Such an effort is mostly a long-term one where specific types of early childhood behaviour (pestering, bullying) are recognised as indications of a possible tendency towards high-risk behaviour once the child becomes a teenager or young adult.[178] The focus for such a preven-

177 TREMBLAY, Richard E. and Wendy M. CRAIG, "Developmental Crime Prevention", in TONRY, Michael and David P. FARRINGTON, eds., *Building a safer society: strategic approaches to crime prevention*, Chicago: University of Chicago Press 1995; p. 151.
178 TREMBLAY, Richard E. and Wendy M. CRAIG, "Developmental Crime Prevention", in TONRY, Michael and David P. FARRINGTON, eds., *Building a safer society: strategic approaches to crime prevention*, Chicago: University of Chicago Press 1995; p. 151–152.

tive strategy is mostly on children and teenagers who are considered to live in a higher-risk environment. Ideally, all teachers in kindergartens and schools should pay attention to those pupils who consistently show anti-social behaviour. By being aware of stress factors that may exist in the child's family or social environment, teachers would then appeal to specialised social, psychological and police services to address the needs of the child and its family.

## Situational crime prevention

"Situational prevention seeks to reduce opportunities for specific categories of crime by increasing the associated risks and difficulties and reducing the rewards" to the potential offender.[179] This crime preventive approach rests upon the assumption that criminal behaviour is responsive to the context of opportunities, risks and rewards which are recognised by (potential) offenders. This means that the offender's perception of opportunities, risks and rewards are to be targeted through a situational approach. The focus here, then, is analysing the opportunities that exist and finding solutions. Such opportunities are not simply of a physical nature. "Rather, a complex interplay between potential offenders and the supply of victims, targets, and facilitators determines the scale and nature of opportunities for crime."[180]

Prevention in this sense implies altering an environment in such a manner that risk behaviour is discouraged. For example, targets for theft or vandalism can be better protected or simply removed. Stores can be monitored by cameras, unlit entrances to residential buildings can be brightened up with lighting. Architectural modifications can provide more space so as to give a sense of security. Also locks can be installed on doors and windows, or automated bank machines can be relocated in busier places where

179 CLARKE, Ronald V., "Situational Crime Prevention", in TONRY, Michael and David P. FARRINGTON, eds., *Building a safer society: strategic approaches to crime prevention*, Chicago: University of Chicago Press 1995; p. 91.

180 CLARKE, Ronald V., "Situational Crime Prevention", in TONRY, Michael and David P. FARRINGTON, eds., *Building a safer society: strategic approaches to crime prevention*, Chicago: University of Chicago Press 1995; pp. 102–103.

users feel never alone. Other opportunities for crime can also be deflected by, for example, locating evening and night-time entertainment ventures as well as bars and taverns in places where supervision will be carried out more effectively. Subtle or natural surveillance can also be enhanced. For example, community programmes such as "neighbourhood watch schemes" can be organised where residents support each other to survey a street or the area around a school. Finally, police surveillance and private security controls can be made more visible in places where minor offences are a problem. The aim each time is to modifying the environment where offending behaviour is possible by reducing both opportunities and rewards for potential offenders.[181]

## Community policing

Community policing implies a community-wide concern with the sources of insecurity and crime. Its approach rests on the principle that communities have crime rates that are characteristic of the resident population. This approach is based on the assumption that disorder and un-civil behaviour in cities or specific communities is at the root of small delinquency and crime.[182]

Many urban areas in Europe suffer from a serious lack of community engagements to build a safe environment. There are suburbs in some cities where the police has completely given up patrolling at certain hours of the day or night. Youth gangs control the streets and throw stones at police vehicles – tensions between the police and the public are interpreted as a provocation to violence.[183] Such situations have also characterised certain large cities in the United States where community policing were already developed in the 1960's. It was argued that if neighbourhoods organise their residents to participate in building security for all, crime could be

181 Situational crime prevention is discussed in more detail in: CLARKE, R. V., ed., *Situational Crime Prevention: Successful Case Studies*, 2nd ed., Albany, New York: Harrow and Heston Publishers, 1997.

182 WYSS, Eva, "Zerbrochene Fenster müssen sofort repariert werden: Die Sicherheit beginnt im Quartier...", in *Neue Zürcher Zeitung*, 21/22 February 1998; p. 82.

183 DUBET, François and Didier LAPEYRONNIE, *Les Quartiers d'Exil*, Paris: Éditions du Seuil, 1992; pp. 177–178.

reduced and residents would again feel safe. The idea is still popular today and finds increasing positive resonance in Europe as well. Greater co-operation between the local police and the civilian community is encouraged and thus publicly-felt security needs could be addressed. This has led to better methods to prevent juvenile delinquency, public disorder and both robbery in private residences and shoplifting.

In this community approach, the police reacts not only to criminal cases when called by victims. Rather, it provides advance preventive services for residents who ask for them (advising on improving self-protection, installing burglar alarms) and in places where higher risks of offending behaviour exist (improve community supervision in shopping malls, parking lots and evening entertainment centres). When necessary, police officers meet with residents to discuss problems and develop solutions. This implies that the police is familiar with the local community so that it can contribute to improving the quality of life for its residents.

The measures to prevent crime and build safety mentioned thus far are relatively general. They include both the behavioural and the public safety approaches mentioned earlier. It remains here to discuss some tools which police offices in European cities are increasingly using or testing. These can be seen as part of the law and order approach; they are "zero-tolerance", "curfews" for youngsters and closed circuit television (CCTV) supervision in public places. While these do not represent a complete list of tools used by police, we choose to briefly present them here because they are most frequently mentioned in the media. They provide an idea of how risks of crime and victimisation can be reduced as well as how subjective perceptions of safety can be developed.


## Zero-tolerance policing

Zero-tolerance policing became fashionable in the late 1990's. It is often taken to mean instant punishment for the smallest forms of improper behaviour (e.g. no light on a bicycle at night, or throwing away chewing gum on the street). However, zero-tolerance is not a police crackdown on very minor misbehaviour. Rather, it is a method based on the idea that serious forms of violent and criminal behaviour develop because the actors are not taught at a very early stage what kind of conduct will not be accepted.[184] "The theory of zero-tolerance policing [...] holds that allowing small crimes to pass unpunished will encourage contempt for the law in larger matters: a city in which people urinate in the streets will also be one in which people rob each other".[185]

If the moral authority of teachers and parents (and perhaps also of the police) has diminished over the past decades, then other socially and politically acceptable methods to teach social values and norms must be thought of. Zero-tolerance is an attempt to impose authoritative order where other forms of moral influence have failed. It deals primarily with the effects of small delinquencies and crime and does not directly address the underlying causes. However, by following up on the small and banal offences with clear policing measures, it is believed that thrill-seeking and irresponsible impulsive behaviour by children and youngsters can be reduced. In the process, youngsters should also become more conscious of the consequences of both, minor delinquencies and more serious offences. The message of zero-tolerance is essentially that clear and consequent law enforcement will help in supporting moral education. The preventive aspect is that by handing out punishment, the perpetrator and other silent observers might not commit the same disorderly or delinquent act. This is essentially "fighting" crime by using repression as a warning signal.

However, as with many law enforcement initiatives that give more powers to the police, there remains one problem. It is that discrimination against specific ethnic groups can become endemic. This problem arises more frequently where ethnic divisions are deep and roughly coincide with the discrepancy between wealthy and poor residents. People who simply "look" like possible offenders become the target of police searches, not because they are officially suspected of an offence, but because they belong to a disfavoured ethnic group which the police and the public may have stigmatised beforehand as "more likely offenders". Wherever police officers obtain the power to search people without warrants or to arrest suspected offenders without having to observe adequate legal protection for the arrested individual, discrimination can become a serious problem.

184 See for example: KILLIAS, Martin, " 'Zero tolerance' ist keine Strategie für die Schweiz", in *Neue Zürcher Zeitung*, 21/22 February 1998; p. 82; and WACQUANT, Loïc, "Ce vent punitif qui vient d'Amerique", in *Le Monde Diplomatique*, Vol. 46, No. 541, April 1999; pp. 1 & 24–25.
185 "The dark side of zero tolerance", *The Economist*, 3 April 1999; p. 12.

# Evening curfews

The idea of imposing evening and night-time curfews for children and teenagers has reached Europe from the USA. It is already widely practised in some European cities, especially in the United Kingdom. The reason for such a drastic measure is usually a sharp rise of juvenile criminal activities and violence. In response, parent associations, local politicians and police offices agree to impose curfews to prevent youngsters from loitering on streets after specific hours in the evening. As the majority of youth delinquencies, crimes and violence are perpetrated in late evenings, the preventive aspect of a youth curfew is two-fold. First, a curfew makes it impossible for children and teenagers to engage in late-night group activities that border on delinquent, thrill-seeking type of behaviour. Second, forcing youngsters to go home reduces the potential market of young and often vulnerable "customers" in the adult crime scene where illegal drugs are the principal commodity. If youngsters are kept away from a drug scene or prevented from frequenting groups of thrill-seeking or aggressive young adults, then the curfew actually provides an effective means to shelter younger and often weaker teenagers from getting involved.

Whether curfews for children and teenagers are a successful from of crime prevention is debatable. It is difficult to know if juvenile crime is actually reduced due to a curfew measure (offences may simply be relocated to daytime). Certain, however, is that curfews respond to locally-felt needs to impose rules on the young and provide a greater sense of subjective safety in the community. If residents and especially parents feel safer with a curfew, then the measure will have contributed positively.

However, merely imposing a curfew from, say, 23:00 to 06:00 is not enough. This measure also requires a far greater input from the police. They have to patrol the community concerned and supervise that after the specified hour, youngsters are not seen on the streets anymore. If they find one, they must either drive him or her home or to the police station and then call the parents to pick up their offspring. This measure requires that more police officers need to be on duty during evenings – a measure which the local community or authority must also be willing to pay for.

# Closed circuit television (CCTV) in public places

Video cameras placed on top of traffic lights at busy intersections, above entrances to office buildings or to shopping centres are gradually becoming a common sight in large metropolitan areas. This effort to prevent offending behaviour can be considered an element of situational crime prevention. England has the highest number of CCTV cameras per capita installed in public places and some 500 are added each week.[186] Germany, the Netherlands, France and other European countries follow this new technological trend.[187] In addition, computer programmes have been developed which automatically compare the human faces filmed by a camera with those on police suspect lists and ring an alarm when matching images are found. With the help of such a high-tech effort British police was able to find a picture taken by a CCTV camera of the man who had planted three nail bombs in London bars that caused considerable damage and human suffering in the spring of 1999.

In communities where crime rates and drug dealing are a serious problem, CCTV provides a fairly simple method to keep away would-be-offenders who might be nervous of being observed and possibly recognised by police. Criticism against such public supervision systems are not to be discounted, however. There are three commonly cited criticisms: (a) the loss of privacy for the general public; (b) the danger that people who simply "look" eccentric or have another skin colour become suspected of crimes simply because of their appearance; and (c), electronic surveillance does not prevent criminals from their activities, it merely displaces them to another community where such cameras are not installed.

Regarding the first criticism, it is quite true that being filmed without explicit agreement is an infringement of personal privacy. Whether CCTV cameras should be installed in a given neighbourhood should be up to the local community of residents, the police, businesses and politicians. Anytime that the police introduces new crime prevention methods that are as obvious for all to see as CCTV, it may be helpful if the residential commu-

---

186 Buse, Uwe, "Wir krigen sie alle", *Der Spiegel*, No. 27, 5 July 1999; p. 124.
187 Junger-Tas, J., "Le 'moyennement répressif' des Pays-Bas", *Le Monde Diplomatique*, Vol. 46, No. 541, April 1999; p. 25.

nity is consulted in order to avoid a backlash of public anger or distrust in the police.

As for the second criticism, the possibility always exists that the police will not only look for persons who are known offenders, but also observe those who merely "look" differently, have another skin colour or who behave in eccentric ways. To prevent the development of discrimination, local police offices have to meet the residents of the community to familiarise themselves with the people that live there, their life-styles and their ethnic characteristics. Here again, technical and objective crime prevention should be combined with the more subjective and humane forms of prevention that rely on building a good rapport between the police and the public.

Finally, the criticism about the displacement of crime to other neighbourhoods where no CCTV is installed is valid, but only to some extent. Determined criminals will pursue their work wherever they can obtain the greatest profits at the least risk. With their investigations, the police will always be a step behind professional offenders who willingly travel to do their work. Rather, CCTV can and will probably discourage only the local youth and potential offenders from disorderly behaviour. It is for them that such camera surveillance is meant. Besides, these electronic eyes have another effect: by chasing away determined criminals or drug traffickers, they also reduce the likelihood that the people who live in the community get easily into contact with offenders. However, it is obvious that not every street and every park bench can be observed by cameras and that CCTV will not replace education and community participation in crime prevention.

The crime prevention methods and tools presented here show that adequate internal security can be achieved without resorting to harsh authoritarian methods. Criticism sometimes expressed of certain, often American, police methods such as zero-tolerance raise fears of the beginnings of a future police state. However, each country and each municipality can apply these methods of policing and security-building in ways that preserve the rights to freedom of individual citizens while improving surveillance and public safety. Most important is that in all approaches to crime prevention, the public is directly involved and consulted. Essentially, communication, mutual understanding and co-operation between the public and the police should be promoted.

## Policing for public safety

The police can take an active part in managing prevention programmes and building a partnership with the public. It represents to many teenagers and young adults what parents and school teachers are for younger children: the representatives of moral authority. Here, the police should not merely enforce law, but also participate in the life of the community and inform school children, teenagers and young adults where the limits of tolerable civil behaviour are. In fact, a German study concluded "that the police (and not schools, politicians, churches or the family) should bring values to the people."[188] The public wants the police to be more present in the educational sphere and always ready to help when asked to do so.

Most often, however, a local or national government undertakes reforms in its public security sector only when it is forced to do so. Pro-active and imaginative reforms of police and other public agencies with a focus on public service are still rare. Pressure for change comes mostly when citizens complain so much that their voices cannot be ignored any longer (often following more radical political arguments and media reports). When the need for reform becomes inevitable, then the first step is often a reappraisal on how the police or another public institution should do its job. One message common in most such studies is that security institutions, including the smallest local police office, must adapt to new public needs and expectations.

Indeed, many European police offices are undertaking deep reforms and retraining their personnel – not only in Western countries, but also in Central and Eastern Europe. Reforms of the police are very much needed in former communist countries where the police was often used as an instrument of power and control. In several Central European countries, the police is completely relearning new approaches to its work with a focus on public service. This often includes holding regular press conferences, rendering their internal organisations and police training methods more transparent to the general public and making use of strategies learned from the business community. For example, "security marketing" strategies are meant to promote

188 FELTES, Thomas, "Police Integrity and the Police Organization", Paper presented at the International Police Integrity Conference (New York University / National Institute of Justice, Washington), La Pietra, Florence, Italy, May 1999; p. 18. (For further information, see: http://www.fhpol-vs.de).

confidence in the government's security services by making objective security measures more understandable to the general public.[189] This requires, of course, that police agencies develop methods to measure public trust and concentrate part of their officers' training on providing services which were often not part of their traditional law enforcement duties.

## Building public security

Where high rates of delinquency and violence have already become part of life in a neighbourhood or city, local residents and the police may also have very little contact with each other. In such places, meaningful communication, confidence and public participation in prevention programmes are often completely missing.[190] The difficulty is often how a better and more secure environment can be established when ever more heterogeneous communities live in close proximity and do not share cultural values or social activities. Here, the police and government authorities must become more familiar with the local population. This is crucial not only for the prevention of offending and criminal behaviour, but also to contribute to better social services and thus prevent poverty and misery in the heart of European cities. Many European police agencies are today employing an increasing number of women officers and especially officers who themselves come from immigrant communities.[191] This is one important step for the police to identify more closely with local residents. It also helps to build confidence and facilitates public participation in crime prevention programmes.

There exist many ideas and community prevention methods to alleviate the risk that young people become involved in crime. Most aim at bringing representatives of all the communities concerned together to discuss their

189 The concept of "security marketing" was devised by *TC Team Consult*, a private consulting agency specialised in designing structural and training reforms of European police forces. See for example: GOTTLIEB, G., KRÖZSEL, K, and PRESTEL, B., *The Reform of the Hungarian Police: Processes, Methods, Results*, Holzkirchen / Obb., Germany: Felix Verlag, 1998.
190 "La violence urbaine? On peut construire avec", *Le Temps Stratégique*, Jan./Feb. 1999; pp. 93–105.
191 See for example: "Das neue Spektrum der holländischen Polizei", *Neue Zürcher Zeitung*, 2./3. October 1999; p. 111; or: "Demain, la police genevoise sera pluriculturelle et multiethnique", *Le Temps*, 27 March 2000; p. 41.

problems and find common solutions. Their objective, on the one hand, is to reduce tensions between the different communities (indigenous and immigrant residents, the police, apartment-building caretakers, school teachers, social workers, citizen associations, sports clubs, city mayors and local businesses) and promote collaboration to prevent insecurity.[192] On the other hand, the prevention of insecurity may consist of programmes for the young which combine school education with vocational training, internship as well as with leisure and "edutainment" activities. These seek to reduce the "empty" leisure time which children and teenagers have after school, on week-ends and during their holidays. For example, in some French *banlieues*, special "summer-heat" programmes proved successful in deflecting the social tensions that build up during the warm season by offering youth sports, outdoor survival training and leisure activities. These have been organised by local government authorities in conjunction with police and the military.[193]

These prevention programmes embrace a form of community service that links social and educational supervision with leisure. Another link that must be made is that between school and employment. The obstacles in the way to move from education to employment are often too high for young people who lack the self-motivation and creativity to compete for jobs. With the development of increasingly specialised industries and the global displacement of low-skill manufacturing, obstacles for young people to find even simple jobs can be daunting. The best school teachers, social workers and youth counsellors cannot, by themselves, shorten the distance between school and employment. This requires the participation of employers' associations, labour unions and appropriate government initiatives.[194] Specialised programmes can help to integrate young people in normal economic activities and thereby prevent them from becoming involved in delinquent and criminal activities.

---

192 "La violence urbaine? On peut construire avec", *Le Temps Stratégique*, Jan./Feb. 1999; pp. 97 & 100.
193 DUBET, François and Didier LAPEYRONNIE, *Les Quartiers d'Exil*, Paris: Éditions du Seuil, 1992; p. 214.
194 In part from: DUBET, François and Didier LAPEYRONNIE, *Les Quartiers d'Exil*, Paris: Éditions du Seuil, 1992; p. 216. Also: JUNGER-TAS, J., *Le Monde Diplomatique*, No. 541, April 1999; p. 25.

Without financial support, however, such youth education, leisure and vocational programmes are hardly possible. It is therefore up to local politicians to solicit parliamentary and public approval for the necessary expenses. Financial support could also be provided in part through local competitions, benefit concerts, lotteries or other public events that directly involve the community. It is also helpful to remember that the cost of prevention is far lower than the cost of an enlarged criminal justice system and incarceration facilities.

An example among many of successful prevention that also cost little in terms of public funds is illustrated in a United Nations report with regard to the Dutch city of Delft. In 1985, city officials and the police mobilised local partners (citizens and businesses) to launch a programme to reduce crime problems and decay in a public housing neighbourhood. The programme included efforts focused on: organising recreational activities for young people and providing a street worker to co-ordinate activities; hiring seven caretakers to intensify surveillance; and altering physical design features to encourage surveillance and decrease the vulnerability to vandalism of buildings and public infrastructure. "A before-after evaluation confirmed a 56 percent drop in reported crime in the housing complex after two years".[195]

In conclusion, then, there is room for optimism:

> In the last decade, crime prevention has achieved a prominent position in crime reduction thinking and practice around the world. Designing out crime, promoting social control and responsibility, investing in youth and family, breaking the cycle of violence, city action and innovative policing and justice approaches have become synonymous with best practice in crime reduction. In many crime-ridden communities where these forms of prevention have been implemented, substantial and lasting reductions in crime have been achieved, a greater quality of life has been realized, and community and economic growth has flourished.[196]

195 Taken from: WILLEMSE, Hans M., "Development in Dutch crime prevention", in R. V. CLARKE, ed., *Crime Prevention Studies*, Vol. 2, Monsey, New York: Criminal Justice Press, 1994, and quoted in: NEWMAN, Graeme, ed., *Global Report on Crime and Justice*, United Nations Office for Drug Control and Crime Prevention, Oxford: Oxford University Press, 1999; p. 202.

196 United Nations, *Global Report on Crime and Justice*, Graeme NEWMAN, ed., Office for Drug Control and Crime Prevention, Centre for International Crime Prevention, Oxford: Oxford University Press, 1999; p. 220.

Chapter 8

# Preventing Crime and Feelings of Insecurity: The International Dimension

It goes without saying that international crime will never be controlled at a purely national level. The traditional system of criminal justice, as maintained by Western countries in the 1990's has less and less relevance in light of changing international criminal developments.[197] Often saturated with the everyday minor crime, police and intelligence agencies in Europe are in need of constant modernisation to keep up with the global developments of transnational crime. Following the approaches discussed in the previous chapter for the prevention of insecurity and offending behaviour, similar principles can be applied at the international level.

Crime prevention was defined earlier as a comprehensive effort to reduce both offending behaviour and public insecurity. This is equally valid with regard to international crime prevention. It implies that crime prevention at the international level can only be accomplished if closer co-operation is established among European security agencies and the national and regional populations who need to feel safe. International crime prevention follows the same objectives as local or national prevention, but approaches them differently. Both share some common elements. The most apparent one is that crime can prosper if opportunities for illegal activities are available. Generally speaking, these exist:

- where regulations on operating businesses or investing capital are not sufficiently controlled to reduce their exploitation for criminal purposes;
- where national populations are willing to purchase goods or pay for services which are either illegal or provided by clandestine migrants;
- where policing efforts are not considered vigilant or sufficiently competent to combat crime that crosses national borders;

---

197 QUELOZ, Nicolas: "International Efforts to tackle Organized Crime: The case of Europe"; paper prepared for the 52nd International Course on Criminology, Univ. of Macao, Faculty of Law, October 1996.

- where politicians, civil servants, border guards or police officers can be bribed;
- where desirable goods (luxury automobiles or electronic equipment) exist in abundance in one country and are in great demand in another, then they are coveted by thieves and traffickers for re-sale (in Eastern Europe, North Africa, etc.);
- where criminal codes, penal law and judicial assistance across regions in a country or among countries in Europe are incompatible. Loopholes make it possible for informed criminals to exploit markets (business investment, financial transactions, fraud with regard to taxation, subsidies, insurance or customs declarations, etc.) or abuse policy inconsistencies (asylum regulations, residency and employment permits, etc.);
- where illegal employment in a European country is possible and profitable. Clandestine migrants from less industrialised countries will always try, often paying exorbitant prices to traffickers, to reach these employment markets; and finally,
- where clandestine migrant smuggling is possible, other criminal activities in connection to the movement of migrants risk being exploited by the traffickers. This may include smuggling of goods through the same networks and routes or offering illegal services such as false identity papers. Also, the migrants themselves will more easily become involved in smuggling and crime to pay their traffickers or earn an income in the host country.

All the instances mentioned here – and this is not a complete list by any means – influence the opportunities which offenders may try to exploit. Another common element shared by both local and international crime is the behavioural element of the individual offender. Offenders assess the possible risks and rewards from a crime regardless of whether their activities touch victims within a single country or across a border. One element which is strongly linked to the motivation to commit crimes is the discrepancy in wealth between communities or countries. If wealth seems abundant in a country, then offenders from poorer countries may consider this an invitation for them to perpetrate procurement crimes such as theft, robbery or kidnapping for ransom.

However, there is also a major difference between local and international crime which affect how the public perceives its safety. The distinction is a subjective one. It lies at the level of perception between those offences which are visible and most spoken about in the media and those which are generally not noticed by the general public and less frequently mentioned in journalistic accounts. Most forms of organised crime and corruption are hidden from public scrutiny and are not often considered as causing acute public insecurity. In contrast, offences such as vandalism, juvenile delinquency, aggression by groups at demonstrations and sports games often have immediate, visible and fear-inducing consequences. We can thus again consider the three approaches to crime prevention mentioned in the previous chapter. This time, however, as they concern the international dimension and address both subjective and objective insecurity:

## The law and order approach
Argument: Crime across borders and public fear of international crime result from the impression that there is "too much crime" and that criminal laws are insufficiently tough. Counter-measures may therefore include:

- More police trained in international criminal investigations and greater collaboration among national police agencies and local police offices at border regions.
- Tough laws that aim to discourage the entry of international crime.
- Stiff sentencing of convicted offenders who engaged in trafficking, money laundering, corruption and fraud.
- Greater harmonisation of national criminal laws and sentencing procedures as well as judicial assistance throughout the European region.
- More emphasis on harmonising business regulations, taxation laws and financial investment policies so as to reduce legal and policy inconsistencies among European countries.
- More exchanges of police data and criminal intelligence to support the pursuit of suspected offenders across national borders.

## The behaviour approach
Argument: Crime across national borders results from a stress-creating context in which expectations and ambitions clash with reality; i.e. poverty or a lack of access to resources contrasts sharply with the wealth of people in other countries; this discrepancy in wealth and living standards motivates poorer populations to search for quick wealth in more affluent countries.

- National and local job creation programmes, vocational training and access to education especially for poorer communities in order to prevent young adults from participating in criminal activities which serve international trafficking and smuggling interests.
- Developmental crime prevention to address integration needs of resident foreign workers and immigrants.
- Economic development and vocational training assistance in less industrialised countries where economic migrants tend to come from with the objective to provide them with better living conditions at home and fewer incentives to emigrate to wealthier countries.

*The public safety approach*
Argument: The subjective fear of crime is no less important than objective crime figures.
- Partnerships between citizens and police forces at the community level is important to promote greater public awareness of international crime and of traffickers who may sell illegal goods or services in the local neighbourhood.
- The more the general public sees that national, bilateral and multinational crime prevention initiatives are having a positive effect in their personal lives, the more the public will feel protected from international crime.
- Public confidence in international crime prevention efforts can be promoted by making co-operation between police forces of different countries (bilateral or multilateral) more visible to the general public through the media, in schools and in entertainment.

# Prevention at the international European level

International crime prevention and the approach to internal security as presented here clearly implies that co-operation between national authorities responsible for security is indispensable. The principal reason is that as markets, information technology and social values characterise the globalisation of European society (including perceptions of public safety), crime will continue to develop across borders wherever marketing opportunities for illegal profits exist and where crime prevention efforts are seen to be inadequate. The political implication of this is that European countries must surrender those aspects of their national sovereignty which traditionally controlled the development of criminal law, migration policy and the development of business and investment regulations (international financial transfers and business investments). In other words, providing public safety can no longer be a purely internal national matter.

In such a large territory as Western and Central Europe, an offender may well think that the police cannot possibly pursue every criminal. But this inability to catch every offender applies to the smallest community as well. Never can every offender be caught. The best police and the most guarded border will never stop all criminals. Law enforcement and the criminal justice system of any country operate on the assumption that if a proportion of offenders get caught, others may become aware of the risks and stay away from criminal activities. However, there are always people who choose to forgo such warnings and pursue illegal activities, especially where opportunities for rapid profits are great.

It is important that national criminal police agencies, their intelligence services as well as magistrates can develop Europe-wide methods of collaboration.[198] The emphasis should be given on dissolving structures and networks of organised criminal groups such as migrant smuggling and drug trafficking networks as well as terrorist activists.

> In the fight against organised crime multilateral co-operation is of crucial importance. Hence, international fora dealing with the fight against organised crime and those dealing with migration should initiate a close co-operation.[199]

In particular, European countries must address suspicious and illegal activities that are managed by the leaders of such groups. These are usually activities that concern finances (the international transfers and laundering of illegally earned profits) or the transportation of illegal goods and services (narcotics, weapons, clandestine migrants, paedophile materials, toxic waste, etc.).

198 THUILLIER, François, *La législation antiterroriste*, Études et recherches, Mai 1999, Paris: Institut des Hautes Études de la Sécurité Intérieure; p. 13–15.
199 PUTTONEN, Riikka, *Draft Study on the Relationship between Organised Crime and Trafficking in Aliens*, Prepared by the Secretariat of the Budapest Group, Vienna: International Centre for Migration Development Policy Development, BG 1/99, January 1999; p. 1.

The other dimension to preventing international illegal activities and violence, as mentioned earlier, concerns internal security as perceived by the general public. We return here to consider the importance of prevention with regard to the subjective perception of safety or insecurity which European populations may feel with respect to various types of international crime. This feeling is usually not as enduring as is the insecurity caused by local delinquency and aggression. The general public does not feel unsafe because of the possibility that terrorists might detonate a bomb in a city. However, when this actually happens, all Europeans quickly demand of their state authorities to ensure that such terrorist acts will not happen again. Similarly, few people feel less safe when they hear or read in mass media that organised crime has infiltrated and corrupted a government of a far-away country. Nevertheless, no European wants such developments in their own country. Public insecurity concerning international organised crime, corruption or terrorism is therefore usually not an acute problem. It becomes a serious challenge only when a violent act, when corruption, or when a politician's collusion with crime is revealed by the media.

What does this mean for the prevention of crime in Europe? First, strategies of prevention at home and abroad as well as emergency reactions to sudden crises must be openly discussed. The public should be informed about prevention strategies because transparency promotes confidence – something that is often lacking between the public and security institutions.

## Challenges to international co-operation

We tend to imagine that security co-operation across borders is based on well designed plans that are strategically and operationally sound to deal with crises or crime-related problems when they arise. However, co-operation between two or more ministries and agencies from different countries can present some serious obstacles to organisers. Not uncommonly, this even applies to co-operation of government agencies within a single country. Some of these problems may appear so simple as to be considered irrelevant (shape and size of a negotiating table) while others are indeed more serious (on which radio frequency will police officers communicate with each other across a border). Still, in emergencies or for clean-up after natural catastrophes, Europeans have shown that it is possible to organise mutual assistance rapidly.

Examples are not difficult to find: An international rescue operation was successful in helping some 1200 passengers off the ferry *Prinsesse Ragnhild* which had caught fire near the Swedish coast in early July 1999. The Swiss military helped in an avalanche catastrophe in the Austrian Alps in early 1999 and a Swiss fire-brigade assisted its French colleagues in extinguishing the fire in the Mont-Blanc tunnel after the fatal accident of 24 March 1999. Less dramatic, but perhaps equally significant for public safety was the large crack-down on persons suspected to be involved in terrorism two weeks before the 1998 World Cup football games in France. Five countries – Belgium, France, Germany, Italy and Switzerland – combined their intelligence and police efforts and arrested nearly 100 people suspected of terrorist activities.[200]

Once a crisis occurs, be it terrorism in a city metro or violent political demonstrations, then the obvious urgency to develop better prevention is there for all to see. However, planning and realising practical co-operation without any crisis in sight has its difficulties. To agree on ways to work together, share information and exchange technological innovations when danger or risks are merely calculated guesses requires a commitment by all parties to arrive at workable solutions. To provide practical safety, train anti-terrorist squads and co-operate in international criminal investigations can only be developed over a long period of time.

Unfortunately, it is often only after a disaster or a violent event which shocks a national population (terrorist attack, large-scale fraud or gruesome human rights abuses such as by paedophile networks) that security agencies begin to think on how to deal with similar conditions in the future. European governments and their police agencies are not all equally sensitive to public voices and sentiments. Neither are they all prepared to undertake institutional and legal reforms when these are deemed useful. Some countries are quick to embrace reforms and introduce new policing techniques (diversifying the ethnic composition of their police officers so as to represent local populations or introducing more education-oriented securi-

200 HOFFMANN, Bruce, "Is Europe Soft on Terrorism?" in *Foreign Policy*, No. 115, Summer 1999; pp. 70–71.

ty services to build public confidence). Others, however, appear to wait until a crisis forces them to review their methods.

One major difficulty for many governments is that new forms of co-operation, be they among police agencies or rescue teams, require that appropriate administrative and possibly legal reforms are undertaken. Also, practical exercises on a regular basis are necessary to ensure that co-operation will be effective in times of need.[201] Futhermore, public subjective feelings of security can also be raised. If common exercises are frequently carried out in such a way that they are visible to the general public, then they can contribute to building public confidence in the capacity of state authorities to handle international challenges that stem from crime or catastrophes.

## International and European Union efforts at crime prevention

Most institutions responsible for enforcing criminal law, exchanging police intelligence or controlling the movement of migrants have been established in reaction to events, usually following the realisation that something must be done to control a problematic situation. European countries are all developing institutions to facilitate the pursuit of offenders across borders, to exchange information on new policing methods or provide education and training for security specialists.

Among these efforts are co-operation agreements among European countries which are neighbours to each other. These agreements encompass legal conventions for mutual assistance, extradition treaties as well as cross-border co-operation between local police and border control agencies. Examples do exist of security collaboration agreements that are considered as being successful. The Scandinavian countries share security and passport control arrangements to facilitate travel and trade and to collaborate in preventing illegal trafficking. Also Switzerland is deepening its co-operation with the police and border guard forces of its four neighbouring countries.

---

201 An example of an exercise for a hypothetical act of terrorism or catastrophe involved 330 French and 1100 Swiss military personnel on 1 July 1999. ("Ein militärischer Brückenschlag mit dem französischen Nachbarn", *Basler Zeitung*, 2 june 1999; p. 9.

A model of a successful bilateral agreement is the German-Swiss Police Agreement of April 1999.[202] It provides not only for practical police collaboration, but also requires of each party to share responsibility in providing security services on each other's territory during engagements across their common border. This agreement was developed mostly on the basis of earlier informal police co-operation efforts founded on pragmatism and mutual trust.

At the multilateral level, crime prevention co-operation is facilitated through organisations such as Interpol and the United Nations. There are also a large number of non-governmental organisations that study issues such as community policing, migrant trafficking, illegal toxic waste dumping and corruption. Finally, another category of crime prevention efforts are those developed specifically by the European Union for its own internal security. Among these are the Schengen Agreement and its Information System (SIS), the Dublin Convention as well as Europol. These institutions and agreements fulfil some security and law enforcement needs. Their contribution to building confidence among the European public is unclear, however.

The difficulty which all international organisations and multilateral agencies face is how to communicate their performance to the general public. The more remote an agency appears from the public's interest, the more difficult it is for the international institution to inspire confidence in its work. The public wants to see results in terms of safer cities, fewer stolen cars and less drug trafficking. For Europeans individually to feel more secure, these international agencies need to bring their "high-level" and often distant multilateral crime prevention efforts closer to the public.

## The United Nations and the OECD

Multilateral efforts to promote crime prevention around the world are being promoted by the United Nations. Since the 1950's, international conferences for government leaders and crime prevention experts have contributed to developing a large body of agreements, recommendations and instruments

202 The "*Schweizerisch – Deutsche Polizeivertrag*" was signed on 27 April 1999. From an interview with Dr. Markus Mohler.

which aim at improving the means by which national governments address their internal security. The Vienna-based UN-Centre for International Crime Prevention and the Commission on Crime Prevention and Criminal Justice have a made the prevention of crime in urban areas as well as juvenile delinquency and violent crime into one of the organisation's priorities. Another office within the UN is the Office for Drug Control and Crime Prevention which analyses the global drug trade and the consequences of drug abuse in terms of procurement theft and public insecurity.[203]

Together, these UN offices and agencies constitute a large resource of expertise and training for state ministries or departments for justice and safety. They attempt to influence national and international police offices and their intelligence services as well as training in crime prevention in cities and communities around the world. In support of this, the UN maintains a Crime and Criminal Justice Information Network in form of an internet service that provides access for security experts to crime statistics, major crime trends and developments of criminal laws. One example is the International Convention against Transnational Organised Crime. On the basis of a common agenda, the member states agree to a legal framework to harmonise their different legal systems and stress the importance of a legally binding instrument to overcome problems traditionally associated with international co-operation and mutual assistance.[204] This Convention is becoming one of the primary legal documents which member countries agree to uphold and implement.

While these UN efforts are noteworthy, it is still up to individual countries to make use of the information supplied by the UN, train their police officers, reform their security institutions and initiate local crime prevention efforts. As long as national governments and municipalities do not transmit information to the public in the form of practical crime prevention and security-building strategies, then the European public remains mostly unaware of the knowledge that is being accumulated at the multilateral level.

In a similar manner and in close collaboration with the United Nations, the Organisation for Economic Development and Co-operation (OECD)

---

203 NEWMAN, Graeme, ed., *Global Report on Crime and Justice*, United Nations Office for Drug Control and Crime Prevention, Oxford: Oxford University Press, 1999.
204 For further information, see: http://www.uncjin.org/CICP/cicp.html

contributes also to the prevention of international crime. It concerns itself especially with illegal business practices, corruption, fraud and money laundering. The organisation establishes guidelines for industrial competition and law enforcement to help countries regulate trade and competition. Accounting reforms are part of these recommendations and directly concern the fight against corruption. For example, its Convention on Combating Bribery of Foreign Public Officials in International Business Transactions represents a step towards international efforts to criminalise bribery and reduce corruption world-wide. It works to stop the flow of bribe money for the purpose of obtaining international business contracts and to strengthen domestic anti-corruption efforts aimed at raising standards of governance and increasing civil society participation.[205]

## Interpol

While Interpol is different in many respects from the UN and the OECD, it is similar in its relative distance from the general public. The organisation acts as a clearinghouse and storage of data on offences of international relevance. More than 170 countries are member to the Lyon-based organisation and most of them make use of Interpol by sending and requesting information on numbers and characteristics of stolen goods. For example, Interpol maintains data bases on stolen cars, stolen art pieces or the identity of offenders which are pursued across national borders. But the office cannot offer help in pursuing criminals or in uncovering intelligence information which is not freely transmitted by member states. Neither can Interpol supply material evidence needed by courts or deliver witnesses.

Given that Interpol is a police institution, its mandate restricts the organisation to supply information on or support investigations of crimes that are of a political nature. This means that it cannot help in locating offenders who are considered "political terrorists" by one country and "freedom fighters" by another. A related problem arises when such political activists claim refugee status and apply for asylum. Furthermore, offences which touch on the political interests of member States, on military matters, religious activities or those which have a racial or ethnic character are also excluded. This

205 See further the OECD's web page: http://www.OECD.org

means that countries have to find their own ways to control or pursue offenders who cause harm for political motives. For obvious reasons, member countries cannot enforce their fight against terrorists or drug trafficking via a world-wide police organisation which includes amongst its members some national governments accused of harbouring suspected terrorists or profiting from the narcotics trade.[206]

Still, Interpol increasingly contributes to police investigations in a proactive manner. It is able to transfer information from one national police agency to another if either of the parties suspect that specific offenders may travel to a known destination. Ideally, offenders may thus be apprehended before they can commit new crimes. However, Interpol is not always the appropriate institution through which to send intelligence information that merely concerns police investigations between two or more countries which are neighbours to each other. In local instances, police officers from neighbouring countries can better agree to work directly together. This is being done between an increasing number of Central and Western European countries.

With the development of the European Union's security institutions, however, co-operation between EU members and non-EU countries presents new problems. The European Union developed new security institutions in the past ten to fifteen years which essentially exclude non-member neighbouring countries. This is problematic with regard to regional developments of crime and security. All of Western Europe and increasingly Central Europe as well are sharing common characteristics of crime and concerns for internal security. However, as the EU's security institutions become more and more integrated, they risk dividing Europe into two regions: those countries who are members of the EU can participate in regional crime prevention while those who remain outside risk becoming increasingly isolated in matters of internal security.

Within the European Union, economic and political integration dynamics present the region with new opportunities and challenges for the prevention of public insecurity and crime. New security provisions have been developed in recent years. Among them, the Schengen Agreement and Eu-

---

206 Paraphrased and transl. from: Wyss, Rudolf, "Die Internationale Polizeizusammenarbeit", in *Solothurner Festgabe zum Schweizerischen Juristentag 1998*; Solothurnischen Juristenverein, p. 700.

ropol – the two establishments most talked about. However, to what degree they respond to objective security needs and to the public's subjective feelings of safety within the Union is not clear nor easy to estimate.

## The Schengen Agreement

The Schengen Agreement is named after the town Schengen in Luxembourg. This agreement was initially signed by five countries in 1985: Belgium, France, Germany, Luxembourg and the Netherlands. It provided for the gradual elimination of identity controls and duties along the borders between member countries and introduced free movement of nationals between these states. Since, in practice, it would have been impossible to offer this freedom to citizens from Schengen member countries only and still control identities of other nationals, the agreement allows all people who enter the Schengen area to travel freely through all the member countries. More countries joined this agreement since its introduction.

But the agreement left many questions open regarding institutional mechanisms in response to changing security needs and public demands. The agreement constituted a kind of "catalogue of general measures" which states could take to advance their common integration at economic and social levels.[207] Its first objective was clearly to free trade and promote a new freedom of travel. As a result, the Schengen member countries had to complement these developments with new security provisions. Thus, the Schengen system today includes a uniform application of a common visa policy, standardised identity checks at the external borders of the Schengen countries, a regime of residency and immigration regulations for persons from outside the Union as well as the allocation of responsibility for the processing of asylum applications. Finally, the Schengen states also elaborated procedures for regulating police co-operation and share a computerised information system (SIS). This information service enables police offices and border guards of all Schengen countries to access data on criminal pursuits, asylum requests and residency permits within the entire "Schengenland" area.

207 KAESER, Philippe, *L'espace Schengen: Des premiers pas au traité d'Amsterdam*, Institut européen, Université de Genève, No. 5, 1997; pp. 3–4.

The Schengen Agreement has now been incorporated in the framework of the EU through the Treaty of Amsterdam. It guarantees free movement of persons, goods and services and is intended to provide a high degree of public safety. This means that since 1 May 1999, when the Treaty of Amsterdam became effective, the Schengen *acquis* (asylum, migration policy, visa regime, standards of police co-operation and judicial assistance) is placed within the framework of the EU itself.

Measures are continuously being elaborated to build public confidence in the EU's security institutions. In general, they include police co-operation and judicial assistance as well as the harmonisation of laws that define and address migration, the trafficking of migrants and transnational crime. The objective is to avoid a weakening of the "protection of the common space". This implies:[208]

(a) The reinforcement of border controls at external Schengen borders through co-operation with regional and national authorities of the countries concerned. This also implies a uniformalisation of methods and tools.

(b) Harmonising visa requirements for short-duration travellers (3 months for tourists) for all persons from countries which the Schengen members agree to submit to visa requirements.

(c) Common regulations regarding migrants who request asylum and the procedures through which their status as refugees is considered. Because many migrants apply for asylum even when they are not refugees, the Schengen members and the EU as a whole have agreed to a convention under which migrants can apply for asylum only in the first EU country they enter to prevent them from applying in several countries one after the other. This is the Dublin Convention which came into force on 1 September 1997.

And (d), the Schengen Information System (SIS). According to Article 7 of the Agreement, the contracting parties assist each other and assure broad and permanent co-operation in the exchange of crime data, criminal police and judicial information. The SIS serves police and border control by storing information relevant to the pursuit of suspected offenders across the

---

208 KAESER, Philippe, *L'espace Schengen: Des premiers pas au traité d'Amsterdam*, Institut européen, Université de Genève, No. 5, 1997; pp. 5–6.

borders of member states as well as the registration of asylum seekers. The information system facilitates cross-border co-operation in matters of criminal and penal law, the analysis of weapons trafficking, of drug trafficking, and of organised groups of thieves (banditry). It also informs about the extradition of apprehended offenders and monitors data on stolen goods.

## Europol

For political reasons as well as practical ones, some members of the EU promoted the establishment of a regional criminal information clearing-house in the early 1990's. Their objective was to incorporate an office with the authority to investigate drug-related crime, trafficking of human beings, car theft and illegal trade in nuclear materials. The political reasons for establishing what today is known as "Europol" were several attempts, forwarded most notably by the German federal government, to overcome international handicaps in matters of criminal police investigations.[209] Another reason for creating Europol was the realisation that open borders would facilitate greater mobility of offenders. The establishment of this European criminal police office was initially agreed upon in the 1991 EU-Treaty of Maastricht. Once the office was set up in The Hague, it operated as the European Drugs Unit (EDU) until it officially became Europol in 1998.

Europol is supposed to contribute to the development of better exchanges of intelligence for both national police and national judicial institutions among all member countries. The organisation has the mandate to conduct criminal investigations and inform on crimes which stretch across the borders of member countries. It is an intelligence gathering, analysing, evaluating and distributing agency with its own data base. Its investigations cover not only traditional crimes, but also those types of politically motivated international violence and crimes which Interpol cannot address. However, Europol does not have executive powers (for the time being). It can only operate when authorised by member countries to investigate crimes in conjunction with national investigators and judicial prosecutors in the EU.

209 BIGO, Didier, *Polices en Réseaux: l'expérience européenne*, Paris: Presse de la Fondation nationale des sciences politiques, 1996; pp. 208–209.

Some EU countries would like Europol to develop more executive powers and co-ordinate international criminal investigations across the territory of the EU and perhaps even of other associated neighbouring countries as well. Perhaps it is self-evident that as EU integration at economic and political levels is deepening, the security aspect may need to follow. The question to ask here, however, is whether institutional developments with regard to internal safety respond to actual lacunae in crime prevention in the larger European region.[210] There is no doubt that international co-operation in judicial and policing matters is necessary. But given that most countries in Central and Western Europe experience very similar criminal developments because of their geographic proximity, one might ask why only EU members should benefit from security institutions that would clearly be of use to all countries in Europe.

## The EU and Europe

Discrepancies among national police agencies, criminal investigation methods, legal instruments and penal proceedings of Western and Central European countries make it still possible for transnational offenders to exploit illegal markets. The objective of national criminal law linked to international jurisprudence and inter-governmental agreements should be the following: to increase the efficiency of penal systems, to bring fugitives to trial, to permit local authorities to have access to evidence in other countries and to have legal authority to call on foreign witnesses and finally, to be able to rapidly block illegally earned profits elsewhere.[211] But for a judge to be able to call on persons or information beyond his own country's national jurisdiction means that the legal authorities of the other country concerned must have agreed to this beforehand.

---

210 This question is aptly discussed by Didier BIGO in relation to the integration of police security structures in the EU in: *Polices en Réseaux: l'expérience européenne*, Paris: Presse de la Fondation nationale des sciences politiques, 1996.

211 In part from: WYSS, Rudolf, "Die Internationale Polizeizusammenarbeit", in *Solothurner Festgabe zum Schweizerischen Juristentag 1998*; Solothurnischen Juristenverein, p. 692.

The incompatibilities that still exist among European judicial systems hamper the work of judges, magistrates and lawyers. Inter-European legal support to investigate international crimes and bring offenders to trial is therefore still very difficult to achieve. Every national criminal law defines certain offences differently, provides for different procedures to bring offenders to trial and hands out different punishments for the same crimes. This leaves Western Europe with an array of sometimes conflicting legal procedures which, for the criminal connoisseur, represent loopholes for crime, fraud, corruption, money-laundering and tax evasion.[212]

It is apparent, that apart from Interpol and international judicial assistance agreements, the EU's institutions offer few possibilities for extended international co-operation between the EU and non-EU countries for the prevention of crime. As in the case of Europol, the question arises here again why, since international crime prevention should respond to the proliferation of crime in Europe, are the new multilateral security structures limited to members of the EU? All of Europe has become "a more and more criminal geographically relevant area".[213] One would like to believe that a concrete interest to maintain and improve internal security beyond the borders of an individual State would require wider co-operation beyond the institutional confines of the EU.[214]

One may argue that the EU as a whole, like any individual country, will not be able to control international crime by itself on its territory. The prevention of international crime can advance only through a development of close collaboration and increasing harmonisation of police training and criminal investigation technologies that reach beyond the borders of the EU to include all countries in the larger European region.[215] It appears evident that multiple creative solutions to face ever new global challenges to inter-

212 In part from Perduca Alberto and Patrick Ramael, *Le Crime International et la Justice*, France: Flammarion, 1998; pp. 47, 53–55.
213 Wittkämper, Gerhard W., P. Krevet and A. Kohl, *Europa und die Innere Sicherheit*, Wiesbaden: Bundeskriminalamt (BKA) Forschungsreihe Nr. 35, 1996; p. 439.
214 In part from Bigo, Didier, "The European International Security Field: Stakes and Rivalries in a newly developing areas of Police Intervention", in Anderson, Malcolm and Monica den Boer, eds., *Policing across National Boundaries*, London: Pinter Publishers, 1994; pp. 162–163.
215 Wittkämper, Gerhard W., P. Krevet and A. Kohl, *Europa und die Innere Sicherheit*, Wiesbaden: Bundeskriminalamt (BKA) Forschungsreihe Nr. 35, 1996; p. 398.

nal security are necessary not only in the EU, but in the entire European region. Success in these efforts

> will be dependent upon more effective law enforcement and more expansive intelligence gathering. Governments must carefully monitor and infiltrate [...criminal] organizations. Intelligence agencies must unravel the complex international web of bank accounts, businesses, and investments that fund these groups. [...] All these efforts will require an unprecedented level of cooperative law enforcement and intelligence sharing.[216]

## Conclusion

Chapters seven and eight on preventing crime and feelings of insecurity attempted to demonstrate that Europeans are not condemned to feel unsafe. Security can be developed through many local, national and international measures. To achieve an acceptable degree of security in society, many different institutions have to co-operate in partnership with the public to develop both aspects of internal security: objective needs and subjective perceptions. Comprehensive crime prevention implies an effort to reduce public feelings of insecurity, to enforce laws and to develop channels of communication and co-operation between the general public and security agencies at local, national and international levels. In this respect, local and small community policing projects are as important as large international criminal intelligence services. Both contribute in different ways to improving public safety.

---

216 HOFFMANN, Bruce, "Is Europe Soft on Terrorism?" in *Foreign Policy*, No. 115, Summer 1999; p. 75.

# Chapter 9

# The Case of Switzerland

This chapter presents a brief overview of Switzerland's internal security situation. The argument here is that however much a national population may wish to preserve its autonomy in matters of security and public safety, the country's position within the wider European region ties it to this region's social, economic and political developments.[217] Included here are those countries from Eastern and Central Europe to the Atlantic coast which share the aspiration to uphold liberal, democratic values along with a free-market economy. They form a distinguishable socio-economic region that, in terms of internal security, has three common characteristics: First, a development of small local and large international crime which is highlighted in public debate and by the commercial media. Second, when one follows the headlines in the media, the impression becomes strong that the general public suffers from rising insecurity. And third, all governments in this region attempt to come to terms with cross-border criminality and with reforms of their crime prevention and law enforcement institutions as spearheaded by the European Union.

The term internal security is distinct from "external" or "international" security in that it implies the safety of the population in any one country. This rests on factors such as the competence of social, political, legal and economic institutions to prevent crime and maintain an acceptable degree of law and order in society. Given that European countries cannot prevent the movement of ideas, people, goods and services from coming across their border, internal security can exist only so long as stability and security also exist in neighbouring countries. In this sense, Switzerland is not isolated from events on the territory of its neighbours. Their security is, in turn, dependent on the internal security and stability of their own neighbours,

---

217 The terms "internal security" and "public safety" are here taken to mean essentially the same thing. The former, however, is more often taken to imply the security of society in a country while the latter refers to the security of individual people.

and so forth. This means that public safety in Switzerland is to varying degrees dependent on the security and stability of Western and Central European countries, including the Balkans, and beyond.

## Internal security in the European context

The political, economic and social changes since the end of the Cold War have meant that no country in Europe can hope to provide security on its own for its citizens. Europe's governments must increasingly find ways to co-operate to prevent transnational as well as local crime. However, Switzerland is, from an institutional perspective with regard to maintaining security and public safety (police, intelligence and crime prevention), relatively isolated from its neighbours. At the same time, Switzerland shares with its neighbours the following concerns:

- The general public in Switzerland and in most European countries share an increased sense of un-ease about public safety from international organised crime and transnational burglary and theft.
- Switzerland, other non-European Union countries as well as EU members must all live with the knowledge that their national borders are not a major obstacle for transnational offenders or for migrant smugglers to ply their trade.[218]
- Like other countries in the wider European region, Switzerland must continuously adapt its security framework so as not to stand out from among its neighbours as a haven for criminal activities. This is no simple matter as adaptation implies doing away with ideas of national independence and autonomy in security matters.

---

218 It is important to note that migrants and asylum seekers (whether they are refugees or economic migrants) do not threaten security. Rather, it is the exploitation of migrants by smuggling networks that must be prevented through transnational crime prevention in the same manner as smuggling and trafficking of other goods and services are to be checked. That economic migrants from poverty-stricken regions seek to find a better livelihood in a Western country must be considered as a natural part of human life and history. Less fortunate individuals, including countless Europeans, have always sought to find better living conditions elsewhere.

Switzerland lies in the middle of a geographic region in which the European Union (EU), rather than individual countries, is becoming the principle player in security matters. Some of its member countries lead the way in developing EU security policy and intra-EU co-operation. Most Central European countries are eager to join the European Union and, with a view to doing so one day, they are gradually adapting their security institutions, legal framework and even their travel and migration policies. Their aim is to better collaborate with the EU as a whole and with its individual member countries in domains needing reform so as to advance their future integration in the EU.

The principal EU initiatives to strengthen internal security and improve controls on the movement of offenders across borders in the Union are the Schengen Agreement, the Dublin Convention and Europol. They provide for co-operation in cross-border policy issues affecting migration, travel visas, asylum and immigration as well as police activities (law enforcement and the pursuit of suspected offenders). Border guard functions and crime-prevention intelligence services are also increasingly being integrated in the EU's security structure. They represent the beginnings of an "EU-internal security regime" that influences even the policies of non-EU neighbours.

Switzerland cannot take part in the security agreements and institutions of the European Union. The only possible exception is Swiss participation in Europol once an agreement has been reached. However, Switzerland cannot contribute to the development of the EU's security policy nor its institutions. At the same time, Switzerland is a full participant in the region's developments of crime. This is also true for Norway and Island – two other determined outsiders of the European Union. However, they will be able to participate more fully than Switzerland in the EU's internal security provisions because they are part of the European Economic Area (EEA) and the Nordic Passport Union.

As for Switzerland, it is not part of the EU because of the insistence by a large proportion of its population to uphold the country's independence and neutrality. The political drive to maintain independence in certain domains of governance may be praiseworthy. However, in matters of security, such a drive may be rather illusive as the prevention of crime and insecurity must increasingly reach beyond the national border. Internal security or public safety cannot any longer be provided by a single country.

183

# International mobility, asylum and immigration

Switzerland is, like all European countries since the end of the Cold War, exposed to an unprecedented volume of travellers of all kinds, including refugees and economic migrants. An average of 700'000 people enter and leave Switzerland every day. The inter-connectedness of global markets inevitably opens new fields of industrial and business activities. Each country in Europe not only competes in roughly similar industrial, labour and financial investment markets. Switzerland's long history of political and economic stability and its now unique position as an outsider in the middle of the Euro currency zone can be to its advantage: this position may contribute to the country's attractiveness for foreign investments well into the future. However, Switzerland's services and stability are not only of interest to investors who bring legally earned money. The added values also attracts investors who come to place criminally earned profits or un-justly earned funds in the country's financial institutions.[219]

Furthermore, Switzerland is also an attractive safe haven for people who flee from political crises and wars in their home countries. As the number of such crises has increased world-wide since the end of the Cold War, the average number of asylum seekers coming to Switzerland has gradually risen. This trend remains valid even if we leave out the "highs" caused by the war in the former Yugoslavia. Between the early 1970's and the late 1980's, Switzerland accommodated a few hundred asylum applicants (about 6'100 registered asylum requests in 1980) – a proportionally similar number as in the other West European countries. But with the end of the Cold War, the numbers began to climb. These figures increased most rapidly each time violent conflicts pushed civilians to flee. As soon as cease-fires and peace agreements brought an end to the fighting, asylum numbers also came down again. The numbers of asylum applicants for some of the years between 1987 and 1999 is as follows:

| 1987 | 1990 | 1991 | 1992 | 1993 | 1994 | 1996 | 1997 | 1998 | 1999 |
|------|------|------|------|------|------|------|------|------|------|
| 10'913 | 35'836 | 41'629 | 17'960 | 24'739 | 16'134 | 18'001 | 23'982 | 41'302 | 46'068 |

219 Von DAENIKEN, Urs, "Organisierte Kriminalität in Osteuropa, Einflüsse auf die Schweiz", in STAHEL, Albert A., ed., *Organisierte Kriminalität und Sicherheit*, Bern: Verlag Paul Haupt, 1999; p 86.

The fluctuations are obvious when looking at the rapid increases and decreases of asylum seekers between 1990 and 1992 as well as from 1992 to 1994 and then again from 1996 onwards. These reflect the political changes in the former communist countries following the end of the Cold War and especially the conflicts in the former Yugoslavia, particularly in Bosnia and Kosovo. Most other EU countries experienced similar fluctuations of asylum seekers during these same years.

However, one difference can be noted with regard to economic instability in Albania, the civil conflict in Kosovo in 1998 and the NATO air campaign in 1999 in the FRY. Switzerland became a preferred destination for a very large proportion of Albanian speaking refugees and migrants from the Federal Republic of Yugoslavia (Serbia, Montenegro and Kosovo). Their arrival in Switzerland led to a sharp increase of the proportion of Albanian-speaking asylum seekers. They represented about 60% of all the asylum seekers in 1999. However, the end of the Kosovo war in the Autumn of 1999 and the return of relative stability in both Kosovo and Albania meant that the numbers of new asylum seekers from this region began to decrease.

A reason for why large numbers of asylum seekers from Kosovo and Albania came to Switzerland is because the country is home to many migrant labourers and immigrants from those regions. From the 1960's to the 1980's, Switzerland employed hundreds of thousands of labourers from Yugoslavia. Many came as seasonal workers and eventually received longer-term residency and work permits. About half of the approximately 300'000 Yugoslavs who reside in Switzerland today are of Albanian linguistic origin. Naturally they maintain contact with their families and friends in the home country and so became the destination addresses for refugees from the war in the home country.

Every time crises elsewhere cause the numbers of asylum seekers in Switzerland to rise sharply, it becomes evident that the Swiss population is easily affected. Protectionist or isolationist political demands to prevent such a vulnerability become more frequent at such times. However, protectionist demands cannot easily be satisfied by political authorities. One reason is that Switzerland, like its neighbours, wishes to benefit economically and socially from the country's openness. Another reason is that Switzerland is attractive for emigrants from countries where political repression or economic instability are endemic.

In reaction to the arrival of large numbers of asylum seekers, social tensions among the Swiss population have come to be expressed through xenophobic violence. Arson fires were set in 1999 to buildings marked to accommodate asylum-seekers in both, the German and the French part the country. This attests to a worrying development. Such acts are usually directed not simply against the arriving asylum seekers, but also towards the local government (canton or municipality). They are attempts to force a change in asylum policies by calling for wide media attention that creates an impression of insecurity.[220]

Indeed, the Swiss government has not remained deaf to public concerns. Over the past years, Swiss reaction to the influx of asylum seekers has led to a reduction of benefits. The aim of most of these reductions has been to render the Swiss asylum system less attractive in comparison to those of other European countries. The hope is that migrants will choose another EU country. But of course, the EU neighbours are also engaged in similar gradual reductions of asylum benefits and therefore they are lowering their own attractiveness as well. Hence, Switzerland was affected, and will also be in the future, by political, economic and humanitarian crises abroad.

This influence is perceptible by the numbers of refugees and migrants who came since the 1960's for find a safe haven or for temporary employment as foreign workers and who end up staying in Switzerland permanently. Among these migrants a growing number eventually apply for naturalisation. The growth of the Swiss population is due almost exclusively to the settlement and naturalisation of new immigrants and the children which they give birth to. The number of persons who became Swiss citizens in recent years is as follows: In 1990, about 8650 persons were given a Swiss passport while in 1997, 19'169, and in 1998, 21'277 immigrants received naturalisation.[221]

Most immigrants are between 18 and 35 years old. They help to lower the average age of the population which is gradually becoming older. The ageing of the indigenous population is also a cause for concern in Switzer-

220 "'Blick': Stimmungsmache sucht Glaubwürdigkeit: Das Boulevardblatt 'Blick' sorgt mit Schlagzeilen und lärmigen Geschichten rund um die Kosovo-Flüchtlinge immer wieder für publizistischen Wirbel", in Basler Zeitung, 2 June 1999; p. 2.
221 Data from Bundesamt für Statistik, "Bevölkerungsentwicklung, Form "T1.26 Erwerb des Schweizer Bürgerrechts"; and "Bevölkerungszunahme auf 7,1 Millionen", Neue Zürcher Zeitung, 13 October 1999; p. 15.

land. In 1980, the largest age group of the population was between 15 and 20 years old. Now, the largest group of Swiss is between 30 and 35 years old.[222] In twenty years, the largest group of the indigenous population will have reached 45 to 50, and if no drastic changes occur, 45% of the Swiss population will be 55 or more by the year 2050. In similar proportions, this ageing of the population is occurring in all Western European countries.

The immigration-population growth factor attests to the influence which the mobility of migrants has. This mobility is also profitable to Swiss industries that continuously need new mostly unskilled labour. The number of foreigners employed in Switzerland has increased in 1999 as the economy began to improve again.[223] Some Swiss cantons are again experiencing a shortage of workers in industries such as tourism and construction. Labour migration, as well as the continuous naturalisation of immigrants and the accommodation of new asylum seekers give a summary idea of the extent to which Switzerland is influenced by events in Europe and beyond. The facility with which migrants arrive in Western Europe remains a fact which neither more protectionist policies nor tighter controls at the border can make disappear.

## Transnational crime and security

An issue which is hotly debated in Switzerland is crimes committed by foreigners. Debates on this topic become most vocal whenever political crises push thousands of people to flee their homes and seek asylum in Switzerland and other European countries. While it is true that offenders can travel across borders and exploit migration channels to do so, the debates about foreigners' crimes are often motivated by political interests to

---

222 Bundesamt für Statistik, Sektion Bevölkerungsentwicklung, "Ständige Wohnbevölkerung nach Altersgruppen, 1980 und 1997"; Sept. 1998.

223 The number of foreign workers grew by 0.8 % in the first three quarters 1999. Of a total of 870'251, there are some 698'640 foreigners with yearly employment permits and about 27'800 with seasonal contracts as well as 143'780 cross-border employees. "Zunahme der Ausländerzahl....", Neue Zürcher Zeitung, 22 October 1999; p. 15. See also: ROULET, Yelmarc, "Permis de travail: Genève et Vaud crient famine", Le Temps, 22 September 1999; p. 2; and "Unveränderte Höchstzahlen für Ausländerbewilligungen", Neue Zürcher Zeitung, 21 October 1999; p. 13.

cause feelings of insecurity. There is no doubt that with the large numbers of people leaving either economically desperate conditions or fleeing from grave insecurity, there are always some individuals who will capitalise on the situation to profit from crime. It is a fact that:

> open borders across Europe have increased population mobility to unprecedented levels, including mobility of those who move in search of criminal opportunities. Given its wealth and concomitantly the excellent opportunity structure for offenders [...Switzerland, like] countries with huge transient populations will necessarily see their crime rates affected by the size of their nonresident population.[224]

Transnational offenders are most often individuals who manage to profit from cross-border networks, often with members of their kin in other countries. The offences they most often are involved in are drug trafficking, the trafficking of migrants or of women for prostitution, theft and burglary of items for resale in other countries, smuggling of goods such as tobacco products (mostly to evade import duties) or financial offences such as fraud and the laundering of illegally earned profits.[225] These offences are committed more often by people who are not long-term residents in Switzerland. They either travel through or reside for only short periods of time the country.

Rarely mentioned, but important to note is that the vast majority of foreigners who reside legally in Switzerland for the long-term are not more likely to engage in crime than the indigenous population. This was shown in a report of the Swiss Federal Statistics office which indicated that of the

---

224 KILLIAS, Martin, "Immigrants, Crime, and Criminal Justice in Switzerland", in *Ethnicity, Crime and Immigration:...*, ed. by Michael TONRY, Chicago: The University of Chicago, 1997; p. 386–387.

225 In part from: KILLIAS, Martin: "Immigrants, Crime, and Criminal Justice in Switzerland". In *Ethnicity, Crime and Immigration:...*, ed. by Michael TONRY, Chicago: The University of Chicago, 1997; p. 377 & pp. 385–388; and STORZ, Renate, et. al., *Zur Staatszugehörigkeit von Verurteilten*, Bundesamt für Statistik, 1996. Important is to note that in such statistics, offences against immigration laws or asylum regulations can only be committed by foreigners and should therefore not be included in crime statistics that look at nationality. This is particularly important as in the figures of condemned asylum seekers, more than half of all condemnations are for offences against the Swiss asylum law/residency regulations (Storz 1996; p. 22).

total 44% of foreign offenders in 1991 (a year of large migration movements), 16% had a place of residence in Switzerland, 7% were asylum seekers, and the remaining 21% were "tourists" of sorts and illegal aliens.[226]

With this in mind, it is possible to explain in part why it is that the numbers of foreigners in police statistics has risen in comparison to indigenous offenders. However, another perhaps more important explanation for the presence of foreigners in police statistics is their age. In any population, offenders are mostly male and between 18 and 35 years old. Migrants and refugees are in their majority also male and in this same age group. Furthermore, the proportion of non-Swiss offenders which increased substantially through the 1990's has been due far more to the illegal activities of non-resident foreigners than it has for legal residents with a foreign nationality. This is particularly so for violent crimes.[227] For example, in 1990, 38.7% of all delinquent and criminal acts cleared by the Swiss police were committed by foreigners. This number has been on the increase to reach a high of 54.9% in 1998. These years correspond roughly to the years of war and serious instability in the Balkans and the migration flows which they produced. As long as no new crisis erupts in this region, a reduction of migration flows of young people in search of jobs and quick wealth can be expected – it may then also lead to a decrease of offences in the coming years.[228]

Crimes committed by people pretending to be or recognised as asylum seekers, whether these are small delinquencies or major offences, inevitably cause two related problems. On the one hand, public outrage is directed against all asylum seekers. Such views, however, can lead to a discrimination against the vast majority of genuine refugees who do not commit offences. On the other hand, federal authorities responsible for internal security and asylum regulations risk losing public confidence. This confidence is crucial for the Swiss federal and cantonal police offices and border guards. Each time reports about criminality by foreigners are publicised

226 STORZ, Renate, et. al., *Zur Staatszugehörigkeit von Verurteilten*, Bundesamt für Statistik, 1996.
227 STORZ, Renate, Simone RONEZ and Stephan BAUMGARTNER: *Zur Staatszugehörigkeit von Verurteilten: Kriminalistische Befunde*. Bundesamt für Statistik, Bern, 1996; pp. 5 & 13.
228 The figure for 1999 is indeed lower than it was in 1998. Bern: Bundesamt für Polizeiwesen, data for 1997, 1998. Bundesamt für Polizei, data for 1999.

through the commercial media, public confidence in authorities responsible for public safety is challenged.

The difficulty is that public confidence cannot easily or quickly be improved. To prevent crimes by travelling offenders is not a matter of simply stationing more personnel at the national border or increasing the number of police officers in the streets. Such visible measures can have a palliative effect on public feelings of insecurity. More officers at the national border can also have a dissuasive effect to potential migrant traffickers. However, determined offenders will always find a way into Switzerland so long as they see attractive opportunities for trafficking, theft, money-laundering, drug trading or other illegal activities.

Finally, crime is not the only challenge that affects public feelings of safety. Others also trigger political debates. For example, the reorganisation of the police in Switzerland at the national and cantonal levels in light of the country's federal structure. This touches on sensitive questions such as whether a federal police authority should have autonomous executive powers or to what extent intelligence can be centrally controlled. Furthermore, the increasing need for cross-border co-operation in matters of border control, legal assistance and crime prevention are also topics that raise questions about Switzerland's neutrality and independence. As is becoming clear, however, in these security policy areas as well as with regard to migration and asylum, Swiss internal security is not free from foreign influence.

## Swiss and European crime prevention

In the 19th century, international co-operation for the pursuit of known offenders developed in the form of bilateral extradition agreements between Switzerland and other European states. These were complemented in the early 20th century with allowances for the collection of criminal information by investigators in each others' countries. Provisions were added to facilitate the calling and protection of foreign witnesses and the exchange of archival and vital statistical information. However, none of these agreements were initially intended to deal with complex criminal cases such as multinational drug or migrant smuggling.

For this purpose, multilateral agreements for criminal investigations have undergone further development. Interpol, established more than 75 years ago, is such a development. As the world's international criminal police organisation, it supports criminal investigations among its 177 member countries whenever such help is requested by national police agencies. Switzerland participated in the foundation of Interpol. The country's membership offers it an important link with other national police offices around the world. Each year, Swiss authorities transfer between 50'000 and 60'000 search requests to Interpol and the office in Bern receives a similar number from other countries. Many investigations via Interpol into the whereabouts of criminals and searches of suspected funds, stolen goods and illegal services are indispensable for Switzerland as there is no other international intelligence information centre to which it can turn.

However, Interpol has some formal and institutional limitations. They restrict the organisation from handling information that is of an explicit political, military or religious nature. Another problem that arises regarding Interpol is its universality. It is a global organisation which must cover very broad needs. This can be a disadvantage when types of crime must be investigated which are characteristic of a particular geographic region. European countries share many of the same crime characteristics and therefore need to collaborate fighting these – not only in terms of exchanging intelligence, but in practical ways as well.

Europe's larger region, including the territory covered by the European Union, forms a criminally specific area. International offenders pay less and less attention to individual countries. Rather, trafficked drugs or migrants enter this region and stolen automobiles leave it regardless of whether the entry or exit points are in Finland, the Netherlands, Slovenia, Poland or Portugal. In other words, this entire European area increasingly shares the same consequences from international crime and must therefore develop common prevention strategies. This is true for trafficking as well as for financial crimes. With the gradual harmonisation efforts in monetary and taxation policy for economic reasons, this European region is also becoming an increasingly homogenous place in which the fight against money laundering and fraud must be co-ordinated as much as possible. Interpol cannot sufficiently respond to these specific regional needs which Europeans in general, and specifically the European Union members express.

Already in the 1980's, member countries of the then European Community recognised that because of regionally specific developments in crime, new ways to maintain internal security were called for. The need to gain better control over transnational crime that affected two or more member countries became especially clear in the 1990's as the Schengen Agreement was elaborated. The gradual elimination of national border controls among the Schengen member states to facilitate economic trade and the mobility of their citizens meant that compensatory security measures had to be developed.[229] The Schengen Agreement today provides for security measures which go well beyond the capacities of Interpol. Under this Agreement, new forms of co-operation among the Schengen members have been agreed to as well as methods for judicial assistance and the pursuit of offenders across internal borders. The European Union's Schengen members individually still call upon Interpol to relay information on criminal investigations which are of a wider international character. Nevertheless, these same countries are increasingly making use of their Schengen Agreement's police information service and Europol, the EU's common criminal intelligence agency, to exchange police data which previously was channelled through Interpol.[230]

## The EU and Switzerland

As a "third State" outside of the EU, Switzerland stands equal with other non-EU member countries in Europe. The border around Switzerland is an external Schengen border at which the four neighbouring countries can apply the same strict controls which Schengen members also apply on their external border elsewhere. It appears today that the associated States and possible next members of the EU such as Poland, the Czech Republic, Hungary, and the Slovak Republic are eager to harmonise their security and migration policies as well as their economic policies with those of the EU.

---

229 Wyss, Rudolf, "Die internationale Polizeizusammenarbeit", Solothurner Festgabe zum Schweizerischen Juristentag 1998, Solothurn: Solothurnischen Juristenverein, 1998; p. 697.

230 Mohler, Markus H. F., "Sicherheit hat mit Solitarität zu tun", Neue Zürcher Zeitung, 21 March 2000; p. 15.

In contrast to the populations in most Central European countries, however, many Swiss would not welcome Switzerland's membership in the European Union. The reasons for this need not to be discussed here, except that with regard to internal security, membership in the EU would imply full participation in the Schengen Agreement. To many Swiss police officers, this would be a welcome development. However, for a large section of the country's population, becoming a member might imply an unwelcome abolishment of Swiss border controls. To surrender these and leave the control of borders to others at the external Schengen border amounts to a question of confidence on the part of the Swiss in the EU and its institutions. This raises not only political sensitivities among some Swiss political parties, but also misgivings about losing control over what is the most visible and symbolic aspect of national security. The situation regarding policing across the country's territory is similar. The notions of national independence and neutrality ring deep chords in the hearts of many.

However, the numbers of crimes committed by non-resident foreigners in Switzerland and the coming and going of large numbers of refugees and economic migrants over the past decade indicate that Switzerland cannot but be influenced by what goes on beyond its national border. Collaboration in matters of policing with the EU and other Western and Central European countries is the only way forward. In fact, far more than mere collaboration with other national security agencies is recommended. Some experts want Swiss policing, border control and other security institutions, including the military, to collaborate far more closely with those of neighbouring countries and of the EU. This would principally be to prevent both small transnational crime and international organised crime, fraud, tax evasion and money laundering.[231]

In light of the accepted need for some forms of closer collaboration, the Swiss government has, since the early 1990's, tried to open negotiations on security collaboration directly with the EU. So far, however, these have been without success. Only at the bilateral level has Switzerland obtained support for greater security collaboration. The four neighbouring EU mem-

---

231 For example: DÄNIKER, Gustav, "La Suisse est dans le 'Partenariat pour la paix', ni plus, ni moins", *Le Temps*, 10 December 1999; p. 15; and MOHLER, Markus H. F., "Sicherheit hat mit Solitarität zu tun", *Neue Zürcher Zeitung*, 21 March 2000; p. 15.

ber states (Austria, France, Germany and Italy) supported Swiss requests to participate in some of the security provisions that touch on aspects of the Schengen Agreement. These included the exchange of police data and information on asylum seekers who are suspected of offences. The four neighbours have a clear interest in seeing that Switzerland is tied into their increasingly integrated security structure. However, other EU countries spoke out against a selective or partial participation by Switzerland in the Schengen provisions.[232]

Thus far, the Schengen Agreement provides for free movement across internal borders, close collaboration in the creation of policies on asylum, visa and immigration as well as the exchange of information on judicial matters and criminal intelligence. With regard to asylum, the EU Schengen members agreed, through the so-called Dublin Convention, to limit the countries in which migrants can request asylum. All who apply for asylum can do so only in the first member country through which they enter the European Union. This provides for a measure of control on where asylum applications are made and how many applicants there are. With the help of the Schengen Information System (SIS), records of asylum applicants can be checked on an EU-wide computer database. The objective is to reduce both "asylum tourism" as well as the lucrative trafficking of migrants. Through the SIS, the national police agencies and border control forces of the EU, member states can collaborate more effectively to pursue migrant traffickers and other suspected offenders.

With the entry into force in 1999 of the European Union's Treaty of Amsterdam, the Schengen Agreement is placed firmly within the Union. Switzerland's isolation from the EU means that it cannot participate in policing and crime prevention matters. It therefore had to seek compensatory ways to bridge this co-operation lacunae. As is explained further below, this has been possible only at the bilateral level between Switzerland and its four EU neighbours. For Swiss participation in the Schengen provisions as well as for accession to the Dublin Convention, Switzerland would have to become a member of the EU. The EU has been unwilling to offer a partial "*à la carte*" participation for Switzerland in EU provisions. In contrast to the EU position vis-à-vis Switzerland, other non-EU and EU coun-

232 KRIMM, Roland, "La Grande-Bretagne adhère aux Accords de Schengen..." in *Le Temps*, 30 May 2000.

tries have managed to negotiate agreements for partial participation in Schengen. For example, Great Britain maintains its border controls even though it is a member of the Schengen Agreement. It can thus collaborate with the EU in matter of criminal intelligence, law enforcement and police investigations. Norway and Island can, as outsiders of the EU, negotiate their future participation in the Dublin Convention and thus take in aspects of the EU's migration policy. For Switzerland, to participate in some of these same aspects of the Schengen Agreement or the Dublin Convention remains impossible. Some EU states consider that for any form of participation, Switzerland would need to make some political and practical concessions in terms of relinquishing national sovereign control over aspects of security policy. However, that is something on which many Swiss have not been able to agree.

Remaining independent from the EU, Switzerland is obliged to accept all asylum applications regardless of where the applicants come from or how long they may already have travelled in the EU. To prevent both "asylum tourism" and the abuse of asylum regulations by migrants who know they have no chance of staying in an EU country, Switzerland has little choice but to adapt its laws and policies to those of its four EU neighbours. This not only amounts to a Swiss participation without an equal return of benefits from the Schengen member states. It also means that for reasons of trying to keep abreast with all the policy changes and reforms among the Schengen members, Switzerland has less sovereign autonomy left in matters of asylum and migration. Furthermore, adapting security or migration policies to those of the EU is not a simple matter. Nor can one be certain that this effort will benefit Switzerland's security needs in the long-term. Unilateral policy adaptations may reduce Switzerland's attractiveness for international offenders in comparison to EU countries, but they will not help the country harmonise its police and border control work with those of the EU.

At present, Switzerland comes to feel its institutional isolation in particular instances. An example can be illustrated with regard to the control of the movement of migrants. In 1999, Switzerland unexpectedly became the asylum country of choice for migrants from Iraq. This is because the EU tightened its restrictions with regard to all Iraqi migrants. This brought about a re-orientation among migrants from that country who chose Switzerland instead. The result is that in 1999, Iraqi asylum seekers made up the second largest national group after migrants from the Federal Republic of Yugoslavia.[233] Thus, in 1999, the countries of origin of the largest groups of asylum seekers that arrived in Switzerland were as follows:[234]

Federal Republic of Yugoslavia
(mostly asylum applicants from Kosovo, Serbia and Montenegro): 28'913
Iraq (mostly asylum seekers of the Kurdish minority): 1'658
Bosnia and Herzegovina 1'513
Sri Lanka 1'487
Turkey (mostly asylum seekers of the Kurdish minority): 1'453
Albania 1'386

This tells us that Switzerland is not only influenced by political crises or economic instability in countries beyond Western Europe, but that EU migration regulations also affect Swiss internal policy. In this respect, Switzerland will remain isolated from the EU's instruments for the foreseeable future. However, with regard to criminal investigations, a possibility for Swiss-EU collaboration does exist with Europol.

Based in The Hague, Europol acts as a central intelligence police information centre for crimes that reach across borders within the EU as well as for international crime from outside the Union. Europol became operational in October 1998. It offers all member states the possibility to exchange intelligence information and participate in its analysis for police investigation and criminal pursuit. The information processed concerns drug trafficking-related crimes, the smuggling of nuclear and other illegal or dangerous industrial materials, migrant smuggling, theft and trafficking of stolen motor vehicles and the trafficking in human beings. Europol does not have independent executive police powers to pursue offenders anywhere in Europe. Rather, each EU country stations liaison officers at Europol who then collaborate with the centre's staff and with their national criminal police office to co-ordinate the search and pursuit of offenders.

Even though Switzerland will not soon, if ever, become a member of the EU, Article 42 of the Europol Convention stipulates that third States can enter upon co-operation agreements directly with Europol. Given that

233 "Asile: la Suisse contrainte à la fermeté?", in *Le Temps*, 13 September 1999.
234 "Asyl Suchende nach Herkunftsländern", 1999. Bundesamt für Flüchtlinge, Januar 2000.

Switzerland is surrounded by the EU, transnational crime that touches Swiss territory almost always affects one or more EU countries as well. From a geographical and criminal perspective, co-operation with Europol is a logical step forward. Collaboration between Europol and the Swiss police could take the form of an exchange of police/intelligence information, co-operation in police investigations, as well as for training and technical support.[235] Furthermore it may be possible in the near future for the Swiss Federal Police to station a liaison officer in Europol. Such an approach to collaborating with the EU may also be acceptable to members of the Swiss population and some politicians who are particularly sensitive that traditional notions of national sovereignty and independence are not explicitly compromised.

## Bilateral security agreements

Besides planning ways to participate in some internal security institutions and agreements, Switzerland co-operates already with its four neighbouring countries. Bilateral negotiations were launched in 1995 to overcome difficulties in cross-border collaboration. It was important that the most serious legal, policing and criminal investigation lacunae be bridged by new agreements at the bilateral level.

Collaboration between Swiss and neighbouring border guards and some cantonal police offices has existed since the beginning of the 20th century. However, no formally binding agreements regulated such policing across the border. Formalising this became increasingly necessary in the 1990's due to the increased movement of people across Europe. In 1995 the Swiss federal government began to discuss methods of practical security co-operation with its four neighbours in which their police and border guards were automatically included in the negotiations.

---

235 In part from STORBECK, Jürgen, "Die Rolle von Europol bei der Bekämpfung der organisierten Kriminalität", in Hanns-Seidel-Stiftung e. V., *Dokumentation der 16. internationalen Fachtagung zum Thema 'Demokratie in Anfechtung und Bewährung – die Bekämpfung von organisierter Kriminalität und Drogenhandel'*, Schriftenreihe 3.47, München, 1998; pp. 49–50.

The common purpose to which all agreed was to prevent that Switzerland becomes a turntable for illegal trespassing and customs fraud. The entry of illegal migrants who mostly come with the help of trafficking networks is a concern for both, the four neighbours and Switzerland. It affects asylum provisions intended for refugees and crime prevention in the territory of both. Also the pursuit of offenders across the national border in either direction was to be facilitated. The first bilateral agreement was signed with France on 11 May 1998. The second one was agreed to with Italy and signed on 9 September 1998. As for Germany and Austria, agreements were negotiated and agreed to in April 1999. These four agreements provide for intensified cross-border police and border guard collaboration and place this on a more solid legal footing. The provisions in these agreements can be summarised in two groups of activities: First, admitting their neighbouring police investigations on their own territory in collaboration with their own police forces; and second, facilitating police intelligence information exchanges in support of international investigations.

Although these four bilateral agreements are an innovative development that is still in its infancy, practical collaboration at several Swiss border areas such as Basel and Geneva is already well established. The advantage of the four agreements is that they now provide a basis upon which closer collaboration can be built and a common sharing of policing responsibilities can be secured. These agreements are a small but important step away from considering internal security as a purely internal matter.

The prevention of crime at the local level across a border must, however, not exclusively be a matter of practical police co-operation. Internal security is not only to be considered in objective terms. It is frequently more a subjective assessment – a feeling – of safety by the general public. This is often reflected in concerns about insecurity which public opinion polls and the media express. They include a fear of transnational crime and of "floods of migrants who may drown the boat" as well as a frustration about a seeming inability on the part of government authorities to control these phenomena to everyone's satisfaction. In light of these rather subjective views and expectations, police and government authorities need to have a good understanding about what influences public sentiments. How are feelings of insecurity best reduced and how can information about policing reforms and international collaboration contribute to this.

# Switzerland's changing internal security provisions

Public security institutions and services, such as the military, border guards, civil protection and police forces, have been the subject of much discussion about reform in recent years. Security is hotly debated whenever the media or political interest groups complain about crime, foreign offenders or juvenile delinquency. The more international and domestic crime is discussed in the media, the greater demands for better policing and reforms of security institutions become. To these complaints, the Swiss government has not remained deaf. One official response has been to commission studies that outline new security objectives and structures.[236] These have generally argued that national and public security cannot any longer be provided without the collaboration of security agencies in other European countries.[237]

Cantonal police forces as well as the police authorities in the Federal Government are presently in the process of undertaking institutional and professional reforms. Their aim is, on the one hand, to provide better nation-wide and international law enforcement and crime prevention services. On the other hand, police agencies must strive to help individual officers identify more closely with the local population. Public feelings of insecurity, whether real or subjective, must be taken seriously.

---

236 The federal government commissioned several studies to assess security needs. The 1993 "Expertenkommission grenzpolizeiliche Personenkontolle" was the first one that looked at the crime factor across borders. The most recent one which included international crime is the 1999 report entitled "Security through Co-operation". During the 1990's, several working groups and academic studies were also commissioned to evaluate Switzerland's position outside of the EU. See for example: PIETH, Mark, and Dieter FREIBURGHAUS, "Die Bedeutung des organisierten Verbrechens in der Schweiz", Bericht im Auftrag des Bundesamtes für Justiz, October 1993; TINGLUELY, Florence E., "Coopération transfrontalière locale ... L'exemple du canton de Genève", in FREIBURGHAUS, Dieter, ed., *Die Kantone und Europa*, Bern: Haupt Verlag, 1994; pp. 291–306; BIEBER, Roland, A.-C. LYON and J. MONAR, eds., *Justice et affaires intérieures – L'Union européenne et la Suisse*, Berne, Staempfli Editions SA, 1997. Also, "Nach den Einzelschritten die Gesamtanalyse: Reorganisation des Systems der inneren Sicherheit", *Neue Zürcher Zeitung*, 5 November 1999; p. 13.

237 Most notable is the report entitled "Security through co-operation" (SIPOL B 2000) of 7 June 1999, was published by the Federal Council to the Federal Assembly on the Security policy of Switzerland. See also discussions in: *Neue Zürcher Zeitung*, 11 June 1999; pp. 13 & 15; *NZZ*, 18 October 1999; p. 12; and *NZZ*, 22 November 1999; p. 13.

Three areas that touch on Swiss internal security are undergoing reform. They concern (1) the military, (2) the police and (3) intelligence information services. Any reforms could theoretically be carried out in complete independence or isolation from Switzerland's neighbours and the European Union. However, tackling cross-border (international) security challenges with purely national (internal) means is as unrealistic as trying to limit criminal police investigations to one single canton when the offenders can travel freely to any other part of the country. Briefly, the three areas of security services include the following:

(1) In the military sector, events in 1998 and 1999 necessitated rapid changes. These were, for example, the need for the military to support city police and security officers at embassies and international organisations in Bern and Geneva, or the call for the military to stand guard at asylum centres and at the Swiss border. Thus, besides being ready at any time to provide emergency help in natural catastrophes (clearing up an avalanche or building sandbag walls when rivers flood), the Swiss army has temporarily been involved in public security beyond of what were its traditional functions.[238] However, such functions will increasingly be left for special police forces to carry out; the army will step in only if public security is threatened in an unusual way.

(2) In almost all police offices in Switzerland, reforms and adaptations to new security needs are underway. Collaboration among Swiss police corps organised under the jurisdiction of cantonal and communal authorities has now become a part of day-to-day work.[239] As already mentioned, the same

---

238 Many newspapers have regularly reported on the temporary services provided by the military. For example: "Subsidiäre Einsätze der Armee an der Südgrenze?", *Neue Zürcher Zeitung*, 2 June 1998; p. 13; "Le canton de Genève ne peut renoncer à l'aide de l'armée lors de conférences internationales" in *Le Temps*, 22 April 1999; "Berne recourt au droit d'exception contre les réfugiés", in *Tribune de Genève*, 1 June 1999. Finally: "Les soldats suisses ne protégerons plus le Palais des Nations", in *Le Temps*, 9 Sept. 1999; p. 16.
239 MOHLER, Markus, H. F., "Les experiences de la Suisse en matière de coopération policière tant entre les cantons qu'entre autorités fédérales et cantonales", in BIEBER, Roland, A.-C. LYON and J. Monar, eds., *Justice et affaires intérieures – L'Union européenne et la Suisse*, Berne, Staempfli Editions SA, 1997; p. 128.

is also increasingly the case for both Swiss police and border patrol in their co-operation with colleagues across the border in Austria, France, Germany and Italy. Overlapping administrative work must be reduced to a minimum across the border and within Switzerland itself. This is no easy task in a country where there are twenty-six cantonal police agencies, a large number of municipal police offices, twenty-eight penal procedures, diverse administrations for equipment, infrastructure and training, as well as various administrative cultures with their own methods and procedures.

In the years the come, Switzerland will adapt its instruments of international police co-operation with the EU and with Central and Eastern European states.[240] To realise this several measures are required such as improving channels of communication between the Swiss authorities and those of other countries as well as restructuring the decentralised police and security competencies within the country.[241] Specifically, Switzerland's crime prevention efforts ought to be co-ordinated at the federal level whenever offences are to be investigated or prevention tools developed that reach beyond the borders of any single canton or of the country. The fragmentation of federal, cantonal and local security agencies (police forces, criminal police, information exchange, border control, etc.) can be a serious handicap if administrative and jurisdictional obstacles hamper smooth collaboration.[242]

To overcome this possible problem, cantonal and federal authorities have agreed to improve the capacities of centralised crime analysis services and to develop more centralised criminal investigation competencies. In this manner, nation-wide and international security problems can be tackled in a more coherent manner when transnational crimes must be investigated. It is in Switzerland's national interest to develop its centralised institutions so

---

240 WYSS, Rudolf, "Die internationale Polizeizusammenarbeit", Solothurner Festgabe zm Schweizerischen Juristentag 1998, Solothurn: Solothurnischen Juristenverein, 1998; p. 702.

241 MOHLER, Markus, H. F., "Les experiences de la Suisse en matière de coopération policière tant entre les cantons qu'entre autorités fédérales et cantonales", in BIE-BER, Roland, A.-C. LYON and J. Monar, eds., Justice et affaires intérieures – L'Union européenne et la Suisse, Berne, Staempfli Editions SA, 1997; p. 130; and "Nach den Einzelschritten die Gesamtanalyse: Reorganisation des Systems der inneren Sicherheit", Neue Zürcher Zeitung, 5 November 1999; p. 13.

242 AEPLI, Pierre, "Pour un nouveau système de sécurité en Suisse", in Le Temps, 26 April 1999; p. 15.

as to be in a better position to contribute to security in the wider European region as well.[243] Parallel to building competencies at the federal level, cantonal penal laws and criminal proceedings need to be co-ordinated more closely so as to facilitate both legal assistance and the prevention of transnational crime.[244]

(3) This brings us to the third area that needs reform to adapt to the wider European context of crime and its prevention. It concerns the growing need for more wide-ranging intelligence services for local police, border guards and federal investigation services. There are two aspects to this service, one which concerns foreign political and possibly economic data and the other which covers criminal investigations for the pursuit of suspected offenders and the prevention of transnational crime. Necessary is that a wider-ranging intelligence service becomes available which is at least compatible with the relevant networks and intelligence services of the European Union.

Preventing transnational crime and addressing challenges to internal security requires international collaboration in matters of policing, criminal investigations, border control and legal assistance. To advance such international collaboration, the country's federally decentralised structure of crime prevention and law enforcement may prove more and more to be an obstacle. International collaboration requires that each country has a centralised agency that acts as the co-ordinator and clearinghouse for criminal investigations and intelligence. For Switzerland, developing such an agency is a difficult task. The country's federal structure, as it stands at present, makes more centralised policing methods difficult if such a central agency is to have its own autonomous executive powers. While the Swiss

---

243 "EG-Gemeinschaftspolitiken – Interessen der Schweiz", in *Nationale und Grenzüberschreitende Probleme im Bereich der inneren Sicherheit*, Expertenkommission Grenzpolizeiliche Personenkontrollen, Diskussionspapier zuhanden des Schweizerischen Bundesrates, Bern, 1993; p. 13; and "Security through co-operation" (SIPOL B 2000), Report of the Federal Council to the Federal Assembly on the Security policy of Switzerland, 7 June 1999; p. 7.
244 DEL PONTE, Carla, "Organisierte Kriminalität und die Schweiz", in STAHEL, Albert A., ed., *Organisierte Kriminalität und Sicherheit*, Bern: Verlag Paul Haupt, 1999; p. 20.

federal structure is deeply part of the Swiss polity and its population's concept of national identity, a change of how these concepts are understood is necessary to prevent the country's isolation in matters of crime prevention.

## Conclusion

International mobility and ease of communications have a profound impact on Switzerland. It is a small country surrounded by open markets and liberal democracies. All of them promote individual liberties, free trade and mobility across borders. Regardless of how many police officers line the streets or how many guards stand at the border, Switzerland cannot guarantee internal security by isolating itself from the economic and political environment that surrounds it. The country depends to a great extent for its security on conditions that exist on the other side of the border. Beyond this line, political and economic conditions inside and outside of the EU increasingly determine the number and character of migrants and transnational offenders.

Switzerland's internal security cannot be regarded as independent from the four neighbouring countries nor from the larger European region. The country needs to find ways towards greater engagement in EU efforts to promote security. This is necessary not only in the crime prevention sector, but also in others. For example, the promotion of peace and stability in regions where refugees and economic migrants come from. There is an enormous need for economic development in these countries. Assistance in the form of financial aid or education and training programmes must not be seen as separate from efforts to prevent transnational crime. Switzerland can support more fully EU initiatives to promote security in other parts of the continent. An example is Swiss participation in peace-building efforts in the Balkans during the late 1990's and in 2000. Solidarity with the EU in facing larger European security challenges is necessary, not merely to develop military security, but also to obtain closer co-operation in matters of crime prevention.[245] The same can be said with regard to collaboration

---

245 MOHLER, Markus H. F., "Sicherheit hat mit Solitarität zu tun", *Neue Zürcher Zeitung*, 21 March 2000; p. 15.

with international organisations that support and promote norms for international law enforcement, crime prevention and the pursuit of offenders across borders. The challenge of providing internal security is not a purely internal matter any longer, it reaches well beyond the borders of any individual country. At the same time, preventing insecurity implies reaching to the heart of any population, namely to the individual person who wants to feel safe in his or her community.

# Concluding Commentary

The 1990's brought great changes to Europe with regard to an opened eastern border and the expansion of trade and communications. The increased mobility of people across the continent and the continuing migration to Western Europe of mostly young people in search of employment from former communist countries as well as from Africa, Asia and Latin America attests to the fact that Europe is an attractive place to live and work. Developments of the past decade have, however, also heightened feelings of instability and insecurity among the public. This is notably the case in European cities where the majority of migrants settle and most crimes are committed. Reports by police agencies that are taken up in the media on offences and violence have made public safety of critical importance to most political parties. Debates about how crime should be fought enliven television talk-shows and fill the news especially at election times.

However, few Europeans are willing to recognise that we face a double-edged dilemma. Objective security problems risk being misunderstood because subjective fears of insecurity and desires for a increasingly liberal life-style risk contradicting each other. We fear crime, but enjoy seeing it in entertainment. We expect security from our governments, but want maximum freedom and privacy. Should we not ask ourselves whether we can continue to demand greater personal freedom in an open and liberal society while at the same time expecting that our national and international security institutions control the movements of individual offenders and the activities of young people where juvenile delinquency is considered a problem? Can internal security be promoted at the same time as we maintain a liberal and open society which is one of Europe's strengths? This is not an easy task. An open society links Europeans to global economic and social influences – to the exchange and sharing of values and norms which we call globalisation. Its main characteristics are perhaps those technological developments which facilitate human mobility and communication. We have to accept that the changes which these bring to Europe are part of its future. Given the prevailing dynamic of these global developments, the co-ordination of security policies among European countries will constitute the principal challenge in the years to come.

The principal objective which must be kept in mind when facing this challenge is that the evolution of security institutions must continue to provide (subjective and objective) reassurances to the public of its safety. This requires that internal security agencies constantly adapt to new public needs and demands. Adaptations and reforms are necessary not only in Central European countries undergoing a transition to liberal democratic politics and free market economics, but also in the West. The entire European region shares similar criminal characteristics and this includes Western states such as Switzerland which are not part of the European Union.

Beyond Western Europe's borders, much can be done to support internal security (in the broader sense of the term). For example: (a) finding ways to relieve migration pressures in the migrant-exporting countries instead of focussing only on tightening border controls around Western Europe; (b) addressing the imbalance of wealth between the "West" and comparatively poorer countries in Europe's periphery in order to reduce their market demand for stolen goods from the West; and (c), provide economic support towards the establishment of more stable societies in these countries. This is especially important, albeit also very difficult, where corruption and organised crime are weakening political authority and hampering public services.

Within Europe's borders, a deterioration of public perceptions of safety is not inevitable. Various crime prevention methods can be experimented with and tailored to local needs. They must not merely focus on repressing persons accused of criminal acts, but also include prevention strategies in education where anti-social and disorderly forms of behaviour can often be addressed more effectively. Early crime prevention efforts targeted at children and youth who show anti-social behaviour are successful as long as these interventions aim at more than one risk factor. This means, not merely addressing the behaviour once it is observed, but developing communication channels for parents, children, teachers and police officers through which counselling and surveillance can be carried out. Such interventions can change human behaviour. From a policy perspective, government money invested in early prevention for children and teenagers, especially those who live in high-risk environments, is far less costly in the long-run than repression through a criminal justice system once juveniles or young adults have committed criminal offences.[246]

However, many government security agencies as well as local police offices find it difficult to support preventive efforts. One reason is that as police work becomes less law-enforcement and more public service or community-oriented, a considerable amount of retraining may be required. Another reason is that actual prevention methods need to be paid for. Public funds are often hard to obtain. This is so because prevention is a rather quiet and often complex affair. Prevention programmes are sometimes difficult to explain to the public which is expected to participate. Furthermore, the effectiveness of prevention programmes may be hard to evaluate and therefore politicians and police agencies may have trouble finding the money to fund them. A complicating factor is often also the little enthusiasm which prevention programmes attract. Problems such as juvenile delinquency, violence at public events or open drug scenes in European cities attract frequent media publicity. To allocate funds to fighting these visible and acute forms of offensive behaviour is often easier for a government to justify. In contrast, the media, and thus politicians, pay little if any attention to less visible prevention programmes.

To conclude, security or safety are vague and subjective concepts which continuously change in the public's mind. Security is perceived as being sufficiently present only as long as citizens, politicians and government agencies responsible for public safety accept that constant adjustments to new needs are necessary in an ever-changing environment. Such acceptance must include the awareness that subjective assessments and objective challenges will never coincide exactly. Accepting this and working to prevent insecurity accordingly is contributing to security. In contrast, wishful thinking about an unchanging society in which human behaviour is predictable and independent of larger socio-economic influences is unrealistic and leads to feelings of insecurity.

---

246 TREMBLAY, Richard E. and Wendy M. CRAIG, "Developmental Crime Prevention", in TONRY, Michael and David P. FARRINGTON, eds., *Building a safer society: strategic approaches to crime prevention*, Chicago: University of Chicago Press 1995; p. 219–225.

# Bibliography

AEPLI, Pierre, Pour un nouveau système de sécurité en Suisse, in: *Le Temps*, 26 April 1999.

ALBRECHT, Hans-Jörg, Ethnic Minorities and Crime – The Construction of Foreigners' Crime in the Federal Republic of Germany, in: Salvatore Palidda, ed., *Délit d'immigration/Immigrant delinquency*. Brussels: European Commission, COST A2, EUR 17472, 1996.

ANGENENDT, Steffen, ed., *Asylum and Migration Policies in the European Union*. Berlin: Research Institute of the German Society for Foreign Affairs (DGAP), 1999.

BATCHELOR, Stephen, *Alone with Others*. New York: Grove Press, Inc., 1983.

BAUHOFER, Stefan and Pierre-Henri BOLLE, et al., *Innere Sicherheit – Innere Unsicherheit? Sécurité intérieure – Insécurité intérieure?* Reihe Kriminologie, Band 13 / Collection Criminologie, Vol. 13. Chur: Verlag Rüegger AG 1995.

BESOZZI, Claudio, *Organisierte Kriminalität und empirische Forschung*. Chur, Zürich: Verlag Rüegg 1997.

BIEBER, Roland, A.-C. LYON and J. MONAR, eds., *Justice et affaires intérieures – L'Union européenne et la Suisse*. Berne: Staempfli Editions SA 1997.

BIERI, Oliver, Unterschiedliche Verlaufsmuster von Homizidraten im Zeitraum 1877 bis 1995, in: Manuel Eisner and Patrik Manzoni, eds., *Gewalt in der Schweiz: Studien zu Entwicklung, Wahrnehmung und staatlicher Reaktion*. Chur/Zürich: Rüegg Verlag, 1998.

BIGO, Didier, The European International Security Field: Stakes and Rivalries in newly developing areas of Police Intervention, in: Malcolm Anderson and Monica den Boer, eds., *Policing across National Boundaries*. London: Pinter Publishers 1994.

BIGO, Didier, *Police en réseaux: l'éxpérience européenne*, Paris: Presses de Sciences Po 1996.

BRANGER, Katja and Franziska LIECHTI, Jugendgewalt und Freizeit, in: Manuel Eisner and Patrik Manzoni, eds., *Gewalt in der Schweiz: Studien zu Entwicklung, Wahrnehmung und staatlicher Reaktion*. Zürich: Verlag Rüegg 1998.

BUSE, Uwe, Wir kriegen sie alle, *Der Spiegel*, No. 27, 5 July 1999.

BUZAN, Barry, *People, States and Fear*. Hertfordshire, UK: Harvester Wheatsheaf, 2nd edition, 1991.

CLARKE, Ronald V., Situational Crime Prevention, in: Michael Tonry and David P. Farrington, eds., *Building a Safer Society: Strategic Approaches to Crime Prevention*. Chicago: University of Chicago Press 1995.

CLARKE, R. V., ed., *Situational Crime Prevention: Successful Case Studies.* 2nd ed. Albany, New York: Harrow and Heston Publishers 1997.

CRIMISCOPE, Newsletter of the Institut de Police Scientifique et de Criminologie, University of Lausanne.

DAHRENDORF, Ralf, Economic Opportunity, Civil Society and Political Liberty, Discussion Paper No. 58. Geneva: United Nations Research Institute for Social Development 1995.

DANGSCHAT, Jens S., Warum ziehen sich Gegensätze nicht an?, in: Wilhelm Heitmeyer, et al., eds., *Die Krise der Städte.* Frankfurt am Main: Suhrkamp Verlag, No. es2036, 1998.

DÄNIKER, Gustav, La Suisse est dans le 'Partenariat pour la paix', ni plus, ni moins, *Le Temps*, 10 December 1999.

DEL PONTE, Carla, Organisierte Kriminalität und die Schweiz, in: Albert A. Stahel, *Organisierte Kriminalität und Sicherheit.* Bern: Verlag Paul Haupt 1999.

DÖRMANN, Uwe, *Wie sicher fühlen sich die Deutschen?* Wiesbaden: Bundeskriminalamt (BKA-Forschungsreihe Band 40) 1996.

DUBET, François and Didier LAPEYRONNIE, *Les Quartiers d'Exil.* Paris: Éditions du Seuil 1992.

EISNER, Manuel, Immigration, Integration und Assimilation, in: Stefan Bauhofer und Nicolas Queloz, eds., *Ausländer, Kriminalität und Strafrechtspflege.* Zürich: Verlag Rüegg 1993.

EISNER, Manuel, *Das Ende der zivilisierten Stadt? Die Auswirkungen von Modernisierung und urbaner Krise auf Gewaltdelinquenz.* Frankfurt: Campus Verlag 1997.

EISNER, Manuel, Jugendkriminalität und immigrierte Minderheiten im Kanton Zürich, in: *Jugend und Strafrecht.* Zürich: Verlag Rüegg 1998.

EISNER, Manuel, Die Zunahme von Jugendgewalt – Fakt oder Artefakt?, in: Manuel Eisner and Patrik Manzoni, eds., *Gewalt in der Schweiz: Studien zu Entwicklung, Wahrnehmung und staatlicher Reaktion.* Chur, Zürich: Rüegg Verlag 1998.

FELTES, Thomas, Pro-active Prevention: An Effective Police Tool?, in: Hans-Heiner Kühne and Koichi Miyazawa, eds., *Internal Security in Modern Industrialized Societies.* Baden-Baden: Nomos Verlagsgsellschaft 1998.

FELTES, Thomas, Policing a Modern Society: Tougher than the Rest?: Fear of Crime, Victimisation, and New Policing Styles, in: *Police Research and Management*, Summer 1998.

FELTES, Thomas, Improving the Training System of Police Officials – Problems of Creating an International Standard for Police Officers in a Democratic Society, unpublished paper prepared at the University of Applied Police Sciences, Villingen-Schwenningen, Germany, August 1998.

FELTES, Thomas, Police Integrity and the Police Organization, paper presented at the International Police Integrity Conference (New York University/National Institute of Justice, Washington). La Pietra, Florence, Italy, May 1999.

FINN, Peter, Crime Wave in Hungary Sets Off Alarm in U.S., *International Herald Tribune*. 23 December 1998.

FOUCHER, Michel, Les nouvelles frontières de l'Union européenne, in: *Revue Internationale de Politique Comparée*. Vol. 2, No. 3, 1995.

GASTEYGER, Curt, Migration: The 'Crisis of our Age'?", in: The Japan Foundation Centre for Global Partnership, *The End of the Century: The Future in the Past*. Tokyo: Kodansha International 1995.

GHAI, Dharam, Economic Globalization, Institutional Change and Human Security, Discussion Paper 91. Geneva: United Nations Research Institute for Social Development 1997.

GHÉBALI, Victor-Yves and Brigitte SAUERWEIN, *European Security in the 1990s: Challenges and Perspectives*. Geneva: United Nations Institute for Disarmament Research 1995.

GILOMEN, Heinz, Die Situation der Ausländischen Bevölkerung in der Schweiz, in: S. Bauhofer and N. Queloz, eds., *Ausländer, Kriminalität und Strafrechtspflege*. Zürich: Verlag Rüegg 1993.

GODSON, Anna, EU Enlargement and Organised Crime, in: *Outlook 99*. London: Control Risks Group Ltd., January 1999.

GOTTLIEB, G., K. KRÖZSEL and B. PRESTEL, *The Reform of the Hungarian Police: Processes, Methods, Results*. Holzkirchen/Obb, Germany: Felix Verlag 1998.

GREGORY, Frank, Policing the Democratic State: How Much Force?, *Conflict Studies*. No. 194. London: The Centre for Security and Conflict Studies 1986.

GREGORY, Frank, Migrants and Transnational Crime, paper prepared for a conference at Chatham House, *Policy Challenges of the New Migrant Diasporas*. London, 22–23 April 1999, unpublished.

HAKKERT, Alfred, Geweld in Nederlandse gemeenten, in: *SEC*. Tijdschrift over samenleving en criminaliteitspreventie, Den Haag: Ministerie van justitie, Vol. 12, No. 3, June 1998.

HASSAL, Mark and Ken MURPHY, *Stealing the State, and Everything Else: A Survey of Corruption in the Postcommunist World*. TI Working Paper. Berlin: Transparency International 1999.

HATALAK, Oksanna, Anna ALVAZZI DEL FRATE, Ugljesa ZVEKIC, *The International Crime Victim Survey in Countries in Transition: National Reports*, Rome: United Nations Interregional Crime and Justice Research Institute (UNICRI), Publication No. 62, 1998.

HEFTY, Georg Paul, Konsumenten in der Verbrechenskette: Organisierte Kriminalität kommt nicht nur aus dem Osten, in: *Frankfurter Allgemeine Zeitung*. 21 May 1999.

HEITMEYER, Wilhelm, Einleitung: Sind individualisierte und ethnic-kulturell vielfältige Gesellschaften noch integrierbar?, in: W. Heitmeyer, ed., *Was hält die Gesellschaft zusammen?* Frankfurt am Main: Edition Suhrkamp 1997.

211

HOFFMANN, Bruce, Is Europe Soft on Terrorism?, in: *Foreign Policy*, No. 115, Summer 1999.

HOVY, Bela, Asylum in Europe: Arrivals, Stay and Gender from a Data Perspective, paper prepared at the UNHCR. Geneva: The Statistics Office of the Programme Coordination Section, UNHCR 1999.

INTERNATIONAL ORGANIZATION FOR MIGRATION, *Trafficking and Prostitution: The Growing Exploitation of Migrant Women from Central and Eastern Europe*. Migration Information Programme, Budapest, May 1995.

INTERPOL, Statistiques Criminelles Internationales des pays européens de 1990 à nos jours. International Crime Statistics Lyon 1998.

JASCHKE, Hans-Gerd, Eine verunsicherte Institution: Die Polizei in der Auseinandersetzung mit Rechtsextremismus und Fremdenfeindlichkeit, in: Wilhelm Heitmeyer, *Das Gewalt-Dilemma*. Frankfurt am Main: Suhrkamp Verlag, No. es1905, 1994.

JOPPKE, Christian, Immigration Challenges the Nation-state, in: Christian Joppke, ed., *Challenge to the Nation-state: Immigration in Western Europe and the United States*. Oxford: Oxford University Press 1998.

JUNGER-TAS, J., Le 'moyennement répressif' des Pays-Bas, *Le Monde Diplomatique*. Vol. 46, No. 541, April 1999.

KAESER, Philippe, *L'espace Schengen: Des premiers pas au traité d'Amsterdam*. Institut européen, Université de Genève, No. 5, 1997.

KANGASPUNTA, K., M. JOUTSEN and N. OLLUS, *Crime and Criminal Justice Systems in Europe and North America 1990–1994*. Helsinki: European Institute for Crime Prevention and Control, affiliated with the United Nations (HEUNI) 1998.

KAPPELER, Beat, Wir und die Ausländer: Wohltätig mit dem Geld von andern, in: *Die Weltwoche*. 23 July 1998.

KEIM, Karl-Dieter, Vom Zerfall des Urbanen, in: Wilhelm Heitmeyer, ed., *Was treibt die Gesellschaft auseinander?* Frankfurt am Main: Suhrkamp Verlag, No. es2004, 1997.

KILLIAS, Martin, Immigrants, Crime and Criminal Justice in Switzerland, in: Michael Tonry, ed., *Ethnicity, Crime, and Immigration: Comparative and Cross-national Perspectives*. Chicago: The University of Chicago Press 1997.

KILLIAS, Martin, 'Zero tolerance' ist keine Strategie für die Schweiz, in: *Neue Zürcher Zeitung*, 21/22 February 1998.

KILLIAS, Martin and Juan RABASA, Weapons and Athletic Constitution as Factors linked to Violence among Male Juveniles, in: *British Journal of Criminology*. 37:3, Summer 1997.

KREVERT, Peter, Europäische Einigung und Organisierte Kriminalität: Konzequenzen für Polizei und Nachrichtendienste, Wirtschaft und Gesellschaft, in: *Europäische Beiträge zu Kriminalität und Prävention*. Vol. 1, 1998. Münster: Europäisches Zentrum für Kriminalprävention.

KRIMM, Roland, La Grande-Bretagne adhère aux Accords de Schengen…, *Le Temps*, 30 May 2000.

KUNZ, Karl-Ludwig, *Kriminologie*. 2nd edition. Bern, Stuttgart and Wien: Verlag Paul Haupt 1998.

LAYCOCK, Gloria and Nick TILLEY, Implementing Crime Prevention, in: Michael Tonry and David P. Farrington, eds., *Building a Safer Society: Strategic Approaches to Crime Prevention*. Chicago: University of Chicago Press 1995.

MIEGEL, Meinhard, Wachsender Wohlstand, zunehmende Enttäuschung, in: *Merkur. Deutsche Zeitschrift für europäisches Denken*, Vol. 52 (Jahrgang), No. 5, May 1998.

*MIGRATION UND BEVÖLKERUNG*, Newsletter of the Lehrstuhl Bevölkerungswissenschaft. Humboldt-Universität, Berlin, issues No. 7, September 1998 and No. 3, March 1999.

MOHLER, Markus, Les expériences de la Suisse en matière de coopération policière…, in: Roland Bieber, A.-C. Lyon and J. Monar, eds., *Justice et affaires intérieures – L'Union européenne et la Suisse*. Bern: Staempfli Editions SA 1997.

MOHLER, Markus H. F., Sicherheit hat mit Solitarität zu tun, *Neue Zürcher Zeitung*. 21 March 2000.

MÜNZ, Rainer, Phasen und Formen der europäischen Migration, in: Steffen Angenendt, ed., *Migration und Flucht*. München: Verlag R. Oldenbourg, Bundeszentrale für politische Bildung, Schriftenreihe Band 342, 1997.

MÜNZ, Rainer, Demographische Vergangenheit und Zukunft der Industrie Gesellschaft Europas, in: *Schweizer Monatshefte*. Vol. 78, No. 11, November 1998.

OBERNDÖRFER, Dieter and Uwe BERNDT, Möglichkeiten der Einwanderungsbegrenzung, in: Albrecht Weber, ed., *Einwanderungsland Bundesrepublik Deutschland in der Europäischen Union: Gestaltung und Regelungsmöglichkeiten*. Osnabrück: Universitätsverlag Rasch 1997.

O'BRIEN, Kevin and Jason RALPH, Using the Internet for Intelligence, in: *Jane's Intelligence Review*. November 1997.

OECD/OCDE Organisation de Coopération et de développement économiques, *Tendances des Migrations Internationales*. Acquisitions de la nationalité dans certains pays de l'OCDE, SOPEMI Rapport annuel 1998.

OECD/OCDE Organisation de Coopération et de développement économiques, *Effectifs de travailleurs étrangers et nés à l'étranger*. SOPEMI Rapport annuel 1998.

*OUTLOOK 99 – BUSINESS, POLITICS, SECURITY*, Corruption in the Spotlight. London: Control Risks Group Ltd. 1999.

OVCHINSKII, Vladimir, Russian Interpol, in: *International Affairs*. Vol. 44, No. 6, 1998.

PALIDDA, Salvatore, ed., *Délit d'immigration/Immigrant delinquency*. Brussels: European Commission, COST A2, EUR 17472, 1996.

PALIDDA, Salvatore, La construction sociale de la déviance et de la criminalité parmi les immigrés: le cas Italie, in: Salvatore Palidda, ed., *Délit d'immigration/Immigrant delinquency*. Brussels: European Commission, COST A2, EUR 17472, 1996.

PELINKA, Anton and Brigitte HALBMAYR, *EU-Osterweiterung und österreichische Sicherheitspolitik*. Endbericht, Wien: Institut für Konfliktforschung, July 1998.

PERDUCA Alberto and Patrick RAMAEL, *Le Crime International et la Justice*. France: Flammarion 1998.

PFEIFFER, Christian, Jugendkriminalität und Jugendgewalt in europäischen Ländern, Hannover: Kriminologisches Forschungsinstitut Niedersachsen, 1997; and summarized as: Trends in Juvenile Violence in European Countries. National Institute of Justice, U.S. Department of Justice, May 1998.

PFEIFFER, Christian, Gruppendrill und Fremdenhass, in: *Schweizer Monatshefte*. Vol. 79/80, No. 12/1, December/January 1999/2000.

PIETH, Mark and Dieter FREIBURGHAUS, Die Bedeutung des organisierten Verbrechens in der Schweiz, Bericht im Auftrag des Bundesamtes für Justiz, October 1993.

PUTTONEN, Riikka, *Draft Study on the Relationship between Organised Crime and Trafficking in Aliens*, prepared by the Secretariat of the Budapest Group. Vienna: International Centre for Migration Development Policy Development, BG 1/99, January 1999.

QUELOZ, Nicolas, International Efforts to tackle Organised Crime: The Case of Europe, paper prepared for the 52nd International Course on Criminology, University of Macao, Faculty of Law, October 1996.

RAMSEYER, Gérard, Security in Geneva, in: *Geneva News*, February 2000, Vol. 21, No. 1.

REBMANN, Matthias, *Ausländerkriminalität in der Bundesrepublik Deutschland*. Freiburg in Breisgau: Kriminologische Forschungsberichte aus dem Max-Planck-Institut für ausländisches und internationales Strafrecht, Band 80, 1998.

ROBERS, Ben, Het wel en wee van de happy 80%, in *SEC*. Tijdschrift over samenleving en criminaliteitspreventie, Den Haag: Ministerie van justitie, Vol. 12, No. 3, June 1998.

ROBERT, P., R. ZAUBERMAN, M. L. POTTIER and H. LAGRANGE, Mesurer le crime: Entre statistique de police et enquêtes de victimation (1985–1995), in: *Revue Française de sociologie*. Vol. 40:2, April/June, 1999.

ROHMER, Hartmut, Kriminalprävention in NRW als gesamtgesellschaftliche Aufgabe, in: *Europäische Beiträge zu Kriminalität und Prävention*. Münster: Europäisches Zentrum für Kriminalprävention, 1998, No. 2.

ROULET, Yelmarc, Permis de travail: Genève et Vaud crient famine, *Le Temps*, 22 September 1999.

RUPESINGHE, Kumar, Forms of Violence and its Transformation, in: K. Rupesinghe, and M. Rubio C., eds., *The Culture of Violence*. Tokyo, New York: United Nations University Press 1994.

214

SANDER, Uwe, Beschleunigen Massenmedien durch Gewaltdarstellungen einen gesellschaftlichen Zivilisationsverlust?, in: Wilhelm Heitmeyer, *Das Gewalt-Dilemma.* Frankfurt am Main: Suhrkamp Verlag, No. es1905, 1994.

SAVONA, Ernesto, European Money Trails, in: *Transnational Organized Crime.* Vol. 2:4, 1996.

SAVONA, Ernesto U. with A. DI NICOLA and G. DA COL, Dynamics of Migration and Crime in Europe: New Patterns of an Old Nexus, Transcrime, Working Paper No. 8. Trento: Research Group on Transnational Crime, University of Trento, School of Law; October 1996.

SCHELTER, Kurt, Innere Sicherheit in einem Europa ohne Grenzen, in: Reinhard C. Meier-Walser, Gerhard Hirscher, Klaus Lange and Enrico Palumbo, eds., *Organisierte Kriminalität: Bestandsaufnahme, Transnationale Dimension, Wege der Bekämpfung.* Munich: Hanns-Seidel-Stiftung, Akademie für Politik und Zeitgeschehen 1999.

SCHELTER, Kurt, Organisierte Kriminalität und Terrorismus: Die Beurteilung aus Deutscher Sicht, in: Albert A. Stahel, ed., *Organisierte Kriminalität und Sicherheit: Ein Zwischenbericht.* Bern: Verlag Paul Haupt 1999.

SCHLOTH, Stephanie, Irgend etwas nimmt immer mehr zu: Kriminalitätsfurcht und Kriminalität, in: *Vorgänge.* No. 124, 32, Jahrgang, Dezember 1993, Heft 4.

SCHNEIDER, Hans Joachim, La violence en milieu scolaire, in: *Interpol: Revue internationale de police criminelle.* No. 456, 1996.

SCHUBARTH, Wilfred, Jugendprobleme in den Medien, in: *Aus Politik und Zeitgeschichte.* Beilage zur Wochenzeitung *Das Parlament*, B31/98, 24 July, 1998.

SCHWIND, Hans-Dieter, J. BAUMANN, U. SCHNEIDER and M. WINTER, *Ursachen, Prävention und Kontrolle von Gewalt* (Gewaltkommission), *Summary of the Final Report of the Independent Governmental Commission the Prevention and Control of Violence.* Berlin: Duncker & Humblot 1990.

SOROS, George, *The Crisis of Global Capitalism.* New York: PublicAffairs, Perseus Books Group 1998.

SPOLAR, Ch., Crime and Unrest in Post-Communist Society, *International Herald Tribune*, 9 February 1998.

STAHEL, A., Organisierte Kriminalität: Eine Herausforderung, in: Albert A. Stahel, ed., *Organisierte Kriminalität und Sicherheit: Ein Zwischenbericht.* Bern: Verlag Paul Haupt 1999.

STEFFEN, Wiebke, Ausländerkriminalität: Notwendige Differenzierungen, in: *Brennpunkt Kriminalität.* München: Bayerische Landeszentrale für politische Bildungsarbeit. 1. Auflage, 1996.

STONE, Martin, Terrorism: Higher Impact, Lower Risk, in: *Outlook 99 – Business, Politics, Security.* London: Control Risks Group Ltd. 1999.

STORBECK, Jürgen, Die Rolle von Europol bei der Bekämpfung der organisierten Kriminalität, in: Hanns-Seidel-Stiftung e. V., *Dokumentation der 16. inter-*

*nationalen Fachtagung zum Thema 'Demokratie in Anfechtung und Bewährung – die Bekämpfung von organisierter Kriminalität und Drogenhandel'*. Schriftenreihe 3.47, München, 1998.

STORZ, Renate, Simone RONEZ and Stephan BAUMGARTNER, *Zur Staatszugehörigkeit von Verurteilten: Kriminalistische Befunde*. Bundesamt für Statistik, Bern 1996.

STRAUBHAAR, Thomas and Achim WOLTER, Aktuelle Brennpunkte der europäischen Migrationsdiskussion, *Wirtschaftsdienst*. 1996/IX.

SWISS FEDERAL OFFICE FOR FOREIGNERS, Die Schweiz und die europäische Sicherheitszusammenarbeit aus der Sicht des Eidg. Justiz und Polizei Departements (EJPD), 20 August 1998.

THUILLIER, François, *La législation antiterroriste*, Études et recherches, Mai 1999. Paris: Institut des Hautes Études de la Sécurité Intérieure.

TINGLUELY, Florence E., Coopération transfrontalière locale ... L'exemple du canton de Genève, in: Dieter Freiburghaus, ed., *Die Kantone und Europa*. Bern: Haupt Verlag 1994.

TONRY, Michael, Ethnicity, Crime, and Immigration, in: M. Tonry, ed., *Ethnicity, Crime and Immigration: Comparative and Cross-National Perspectives*, (Crime and Justice series). Chicago: University of Chicago 1997.

TONRY, Michael and David P. FARRINGTON, eds., *Building a Safer Society: Strategic Approaches to Crime Prevention*. Chicago: University of Chicago Press 1995.

TRAUBHAAR, Thomas and Achim WOLTER, Aktuelle Brennpunkte der europäischen Migrationsdiskussion, *Wirtschaftsdienst*. 1996/IX.

TREMBLAY, Richard E. and Wendy M. CRAIG, Developmental Crime Prevention, in: Michael Tonry and David P. Farrington, eds., *Building a Safer Society: Strategic Approaches to Crime Prevention*. Chicago: University of Chicago Press 1995.

ULRICH, Christopher J., The Price of Freedom: The Criminal Threat in Russia, Eastern Europe and the Baltic Region, in: *Conflict Studies*. London: The Research Institute for the Study of Conflict and Terrorism, No. 275, 1994.

UNITED NATIONS, *Global Report on Crime and Justice*, Graeme Newman, ed., Office for Drug Control and Crime Prevention, Centre for International Crime Prevention. Oxford: Oxford University Press 1999.

VAN DER HEIJDEN, Toon, *Assessing Nature and Extent of Organised Crime in the European Union*. Driebergen: National Police Agency of the Netherlands, 20 March 1998.

VAN DIJK, Jan J.M. and John VAN KERSTEREN, Criminal Victimization in European Cities: Some Results of the International Crime Victims Survey, in: *European Journal on Criminal Policy and Research*. Vol. 4, No. 1, 1996.

VON DAENIKEN, Urs, Organisierte Kriminalität in Osteuropa, Einflüsse auf die Schweiz, in: Albert A. Stahel, ed., *Organisierte Kriminalität und Sicherheit*. Bern: Verlag Paul Haupt 1999.

VON FELTEN, Mirjam, Geschlechtsspezifische Perzeption von Gewalt im Jugendalter, in: Manuel Eisner and Patrik Manzoni, eds., *Gewalt in der Schweiz: Studien zu Entwicklung, Wahrnehmung und staatlicher Reaktion.* Zürich: Verlag Rüegg 1998.

DE WAARD, J., M. SCHREUDERS and R. MEIJER, Geweldscriminaliteit in 15 Europese landen, in: *SEC.* Tijdschrift over samenleving en criminaliteitspreventie, Netherlands Ministry of Justice, Vol. 12, No. 2, April 1998.

WACQUANT, Loïc, Ce vent punitif qui vient d'Amerique, in: *Le Monde Diplomatique.* Vol. 46, No. 541, April 1999.

WASSERMANN, Rudolf, Kriminalität und Sicherheitsbedürfnis: Zur Bedrohung durch Gewalt und Kriminalität in Deutschland, in: *Aus Politik und Zeitgeschichte.* No. B23, 2 June 1995.

WATTS, Alan, *The Wisdom of Insecurity.* London: Rider, Ebury Press, Random House 1993.

WAXMAN, Dov, *Immigration and Identity: A New Security Perspective in Euro-Magreb Relations*, London: Research Institute for the Study of Conflict and Terrorism, September 1997.

WIEVIORKA, Michel, Le nouveau paradigme de la violence, in: *Cultures & Conflits.* No. 29–30, Printemps/été 1998.

WIEVIORKA, Michel, Kritik des Multikulturalismus, in: Wilhelm Heitmeyer, et al., eds., *Die Krise der Städte.* Frankfurt am Main: Suhrkamp Verlag, No. es2036, 1998.

WILLEMSE, Hans M., Development in Dutch crime prevention, in: R. V. Clarke, ed., *Crime Prevention Studies.* Vol. 2. Monsey, New York: Criminal Justice Press 1994.

WITTKÄMPER, Gerhard W., P. KREVET and A. KOHL, *Europa und die Innere Sicherheit.* Wiesbaden: Bundeskriminalamt (BKA) Forschungsreihe Nr. 35, 1996.

WYSS, Eva, Zerbrochene Fenster müssen sofort repariert werden: Die Sicherheit beginnt im Quartier…, in: *Neue Zürcher Zeitung.* 21/22 February 1998.

WYSS, Rudolf, Die Internationale Polizeizusammenarbeit, in: *Solothurner Festgabe zum Schweizerischen Juristentag 1998.* Solothurn: Solothurnischen Juristenverein.

ZVEKIC, Ugljesa, *Criminal Victimisation in Countries in Transition*, Rome: United Nations Interregional Crime and Justice Research Institute (UNICRI), Publication No. 61, 1998.